S0-BZL-074

THREE RIVAL VERSIONS OF MORAL ENQUIRY

Three Rival Versions of Moral Enquiry

Encyclopaedia, Genealogy, and Tradition

*being Gifford Lectures delivered in the
University of Edinburgh in 1988*

by

Alasdair MacIntyre

UNIVERSITY OF NOTRE DAME PRESS
NOTRE DAME, INDIANA

Copyright © 1990 by
Alasdair MacIntyre
All Rights Reserved

Manufactured in the United States of America

Library of Congress Cataloging-in-Publication Data

MacIntyre, Alasdair C.
    Three rival versions of moral enquiry : encyclopae-
dia, genealogy, and tradition: being Gifford lectures delivered in the University of Edinburgh in 1988 / by
Alasdair MacIntyre.
        p. cm.
    ISBN 0-268-01871-5
    1. Ethics–Methodology. 2. Ethics, Modern–
19th century. 3. Encyclopaedia Britannica. 4. Ethics.
5. Nietzsche, Friedrich Wilhelm, 1844–1900. Zur
Genealogie der Moral. 6. Catholic Church. Pope
(1878–1903 : Leo XIII). Aeterni Patris. 7. Thomists.
I. Title. II. Title: Gifford lectures.
BJ37.M23   1990
170′.9′034–dc20   89-29275

For
LYNN SUMIDA JOY
onna kara
saki e kasumu zo
shiohigata
Kobayashi Issa

Contents

Preface

Anyone invited to deliver a set of Gifford Lectures at Edinburgh University is bound to feel daunted by the standards set by his or her predecessors. The great honor conferred by the Gifford Committee is a very welcome burden, but nonetheless a burden. I was and am therefore immensely grateful both to the members of that committee and to many others for the ways in which they did so very much to lighten that burden by their large academic and social hospitality. I owe my warmest thanks to the Reverend Professor Duncan B. Forrester for assistance of more kinds than I can mention. While I was giving the lectures, I was also a Fellow of the Institute for Advanced Study in the Humanities and I am deeply indebted to Professor Peter Jones, the director of the Institute and to the Institute for his and its generosity.

During the lectures in April and May, 1988, a seminar was held at New College and the members of that seminar contributed substantially to the lectures by the pertinacity of their questioning. Often enough I would come away from a seminar knowing that I had to rewrite some passage in a lecture yet to come or to rethink something that I had already said. To all the members of that seminar I give my thanks, especially to Barry Barnes for the exercise of his outstanding ability to give to critical discussion a constructive direction.

During 1988–89 I was the Henry R. Luce Jr. Visiting Scholar at the Whitney Humanities Center of Yale University. One of the duties of a Visiting Scholar is to conduct a faculty seminar, and I used this opportunity to have the text of my Gifford Lectures subjected to further criticism. It was a privilege to be put to the question in this way and I am all too conscious of the inadequacy of my responses both in the seminar and in the resulting final version of the lectures. So much remains to be done. I am peculiarly in the debt of Jonathan Lear and of Joseph Raz for discussion both in the seminar and outside it. And I am delighted to have this opportunity to express, albeit inadequately, to Peter Brooks, Jonathan Spence, Jonathan Freedman, and Sheila Brewer my gratitude for all the help and support that made my time at the Whitney Center so very profitable and so very enjoyable.

Finally I have to thank the National Endowment for the Humanities for financial support, in 1987 and 1988, of extended research on the history of the place of philosophy in the curriculum, research which provided the basis for some of the argument of these lectures, especially in lectures III–VII.

Alasdair MacIntyre
South Bend, Indiana
July 1989

Introduction

Every set of philosophical lectures, both as originally delivered and, if later published, as readdressed to a larger, often more multifarious audience, embodies a standpoint inescapably defined by that particular lecturer's engagement with two sets of issues: those explicitly addressed in the lectures and those which arise from the lecturer's relationships to his or her first and second (and sometimes later on third and fourth and . . .) audiences. There have of course been long periods in the history of the lecture as an academic genre during which no one needed to advert explicitly to this latter type of issue. The relationship between lecturer and audience was in such periods taken for granted by both parties, and the social, moral, and intellectual presuppositions of that relationship did not need to be articulated, perhaps could not have been fully articulated. They embodied extensive and fundamental agreements, both concerning the subject matters conventionally assigned to the lecture as a genre and concerning the point and purpose of lecturing as an academic activity.

There have also however been periods in which such agreements have to some significant degree been challenged or rejected, in which the hitherto accepted definitions of subject matters have become questionable, in which audiences have become heterogeneous, divided, and fragmented, and in which the lecture, by its transformation into an episode in some new, perhaps not or not yet fully recognized form of debate and conflict, can no longer be thought of or delivered in the same way. When I first wrote these Gifford Lectures, I could not avoid remarking, just because of the issues which furnished my subject matter, that the period in which Lord Gifford prescribed their duties to his lecturers was of the former kind, while that in which I had the task of carrying out these duties was of the latter. And passages concerned with this contrast appear in a number of the lectures.

1

But even when so writing I had not yet reckoned sufficiently with the way in which, or the degree to which, the problems and questions arising from it would be raised for me by the characteristically generous and often searching responses of my audiences at Edinburgh and at Yale.

Members of audiences for the most part hear or read a lecture as a contribution to some more extended enquiry or continuing debate or conflict with which they are already to some degree acquainted and in which they may have been already engaged as participant or committed as partisan. Sometimes of course someone will find him or herself introduced by a particular lecture to some quite new form of enquiry or some hitherto unknown debate, so that that lecture is a starting point, rather than an episode in, some already embarked-upon enquiry or debate. At both Edinburgh and Yale, however, it was plain that for the vast majority these lectures were heard as continuations and not as beginnings. Yet within each of these two audiences the differences and divisions were such that different groups in both audiences understood the lectures as episodes within very different enacted narratives of enquiry and debate, thus interpreting and evaluating them from a number of very different standpoints. It was somewhat as if some remarks made by someone standing at the point of intersection of three very different groups, engaged in three distinct conversations, were understood by the members of each group as a contribution to and continuation of the themes and arguments of *its* conversation. Yet this simile, while it communicates the divergent understandings and evaluations of these lectures which emerged both in seminar discussions and in many prolonged private conversations, is inadequate just insofar as it fails to bring out the degree to which each such mode of interpretation and evaluation was in some key way at odds with each other such mode, so that the lectures were a set of differently understood interventions not merely in a continuing set of conversations, but in a continuing quarrel.

What were these differences? They had two dimensions. In the lectures I discuss three very different and mutually antagonistic conceptions of moral enquiry, each stemming from a seminal late nineteenth-century text: the Ninth Edition of the *Encyclopaedia Britannica,* Nietzsche's *Zur Genealogie der Moral* and the encyclical letter of Pope Leo XIII *Aeterni Patris*. When I speak of moral enquiry, I mean something wider than what is conventionally, at least in American universities, understood as moral philosophy, since moral enquiry extends to historical, literary, anthropological, and sociological questions. And indeed among the matters on which the three types of moral enquiry with which I am concerned differ is the nature and scope of moral enquiry. So that those who listened to the lectures from an evaluative standpoint already formed by allegiance to one of those types of enquiry differed in predictable ways from each other and from myself both over how each point of view was to be characterized in terms of its own history—Was I right to take Foucault as a faithful interpreter of Nietzsche? Is Deleuze a faithful interpreter either of Foucault or of Nietzsche? Was I justified in neglecting Garrigou-Lagrange's Thomism? Or Yves Simon's?—and upon how the conflicts between them were to be understood.

Only a little less predictable was the further range of traditions, modes of enquiry, and debates in terms of which others in the audience understood and evaluated the arguments of these lectures. Some of these were more narrowly philosophical: Hegelian, phenomenological, or analytic. Some, although in key part philosophical, represented wider cultural preoccupations. In Edinburgh there happily still exist those whose cultural identification is with what Scottish intellectual and social history have made of the life of their city; so that my lectures were assigned a place in a still ongoing debate in which the remoter participants include Dunbar, Hume, and Stewart, one the terms of which have been redefined for our time by George Elder Davie in *The Democratic Intellect, The Crisis of the Democratic Intellect,* and *The Scottish Enlightenment,* a debate in which there is much at stake for the humanities in Scotland in general and not only for philosophy. In a similar way at Yale I could not avoid being heard as contributing to ongoing discussions about how enquiry and teaching in the humanities ought to be pursued, discussions in which successive chairmen of the National Endowment for the Humanities have taken positions critical of both the theory and practice of some of the more distinguished present and recent members of the Yale faculty, themselves not at all at one on these matters.

The extent and depth of these differences in approaching and reacting to my lectures was by itself enough to raise sharply such questions as: Are the differences and divisions which exist within academic communities by now so great that any notion of addressing the academic community as such, and indeed the wider educated community as such—a notion embodied not only in Adam Gifford's conception of the Gifford Lectures but shared by many others who have endowed public lectures—has become vain and empty? Is it the case that the *de facto* failure to communicate with each other, which is now some-times evident—although still often enough unrecognized—where dif-ferent types and traditions of philosophical enquiry are concerned, is not simply an unfortunate accidental side effect of the specializa-tions of the social structure of the contemporary university, but is grounded in something more fundamental?

These however were not merely questions to be posed after the event *about* the range of differences which I have already described. For in their various ways of articulating those differences and respond-ing to the disagreements and conflicts which resulted from that ar-ticulation, those who participated in the discussions at Edinburgh and at Yale already either presupposed or explicitly argued in favor of rival answers to these two questions and by their different and conflicting answers laid bare a second dimension to their disagree-ments. The key concepts needed to characterize this second dimen-sion of disagreement are *incommensurability* and *untranslatability*. I have in the lectures themselves said a little—as much as, I hope, is neces-sary for my argument—about the former and I have elsewhere said somewhat more about both these concepts and the complexity of the relationship between them (*Whose Justice? Which Rationality?* Notre Dame, 1988, chapter XIX). For my immediate purposes I need do no more than sketch in broad terms two opposed positions on the issues raised by these concepts.

On the one hand are those who hold that in certain cases where two large-scale systems of thought and practice are in radical disagree-ment—such various examples have been cited as the disagreements between the physics of Aristotle and the physics of Galileo or New-ton, those between the beliefs in and practice of witchcraft by some African peoples and the cosmology of modern science, and those be-tween the conceptions of right action characteristic of the Homeric world and the morality of modern individualism—there is and can be no independent standard or measure by appeal to which their rival claims can be adjudicated, since each has internal to itself its own fundamental standard of judgment. Such systems are incom-mensurable, and the terms in and by means of which judgment is delivered in each are so specific and idiosyncratic to each that they cannot be translated into the terms of the other without gross distortion. This type of view has been held by some philosophers and historians of science and by some social and cultural anthropologists.

On the other hand are those, chiefly if not only philosophers, who have argued that the alleged facts of incommensurability and untranslatability are always an illusion. To be able to recognize some alien system of belief and practice as in contention with one's own always requires a capacity to translate its terms and idioms into one's own and an acknowledgment of its theses, arguments, and procedures as susceptible of judgment and evaluation by the same standards as one's own. The adherents of every standpoint in recognizing the existence of rival standpoints recognize also, implicitly if not explicitly, that those standpoints are formulated within and in terms of common norms of intelligibility and evaluation.

To have sketched these two positions in so bare an outline does a gross injustice both to the complexity of detail with which each has been developed and to the variety of attitudes which have been taken up towards them. More particularly, the brevity of this exposition might lead some readers to conclude that, were two opposed systems of thought and practice to be to some significant degree genuinely incommensurable and untranslatable, rational debate between the adherents of those two systems would be to that same degree rendered impossible. And some philosophers have of course so concluded. But these lectures have as one of their aims to show that this is not the case, that an admission of significant incommensurability and untranslatability in the relations between two opposed systems of thought and practice can be a prologue not only to rational debate, but to that kind of debate from which one party can emerge as undoubtedly rationally superior (see *Whose Justice? Which Rationality?* chapters XVII, XVIII, and XIX), if only because exposure to such debate may reveal that one of the contending standpoints fails in its own terms and by its own standards.

My concern at this point however is not to do justice to the detail of the various contending positions on this matter, but rather to remark how in the debate between the two principal opposing positions and the variety of alternatives to them which have been offered, the resolution of first-order differences on the substantive questions has been, so it seems, indefinitely deferred. For rival views on the issues of incommensurability and untranslatability provide rival interpretations of how those first-order differences are to be formulated, rival accounts of how the key texts of opposing parties are to be construed, and rival proposals concerning how debate should proceed further. So disagreements about disagreements are multiplied.

One effect of this, apparent at some key points in discussions both at Edinburgh and at Yale, is that premature attempts at debate between fundamentally opposed positions on fundamental issues are rendered sterile. Questions of detail can often be profitably pursued and were profitably pursued. But a large inability to use what was learned in such discussions in a way that could immediately reopen fundamental issues was evident, an inability which however derives not only from the variety of stances on issues of incommensurability and untranslatability.

It is always important not to confuse the consequences of intellectual positions with those of institutional arrangements. What appears to be an *impasse* resulting from the theoretical commitments of those involved in debate may sometimes, in part at least, be one brought about by institutional arrangements and social habits. And this is particularly important to remember when the effects of these latter reinforce attitudes stemming from and defined by theoretical and philosophical commitments—as is the case in the university today.

Whatever their origin, and it is certainly complex, nothing is more striking in the contemporary university than the extent of the apparently ineliminable continuing divisions and conflicts within *all* humanistic enquiry and not only on the questions raised in and by my lectures. In psychology psychoanalysts, Skinnerian behaviorists, and cognitive theorists are as far from resolving their differences as ever. In political enquiry Straussians, Neo-Marxists, and anti-ideological empiricists are at least as deeply antagonistic. In literary theory and history deconstructionists, historicists, heirs of I. A. Richards and readers and misreaders of Harold Bloom similarly contend. And in my lectures I have remarked upon the corresponding conflicts of contemporary philosophy.

From time to time, of course, attempts at synthesis or reconciliation between two or more such standpoints are announced, but never, it turns out, in terms acceptable to all contending parties and sometimes in terms acceptable to none. And more generally, what is striking about all these continuing divisions is the extent to which, whether in advancing their own enquiries or in criticizing their rivals, the adherents of each point of view tend to discuss in any depth only with those with whom they are already in fundamental agreement. One consequence is that within each partisan camp there has emerged a rough and ready agreement as to what weight is to be assigned to different types of reason in different types of context, but there is no general academic consensus on this within whole disciplines, let alone between disciplines. Yet at the same time there is an equally rough and ready general academic consensus, both within and between disciplines, as to what is to be accounted as at least some sort of relevant reason for upholding or advancing any particular conclusion.

Hence debate between fundamentally opposed standpoints does occur; but it is inevitably inconclusive. Each warring position characteristically appears irrefutable to its own adherents; indeed in its own terms and by its own standards of argument it *is* in practice irrefutable. But each warring position equally seems to its opponents to be insufficiently warranted by rational argument. It is ironic that the wholly secular humanistic disciplines of the late twentieth century should thus reproduce that very same condition which led their nineteenth-century secularizing predecessors to dismiss the claim of theology to be worthy of the status of an academic discipline.

The outcome can be summarized as follows. We have together produced a type of university in which teaching and enquiry in the humanities (and often enough also in the social sciences) are marked by four characteristics. There is first a remarkably high level of skill in handling narrow questions of limited detail: setting out the range of possible interpretations of this or that short passage, evaluating the validity of or identifying the presuppositions of this or that particular argument, summarizing the historical evidence relevant to dating some event or establishing the provenance of some work of art. Secondly, in a way which sometimes provides a direction for and a background to these exercises of professionalized skill, there is the promulgation of a number of large and mutually incompatible doctrines often conveyed by indirection and implication, the doctrines which define the major contending standpoints in each discipline. Thirdly, insofar as the warfare between these doctrines becomes part of public debate and discussion, the shared standards of argument are such that all debate is inconclusive. And yet, fourthly and finally, we still behave for the most part as if the university did still constitute a single, tolerably unified intellectual community, a form of behavior which testifies to the enduring effects of the encyclopaedists' conception of the unity of enquiry.

So there is still a reluctance, evident in some of the discussions at both Edinburgh and Yale, to allow that our divisions run so deep that we confront the claims of genuinely rival conceptions of rationality. And yet what those same discussions made plain was that nothing less than the question of what rationality is, in respect of all those subject matters of enquiry with which the humanities are concerned, is now posed by our conflicts. What I tried to achieve in these lectures was not only to present and to argue for one particular point of view in some of these conflicts, but also to give something at least of an overall view of the contending parties and of the terrain of conflict. What I had failed to appreciate as fully as I should have done when I first wrote the lectures, and what I learned to understand better from their reception at Edinburgh and at Yale, is the degree to which and the reasons why this too cannot be achieved in any way likely to secure general assent.

The experience therefore of participating twice over in the discussion of these lectures strongly reinforced the conclusion that such lectures can no longer be presented either on the basis of presupposed agreements or with the purpose of securing general agreement. The most that one can hope for is to render our disagreements more constructive. It was with that aim that I delivered these Gifford Lectures; it is with the same aim that I publish them.

I

Adam Gifford's Project in Context

It is a question of some interest to me, and I hope also to you, whether or not these lectures which I am about to deliver are in fact going to be Gifford Lectures. An answer will emerge only a good deal later, but the point of posing the question at the outset is clear. A Gifford lecturer is someone who is engaged in trying to implement Lord Gifford's will. And Adam Gifford's will is a document from a cultural milieu sufficiently alien to our own that the question of what fidelity to Adam Gifford's intentions would require may be somewhat more difficult than it has often been taken to be. A few early lecturers did explicitly concern themselves with the precise nature of those intentions: F. Max Muller, J. H. Stirling, Edward Caird, and Otto Pfleiderer. But for them a response was not difficult. Disparate as their standpoints were, they shared to some large degree Adam Gifford's presuppositions, just because they were participants with him in a common culture. But after those earliest lecturers, with a very few honorable exceptions the attention paid to Adam Gifford's intentions has commonly been at best cursory, perhaps because to do otherwise than to ignore them would have been embarrassing.

"I wish," wrote Adam Gifford in his will, "the lecturers to treat their subject as a strictly natural science . . . I wish it to be considered just as astronomy or chemistry is." Both F. Max Muller and Edward Caird addressed this issue, asking what would be involved in so doing. Both clearly took it to be one mark of a natural science that its history is one of rational progress in enquiry. And certainly in the hundred years which have elapsed since Adam Gifford's death, astronomy and chemistry have both exhibited continuous progress, so that it is possible to say relatively uncontroversially in what respects the astronomy and chemistry of 1988 are superior to those of 1888 and how this superiority was achieved. But with the subject matter prescribed for Gifford lecturers—that is, natural theology under-stood as comprehending within itself enquiry into the foundations of ethics— it has of course been quite otherwise. Not only has there been no progress in respect of generally agreed results of such en-quiries, but there is not even agreement as to what the standard of rational progress ought to be.

The evidence for this assertion is provided by a reading of the Gifford Lectures of the last hundred years, which collectively pro-vide a magnificent array of fundamental and unresolved disagree-ments, a kind of museum of intellectual conflict. Merely to rehearse the names of some of the lecturers is to reveal this: Josiah Royce, William James, and John Dewey; W. R. Sorley, A. E. Taylor, W. D. Ross, and A. MacBeath; A. C. Fraser, Karl Barth, and Rudolf Bult-mann; Etienne Gilson and Gabriel Marcel. To add to the list would only strengthen the impression that there is no conclusion arrived at by any Gifford lecturer upon almost any major topic which has not been denied by some other. What are the sources of this multi-plication of unresolved and apparently unresolvable disagreements? They are at least threefold.

First there has been and is among Gifford lecturers no generally accepted starting point for the enterprise, no set of first premises or principles upon which there is any consensus. Hence even when the arguments proceed, each from their own particular starting point, with some rigor, their conclusions are such as to compel rational as-sent only from those who were already in agreement upon where to begin. This particular source of disagreement is rooted in the multi-plicity and heterogeneity of the intellectual traditions and backgrounds of those selected as Gifford lecturers. Too many different and con-flicting philosophical and theological positions have found some voice in the lectures: idealism, empiricism, fideism, existentialism, Thom-ism, Calvinism. So the overall effect is one of controversy without *any* apparent movement towards a decisive outcome.

A second source of disagreement lies in the way in which char-acteristically the arguments in Gifford Lectures are organized. A set of relevant considerations are adduced which point towards rather than entail some conclusion which that particular lecturer wishes to establish. That those considerations are relevant and that, if a par-ticular kind of weight is attached to them, they do indeed provide support for the conclusion in question is generally not in doubt. But

as to why such weight or importance should be attached to this particular set of considerations but not to the members of certain other sets, the lecturers have generally been silent. And in this as in the range of their disagreements, they are typical of their culture. They speak as members of a culture in which the relevance of a wide range of disparate and often mutually incompatible considerations to conclusions concerning natural theology and the foundation of ethics is recognized, but in which there is no established agreement upon how these are to be ranked in importance or weight, such ranking being in practice largely a matter of individual preferences. And the degree of disagreement in such preferences is then reflected in the range of arguments with incompatible conclusions which are deployed.

Moreover it is important to remind ourselves that even the most rigorous logical analyses in and by themselves compel assent only to narrowly limited conclusions. For when it has been demonstrated that by affirming such and such *and* so and so, one has thereby logically committed oneself to affirming such and such else, the question of whether this consequence is or is not of such a kind as to provide one with sufficient grounds for rejecting the premises which entail it, always remains to be asked. By discovering what is entailed by a given set of statements we can discover what cost in additional commitments is attached to affirming that set of statements; what we cannot learn thereby is how to evaluate that cost or any corresponding benefit. And a reading of the Gifford Lectures of the last hundred years reveals that there has been among the lecturers no shared standard of value by which such intellectual costs and benefits may be evaluated.

Yet this is of course not merely the condition of those who have delivered sets of Gifford Lectures. It is more generally the condition of mid and late twentieth-century academic philosophy. The resources of such philosophy enable us to elucidate a variety of logical and conceptual relationships, so that we can chart the bearing of one set of beliefs upon another in respect of coherence and incoherence and in so doing exhibit as the shared inheritance of the discipline of academic philosophy a minimal conception of rationality. But whenever and insofar as philosophers proceed to conclusions of a more substantive kind, they do so by invoking one out of a number of rival and conflicting more substantial conceptions of rationality, conceptions upon which they have been as unable to secure rational agreement in the philosophical profession as have Gifford lecturers in expounding *their* rival and competing claims concerning natural theology and the foundations of ethics.

This inability to secure more than minimal agreement within philosophy upon how it is rational to proceed in respect of the formation and criticism of beliefs is rooted in the same three factors which underlie the lack of consensus among Gifford lecturers: the absence of any agreement upon where the justification of belief ought to begin, the *de facto* ineliminable conflicts as to how various relevant types of considerations ought to be ranked in weight and importance as reasons for holding particular sets of beliefs, and the limited resources provided for reasoning about the justification of beliefs by even the most subtle and rigorous analysis of entailment relations.

It is not of course that philosophers of each particular contending school and party do not supplement the inadequate resources of a shared minimum rationality by schemes of argument which enable them to transcend the limitations of that shared minimum. Scientific materialists, Heideggerians, possible-worlds theorists, phenomenologists, Wittgensteinians, and a host of others all do so; but there exists no generally agreed way of resolving the issues which divide the protagonists of these alternative and incompatible standpoints. Consider just how wide the range of their disagreements is, not only between the adherents of such rival standpoints, but also between the protagonists of rival formulations and arguments within such standpoints. The subjects of such disagreements include: questions about the methods and style appropriate to philosophical inquiry, issues concerning which concepts are to be assigned a fundamental and central place in framing philosophical theories, accounts of meaning, reference, and the place of language in the natural and social world, the way in which the relationship of mind to body is to be understood, and—inseparable from all of these and from the bearing that theses and arguments on each of these topics has on at least some of the others—the standards by which one particular mode of procedure and inquiry or one particular theory or account is to be judged rationally superior to others.

The *de facto* unresolvable character of these conflicts and disagreements supports a conclusion parallel to one already arrived at in respect of other subject matters by some historians and philosophers of science and by some anthropologists. For just as some historians and philosophers of science have identified in different periods of the history of physics different and incompatible standards governing rational choice between rival theories and indeed different standards concerning what is to be accounted an intelligible theory, so that between those rival claims there is no way of adjudicating rationally by appeal to some further neutral standard, and just as some social anthropologists have identified rival moral and religious systems as similarly incommensurable, so it appears that within modern philosophy there occurs the kind of irreconcilable division and interminable disagreement which is to be explained only by incommensurability. So general is the scope and so systematic the character of some at least of these disagreements that it is not too much to speak of rival conceptions of rationality, both theoretical and practical.

This is a thought not at all unfamiliar in recent French writing about the history of ideas. But it is one which has too rarely been entertained by English-speaking philosophers about their own discipline. One outcome of education into professionalization has been that philosophers generally treat every philosophical disagreement as somehow or other and in the end rationally resolvable, without asking how far off that end may be. Their attention is for the most part focussed upon, and their colleagues are generally evaluated with reference to, the kind of immediate progress that can be made within some local framework of agreement about particular well-defined problems or issues. About those with whom their larger disagreements are inescapably obvious they are all too often either dismissive ("*That* is not really philosophy") or assimilative ("A careful reading of Heidegger reveals that he is *really* only saying what Wittgenstein said"). And of course incommensurability itself has become one more topic for standard philosophical discussion, its very occurrence denied by some philosophers. So the facts of intractable and systematic disagreement are simultaneously all too familiar and yet all too readily passed over in practice. And this condition of contemporary philosophy in which systematic disagreement upon fundamental issues extends to disagreement over how such disagreements are to be formulated and characterized, let alone resolved, is clearly the same condition which was already beginning to manifest itself in the fields of natural theology and the foundations of ethics in all but the earliest series of Gifford Lectures and whose presence has become all the more evident during the ten decades in which Gifford Lectures have since been delivered.

To understand this is already to have recognized one major respect in which the culture of later Gifford lecturers is so radically different from that of Adam Gifford himself as to put in question the possibility of *their*, of *our* being able to give effect to the intentions expressed in *his* will. For Adam Gifford and almost all his educated Edinburgh contemporaries it was a guiding presupposition of thought that substantive rationality is unitary, that there is a single, if perhaps complex, conception of what the standards and the achievements of rationality are, one which every educated person can without too much difficulty be brought to agree in acknowledging. The application of the methods and goals of this single and unitary conception to any one particular distinctive subject matter is what yields a science. And that natural theology and the study of the foundations of ethics jointly constitute in this sense a science, just as astronomy does and just as chemistry does, Adam Gifford, once again like the vast majority of his educated Edinburgh contemporaries, had no doubt.

It is therefore important to spell out in more detail this conception of a science and how it dominated intellectually Adam Gifford's immediate society; to do so we need to place that conception in its social and intellectual context. About Gifford's own views and standpoint we have two sources. One is a memoir by his brother, John Gifford; the other a collection of *Lectures Delivered on Various Occasions* put together after the author's death by his niece and his son (for the memoir and extracts from the lectures see Stanley L. Jaki *Lord Gifford and His Lectures*, Edinburgh, 1986). If we add to these two books the text of the will, we confront an intellectual portrait of Adam Gifford which reveals him as, although his own person, still also a representative figure of his cultural time and place. He was, for example, until finally stricken down by paralysis in 1881, in demand as a speaker on literary and philosophical topics to a variety of local groups and societies, as must have been many of his legal, academic, and clerical contemporaries. For such societies and their meetings were important to a nineteenth-century culture informed by a widespread discussion of and respect for general ideas. Scotland's was not the only such culture; a similar mode of intellectual and social life was also to be found in French provincial towns. In Scotland these societies represented the wider democratization of a distinctive habit of mind, cultivated through a type of university education in which student discussion and debate on philosophical and cultural topics played a key part. Especially important were the societies which, particularly in Edinburgh, perpetuated into postuniversity life among lawyers, professors, and other teachers and the clergy the same kind of intellectual experience. In Adam Gifford's maturity the most important example was the New Speculative Society, which was founded in Edinburgh, but as William Knight, professor of philosophy at St. Andrews, recorded, "afterwards divided into three sections which met at Edinburgh, Glasgow, and St. Andrews." Its members "desired that the ultimate questions of human existence should be freely discussed on philosophical grounds. . . ." The force of "freely" is clear. John Inglis, Lord President of the Court of Session and chairman of the commission set up by the Universities of Scotland Act of 1858, had chided his fellow-countrymen in 1868 for believing falsely that before the repeal of the tests which had excluded dissenters from university teaching posts until 1852, philosophy in Scotland had been in any substantial way the victim of religious intolerance. But however justified Inglis's reminder of the real freedom of the past may have been, it is clear that many of his contemporaries did believe, and with perhaps some warrant, not only that it was they alone who had at last in their generation freed themselves from the imposed dogma of the past, but that from time to time the reassertion of that freedom was still required.

After all, paradoxically the campaign to eliminate religious tests had been designed to enable a philosophical nonentity, Patrick Campbell Macdougall of the Free Church, to occupy the Edinburgh chair of moral philosophy, and the preference for the unqualified Macdougall over the highly qualified Ferrier had been entirely a matter of the former's evangelical orthodoxy. In 1881 a five-year long investigation of William Robertson Smith's alleged heresies concerning the Bible terminated with his removal from the Old Testament chair in the Free Church college of Aberdeen. (See J. S. Black and G. W. Chrystal *The Life of William Robertson Smith,* London, 1912). And one consequence of F. Max Muller's first series of Gifford Lectures at Glasgow was an unsuccessful attempt to bring not dissimilar charges before the Glasgow presbytery of the Church of Scotland, proceedings which Muller ascribed to the hostile propaganda of local Roman Catholic priests.

It is important to recognize that in all these proceedings, and in the consequent assertiveness with respect to freedom from the imposition of religious tests which we find exemplified in the provisions of Adam Gifford's will, two distinct kinds of issue were at stake. That the particular actions of those who installed Macdougall in his chair, ejected Robertson Smith from his, and attempted to exercise ecclesiastical control of the Gifford Lectures were in fact bad actions, fettering and thus damaging enquiry to no good purpose, is something with which it is not difficult to agree. But in making the further assumption that the imposition of religious tests as such, the requirement of a certain type of commitment and of the acceptance of a certain type of authority as a precondition for entering upon enquiry, had thereby been shown to be unjustified, the Edinburgh *bien-pensants* of that age adopted a principle which not only can be put in question, but which needs to be put in question if we are to understand the culture of Adam Gifford and his circle.

What was rightly objected to in the condemnation of Robertson Smith was the invocation of orthodoxy in order to effect an arbitrary exclusion from enquiry of the consideration of certain kinds of data, data relevant, in his case, to determining the chronology and authorship of the Pentateuch. But accompanying this justified objection was an unargued belief that in all enquiry, religious, moral, or otherwise, the adequate identification, characterization, and classification of the relevant data does not require, and indeed may preclude any prior commitment to some particular theoretical or doctrinal standpoint. The data, so to speak, present themselves and speak for themselves. Hence of course was derived belief in the wrongheadedness of imposing any test of commitment to any theoretical or doctrinal standpoint upon those who are to consider such data.

What was at issue here is perhaps easier for us to recognize now than it was for Gifford and his contemporaries. They had indeed learned both from the philosophical influence of the successors of Reid and Stewart and from the heirs of Kant, especially through the teaching of Sir William Hamilton, that what is given to perception and observation is always already informed by concepts and judgments. They were not empiricists in the mode of either Hume or Mill and they did not believe in what Sellars has called the myth of "the given." But it was part of what I am calling their unitary conception of rationality and of the rational mind that they took it for granted not only that all rational persons conceptualize data in one and the same way and that therefore any attentive and honest observer, unblinded and undistracted by the prejudices of prior commitment to belief, would report the same data, the same facts, but also that it is the data thus reported and characterized which provide enquiry with its subject matter.

We by contrast have learned from Gaston Bachelard, Thomas Kuhn, and others that, relative to any particular type of enquiry, there are always at least two modes of conceptualizing and characterizing the data which constitute its subject matter, a pretheoretical (although not of course preconceptual) prior-to-enquiry mode and a mode internal to that particular type of enquiry which already presupposes one particular theoretical or doctrinal stance and commitment rather than another. So, to use Kuhn's example, where those innocent of enquiry see and report a stone swinging from a line, a theoretically committed Aristotelian will observe an instance of constrained natural motion, an adherent of Galileo a pendulum. The criteria for the identity of everyday objects and persons are indeed pretheoretical, so that we are able to assert that it is one and the same swinging stone which is observed by both Aristotelian and Galilean physicists. But there is no way of identifying, characterizing, or classifying that particular datum in a way relevant to the purposes of theoretical enquiry except in terms of some prior theoretical or doctrinal commitment (see Thomas S. Kuhn *The Structure of Scientific Revolutions,* second edition, Chicago, 1971, chapter X).

What is true of physical enquiry holds also for theological and moral enquiry. What are taken to be the relevant data and how they are identified, characterized, and classified will depend upon who is performing these tasks and what his or her theological and moral standpoint and perspective is. In what ways and respects this is so it will be important at a later point in the argument to specify in some detail. What has to be noticed immediately is that the hostility to the imposition of religious tests which Adam Gifford shared with so many of his contemporaries prevented any recognition even of the possibility that commitment to some particular theoretical or doctrinal standpoint may be a prerequisite for—rather than a barrier to—an ability to characterize data in a way which will enable enquiry to proceed. So there is an intimate connection in Adam Gifford's will between the clauses prohibiting religious tests and his particular conception of natural theology and of the study of the foundation of ethics as a natural science, a conception which not only informed Adam Gifford's private convictions but was generally presupposed in the milieu constituted by the societies and groups in whose discussions he participated.

That there was such a large identity between Adam Gifford's views and those generally dominant in his culture is evident if we compare what we know of the former from his own writings and from the memoir by his brother with what became the canonical expression of the Edinburgh culture of Adam Gifford's day, the Ninth Edition of the *Encyclopaedia Britannica*. It was a leading member of the New Speculative Society, Thomas Spencer Baynes, who edited the Ninth Edition in Edinburgh from 1873 onwards, together after 1880 with none other than William Robertson Smith, whose indictment for heresy had been first directed against the articles 'Angel' and 'Bible' which he had contributed to the second and third volumes. When Baynes died in 1887, the year also of Adam Gifford's death, Robertson Smith succeeded him as editor.

Baynes was one of that long line of English dissenters who had come to Edinburgh for their education; here he became Hamilton's favorite pupil and assistant. He had an admirably comprehensive view of the British intellectual scene, probably understanding more of the strengths and weaknesses of the universities in both Scotland and England than did any of his contemporaries. And his own versatility was exhibited by his chair at St. Andrews in logic, metaphysics, and English literature, his Hamiltonian treatise on *The Analytic of Logical Forms,* the article on 'Shakespeare' which he contributed to the Ninth Edition, and his translation of the Port-Royal *Logic.* In his preface to the first volume of the Ninth Edition, Baynes made it clear that he intended his contributors not merely to provide detailed information on every major topic but to do so within the framework of a distinctive architectonic of the sciences as that had emerged in the late nineteenth century. The subdivisions of biology were to be organized in terms of new conceptions of the transformations of species; here Baynes's adviser was T. H. Huxley, whose botanist assistant W. T. Thiselton-Dyer wrote the article 'Biology.' The subdivisions of physics were to be organized with an eye to equally new conceptions of kinetic energy; here Baynes was advised by J. Clerk Maxwell, who before his death in 1879 wrote a paper for Baynes on the classificatory ordering of the physical sciences which appeared in volume 19 as the article 'Physical Sciences.'

Those sciences which study what is distinctively human also exhibit what Baynes called "the progress of science," and in this case the encyclopaedia articles, he claims, will not merely report, but will themselves advance that progress: "The available facts of human history, collected over the widest areas, are carefully coordinated and grouped together, in the hope of ultimately evolving the laws of progress, moral and material, which underlie them, and which will help to connect and interpret the whole movement of the race" (vol. 1, p. vii). What the Encyclopaedia presents "has to do with knowledge rather than opinion" (p. viii). And that is to say, although Baynes would certainly have hesitated to say it, that the Ninth Edition pointed its reader towards some future edition in which the *Britannica* would in an important way have displaced the Bible by offering a more comprehensive overview, within which the writings of the Bible, duly scrutinized by the relevant scholars, would be understood as sources of data both for particular sciences and for the overview afforded by the architectonic ordering of the sciences. The Encyclopaedia would have displaced the Bible as the canonical book, or set of books, of the culture.

I do not want to give the false impression that Baynes's contributors all agreed entirely with him or each other. The most important of them were men and women – the women contributors were few but notable, among them Hamilton's daughter, who wrote the article on her father – whose own thought was in movement and who in the future would move in very different directions. Nonetheless, Baynes represents a distinctive moment in the history of nineteenth-century thought in which it did appear to a great many otherwise very different thinkers that a comprehensive scientific synthesis was at hand. So Baynes articulated both for his contributors and for his readers a powerful ideological vision of the nature and outcome of enquiry. It is a version within which sciences such as astronomy and chemistry on the one hand and natural theology and the study of the foundation of ethics on the other are assigned coordinate places. And to read Adam Gifford's will, as well as other expressions of his views, alongside the Ninth Edition is to recognize a large coincidence of vision in this respect.

What then was a science taken to be within this particular framework? Sciences were generally taken to be individuated by their subject matter, not by their methods. In the Ninth Edition there was only one example of a science in good standing and good order (the only science not in good order was 'Political Economy,' which J. Kells Ingram diagnosed as in grave crisis both as regards methods and subject matter) not so individuated, that treated of in the article on 'Logic' by Robert Adamson. And this is because Adamson identifies the province of logic with that of what he calls "the critical theory of knowledge," a science whose subject matter consists of the methods of the sciences, including its own, so that it is definable indifferently by subject matter or by methods. In all sciences there seem to be four constitutive elements: first there are the data, the facts, and here the sciences of the nineteenth century were held to have at last provided the degree of comprehensiveness necessary to reason adequately from the facts. Secondly there are the unifying synthetic conceptions supplied by methodical reflection upon the facts; if such reflection begins from a true and adequate comprehension of the facts and if it is informed by adequate inventiveness, it will supply unifying conceptions which order the facts by making them intelligible as exemplifying laws. And thirdly there are the methods so employed, the methods by which we move from facts to unifying conceptions in theoretical discovery and from such conceptions back to the facts in the work both of explanation and of confirmation of our theories. Fourthly, as we noticed earlier, it was taken to be the outcome of the successful application of methods to facts that there is continuous progress in supplying ever more adequate unifying conceptions which specify ever more fundamental laws. So it is characteristic of genuine science, as contrasted with the thought of the prescientific and the nonscientific, that it has a particular kind of history, one of relatively continuous progress.

It is important to remark that an understanding of science thus conceived, an understanding both of at least the central details of each science and of the significance of the architectonic ordering of the sciences, was taken by Baynes and by many of his contributors to be an essential part of the general culture of the educated person. There was not for them, as there is for us, a large gap between the science of the professional scientists and science as it is presented to outsiders. For them a properly organized account of the science of the scientists spoke both to the scientists themselves and to those outside. T. H. Huxley's writings were in some ways their model, but nearer home in Edinburgh was Agnes Mary Clerke, author of *A Popular History of Astronomy during the Nineteenth Century,* published in

1885, and of the lives of the astronomers in the Ninth Edition. Clerke endorsed the educational views of Baron Friedrich Heinrich Alexander von Humboldt—she wrote the article on him in the Ninth Edition while his brother, Karl Wilhelm, at that period treated as a less notable figure, was the subject of a much shorter article by A. H. Sayce—and it was Humboldt's vision of the ordering of the academic disciplines as mirroring the order of the cosmos itself (he had published the two volumes of *Kosmos* in 1845 and 1847), an ordering progressively revealed by the history of science, which informed not only Clerke's own historical and scientific work but the whole enterprise of the Ninth Edition.

Clerke's life must have seemed to her contemporaries to exhibit just the kind of moral progress which they took to accompany scientific progress. She had moved from the sheltered life of a girl in a Protestant family in West Cork—two decades earlier and one social class lower than Edith Somerville and Martin Ross—to private study in Italy, which culminated in her submitting an article on 'Copernicus in Italy' to the *Edinburgh Review* in 1877. She took her place among the foremost minds of the age and when Adam Gifford wrote of the sciences of astronomy and chemistry in his will, it may well be that it was her book of the same year which he had in mind.

What the human sciences explained was how someone like Clerke had become possible. To the four elements of the sciences of nature—data, unifying conceptions, methods, and a history of continuous progress—they added a fifth self-referential characteristic. The human sciences, like all natural sciences, exhibit progress in enquiry, but progress of all kinds, moral, scientific, technological, theological, is their central subject matter and conceptions of progress and of its inevitability are among their most important unifying conceptions. So the sciences concerned with the distinctively human were taken to reveal to us a law-governed history whose climax so far is their own emergence. Where once the savage, the primitive, and the superstitious prevailed, there are now Adam Gifford, Thomas Spencer Baynes, and Agnes Mary Clerke.

In all history but perhaps particularly in the history of moral beliefs and practices the primitive, the savage, and the superstitious are thus seen as the inferior precursors of enlightenment. J. G. Frazer's article on 'Taboo' provided a backcloth to Henry Sidgwick's account of the history of reflective moral thought in the article 'Ethics,' and

Edward Burnett Tylor in the article 'Anthropology' provided a key part of the framework within which both are to be understood. In a not dissimilar way Robertson Smith's article 'Bible' provided a backcloth to Robert Flint's article 'Theology.' Robert Flint is the most unjustly forgotten philosopher of the nineteenth century. He had been Baynes's colleague at St. Andrews in the chair of moral philosophy before he moved to the chair of divinity in Edinburgh in 1876. He was at home in French and Italian philosophy at a time when Scots philosophers commonly looked to Germany. And he wrote the first book in English, and a remarkably good book, on Vico. It is all the more impressive to find how much he, despite his atypicality, agreed with the consensus of the Ninth Edition. The question to which Flint aspired to give an answer in the article 'Theology' he expressed as "What . . . is truly scientific knowledge in Theology?" And in his conception of a science he was at one with his fellow contributors, his editor, and Adam Gifford. So he begins with the data, both the data of nature which furnish the starting point for natural theology and those provided by the Bible which furnish the starting point for a theology of revelation. The subject matter of theology is religion, but that delimitation does not exclude God from that subject matter. For religious experience is experience *of* God and the inescapability of the objectivity of God as the object both of religious experience and of theological reflection is reported as one of the findings of theology as a science. Failure to appreciate this by agnostics and atheists is due to a distorting one-sidedness in their mode of apprehending that whole whose parts are the data of theology.

Natural theology, for Flint as for Gifford, was a science still in the making. And to a very large degree the project set out in Adam Gifford's will, if further understood in the light of his own writings and of his brother's reports of his views, is, as I have already suggested, at one with the conceptions of science and of rational progress in enquiry shared by the editors of and contributors to the Ninth Edition. In one of his *Lectures* Adam Gifford too spoke of there being inevitable progress in "the advance and improvement of ethics" (p. 273). And he laid the same emphasis as did the contributors to the Ninth Edition on a method which begins at the right point: "If first principles have not been truly carried out . . . then be sure that sooner or later we must begin again, for nature will find out our failure . . ." (p. 250). But there is one respect in which, while he agreed with

Robert Flint, he and Flint together are at odds with the central positions of the Ninth Edition.

For Baynes the whole of which the subordinate sciences are parts is the encyclopaedia itself. The organizing discipline which from the separate sciences yields the encyclopaedic whole is philosophy. So Andrew Seth (later A. S. Pringle-Pattison) wrote in the article 'Philosophy' that "Philosophy claims to be the science of the whole . . . the synthesis of the parts is something more than that detailed knowledge of the parts in separation which is gained by the man of science." For Adam Gifford, as for Robert Flint, this overarching view is to be provided not by philosophy, but by theology, and for Adam Gifford more specifically by natural theology. This was why in his will he called natural theology "the greatest of all possible sciences, indeed, in one sense, the only science . . ." The idiom which he used in his will is reminiscent of Spinoza's and this was no accident. Although his brother makes it clear that Adam Gifford was not himself a Spinozist, he saw in Spinoza's conception of a science which comprehends both God and nature the forerunner of the kind of all-inclusive understanding which is, on his view as on that of the major contributors to the Ninth Edition, the goal of enquiry.

This understanding of natural theology made it appropriate for the implementation of Adam Gifford's will to be entrusted to those who shared to some large degree at least the conception of science and of the ordering of the sciences which had dominated the Ninth Edition. So that it is unsurprising to find among the earliest Gifford lecturers so many of the *Britannica* contributors; F. Max Muller, Edward Caird, Edward Burnett Tylor, R. B. Haldane, Andrew Seth, J. G. Frazer, James Ward, A. H. Sayce, and Robert Flint were all both contributors to the Ninth Edition and Gifford lecturers. But of course it is just that in their thought which made it appropriate for them to implement Adam Gifford's will which suggests that it may be inappropriate for us to undertake the same task. The key beliefs and concepts which they shared to at least a significant if varying degree with Adam Gifford are what separate us from both him and them.

What divides our culture from theirs is, as we have seen, at least threefold. They assumed the assent of all educated persons to a single substantive conception of rationality; we inhabit a culture a central feature of which is the presence of, and to some degree a debate between, conflicting, alternative conceptions of rationality. They understood the outcome of allegiance to the standards and methods of such a rationality to be the elaboration of a comprehensive, rationally incontestable scientific understanding of the whole, in which the architectonic of the sciences matched that of the cosmos. We are confronted with a multiplicity of types of enquiry and of interpretative claims on their behalf, so that the very concept of an ordered whole, of a cosmos, has been put radically in question. And finally they saw their whole mode of life, including their conceptions of rationality and of science, as part of a history of inevitable progress, judged by a standard of progress which had itself emerged from that history. The progress of science and reason had on their view been uneven, interrupted by external factors; but rupture and discontinuity were always the result of temporary alien intrusion into that history. That the history of rationality and science might itself *be* a history of ruptures and discontinuities was for them an unthinkable thought. So that in recognizing the occurrence, and in the light of the work of Bachelard, Polanyi, Kuhn, and Foucault, the importance of rupture and discontinuity, we are once again exhibiting an awareness that Adam Gifford's project for his lecturers was devised on the basis of assumptions and within the context of a culture which are not and cannot be our assumptions and our culture. So the question arises: are Gifford lectures any longer possible? But this question is ambiguous. If it means 'Is a systematic enquiry concerning the subject matter of natural theology and of the foundation of ethics of the kind envisaged by Adam Gifford still possible?' the evidence already provided compels the answer 'No.' If however it means 'Is a systematic and fruitful enquiry, historically continuous with those of traditional natural theology, including the foundation of ethics, but of some other very different kind from that envisaged by Adam Gifford still possible?' then we are confronted with an impressive contemporary case for answering 'No,' but also with a contemporary case, albeit necessarily a very different one from Adam Gifford's, for answering 'Yes.' And the central issue with which I shall be concerned in these lectures is what it is that divides the protagonists of these rival answers. Both those contemporary contending parties agree in rejecting the assumptions and beliefs characteristic of the Ninth Edition of the *Encyclopaedia Britannica,* but while the one points us towards the possibility of a radical renovation of a project which Adam Gifford, had he lived to the age of one hundred and sixty-eight, might perhaps after all have recognized as corresponding in some significant way to his own, the other aspires to write an epitaph for such enquiry once and for all.

Each of these two contending parties has its own foundation document. For the latter it is *Zur Genealogie der Moral* published by Nietzsche in 1887, the year of Adam Gifford's death. What *Zur Genealogie der Moral* provided was not only an argument in favor of, but a paradigm for, the construction of a type of subversive narrative designed to undermine the central assumptions of the Encyclopaedia, both in content and in genre. Where the encyclopaedist aspired to displace the Bible as a canonical book, the genealogist intended to discredit the whole notion of a canon. For the other rival party its charter document is the encyclical letter *Aeterni Patris* published by Pope Leo XIII in 1879, four years after the Ninth Edition commenced publication. *Aeterni Patris* summoned its readers to a renewal of an understanding of intellectual enquiry as the continuation of a specific type of tradition, that which achieved definitive expression in the writings of Aquinas, one the appropriation of which could not only provide the resources for radical criticism of the conception of rationality dominant in nineteenth-century modernity and in the Ninth Edition, but also preserve and justify the canonical status of the Bible as distinct from, yet hegemonic over, all secular enquiry. Each of these two documents bears the marks of its time and place of origin as clearly as does Adam Gifford's will. It will therefore be important to ask why, after the transformations of the intervening hundred years, they are able to play a part in defining the conflicts of the present in a way in which Adam Gifford's will is not. But in order to ask and answer this question effectively, it is necessary to focus the enquiry further by delimiting it.

When Adam Gifford in his will put in last place in the list of topics prescribed for his lectures "the Knowledge of the Nature and Foundation of Ethics or Morals, and of all Obligations and Duties thence arising," he did not intend to specify an area of enquiry distinct from or independent of the enquiries of natural theology. For in his lecture on 'The two Fountains of Jurisprudence' he had declared that he took it to be a matter of demonstration "that there is an eternal and unchangeable system and scheme of morality and ethics, founded not on the will, or on the devices, or in the ingenuity of man, but on the nature and essence of the unchangeable God."

If therefore in these lectures I focus upon questions about the nature and status of morality and about the nature of enquiry into such questions, Adam Gifford would not have supposed that in so doing I was departing from the area in which natural theology is sovereign; and I shall later suggest that about this he was in the right and that, even when we have rejected, as we cannot avoid doing, some of the central beliefs of Adam Gifford and of his Edinburgh contemporaries, we shall discover that it is in part because he held that enquiry into God and enquiry into the good are not separable that we are still able to identify a project not Adam Gifford's own but one which a later Adam Gifford *might*—just possibly—have been able to recognize as his own.

I begin then by asking what morality was for Adam Gifford's culture. It had five important characteristics. First, morality was a distinct and relatively autonomous area of beliefs, attitudes, and rule-following activity, ordered in accordance with a scheme of rigid compartmentalization of life. *The* moral was sharply and clearly distinguished from *the* aesthetic, *the* religious, *the* economic, *the* legal, and *the* scientific. Secondly, morality was primarily a matter of rule-following and of ritualized responses to breaches of rules: to others by utterances of moral condemnation, especially by those who were fathers or clergymen, to oneself by reproaches of conscience. Thirdly, the rules, breaches of which chiefly invited such condemnations and reproaches, were *negative* prohibitions. There were of course positive injunctions as well, but the penalties of condemnation and of exclusion from particular areas of social life were peculiarly attached to breaches of the negative rules. Fourthly, this was a culture in which strong notions of impropriety attached to violations of the compartmentalizing boundaries of social life. To know what conversation, what manners, what clothing was appropriate and proper to whom, where, and when was indispensable social and moral knowledge. Euphemism and circumlocution safeguarded these proprieties. And impropriety was itself understood to be a species of immorality. Fifthly and finally, social agreement, especially in practice, on the importance and the content of morality coexisted with large intellectual disagreements concerning the nature of its rational justification, both agreement and disagreement being underpinned by a shared conviction that morality, thus understood, must be such as to be rationally justifiable somehow or other.

The evidence for this characterization of morality as a phenomenon of the Scottish, and not only of the Scottish, late Victorian bourgeoisie has been provided by social historians; but its presence, both in what was said and in what was left unsaid, is in any
case pervasive and evident in many articles of the Ninth Edition. Both
in characterizing it as I have, and in identifying its presence in the
Ninth Edition, I have been guided by what Franz Steiner wrote in
his posthumously published lectures on *Taboo* (London, 1956). It
was, so Steiner claimed, significant that the nineteenth-century discovery by Europeans of taboo customs in Polynesia and the attempt
to understand them as examples of a type of custom found in other
societies classified by them as primitive were first made by Protestants
and then by Victorian rationalists, some of them, like Robertson
Smith, Protestants engaged in transforming themselves into rationalists. "The problem of taboo," Steiner wrote, "became extraordinarily
prominent in the Victorian age for two reasons: the rationalist approach to religion and the place of taboo in Victorian society itself "
(p. 50). Taboo was both a problem and a solution for the Victorians, because in the taboo customs of Polynesia they saw what they
took to be primitive anticipations of their own scheme of rational
ethics, but in a form disfigured by superstitious conceptions of the
sacred and of sacred power and by a failure to distinguish genuine
moral rules from arbitrary and irrational prohibitions. When therefore they read in the Old Testament—a set of texts which they took
to represent some earlier stages in the progress from the primitivism still to be found in Polynesia to the high morality of the late
nineteenth-century Edinburgh drawing room—rules, attitudes, and
practices alien to that high morality, they followed Robertson Smith
in using Tylor's concept of a survival in order to distinguish what were
mere crude survivals from primitivism from what were genuine anticipations of, or already identical with, their own apprehension of
what they took to be the timeless truths of morality. Taboo was thus
something from which the Victorians of the Ninth Edition believed
that they had separated themselves. And they saw in the less enlightened persons to be found in the Free Church and among Roman
Catholics—the sort of person who had supported the charges against
Robertson Smith or had objected to F. Max Muller's Gifford Lectures—beliefs and attitudes that were still infected with the contagion of primitivism and superstition in the form of taboo.

In this they were, so Steiner argued and so I shall want to argue in a way that goes beyond Steiner's thesis, profoundly self-deceived. For they had only been able to understand Polynesian taboo as a primitive and deformed anticipation of their own morality because, in their characterization of the Polynesians and others, they had in key respects projected upon the Polynesians and others a variant of their own moral scheme. They misunderstood taboo rules of the Polynesians as primarily negative prohibitions, rather than as merely the negative side of enabling prescriptions, just because their own rules were primarily negative; they saw the connections between the rules and other elements in taboo customs as an arbitrary mingling of what to rational persons should have been discrete and separated, because they took for granted their own compartmentalization of social life. And they were blind to the local and parochial nature of their own assimilation of impropriety to immorality, just because they imputed to contingent features of their own morality a universality which they took to be the mark of rationality. All cultures are of course ethnocentric and few are genuinely aware of the degree of their own ethnocentricity. In both respects educated Edinburgh of the Ninth Edition was no exception to the human norm.

What was thereby obscured from their view was the possibility of posing two questions about their own morality. Those questions can be formulated in terms of Henry Sidgwick's *Britannica* article on 'Ethics.' That article is almost entirely historical and the history is written in such a way as to presuppose just that distinctness of morality as a phenomenon which was so characteristic of the age. Nowhere does Sidgwick take notice, for example, of the fact that the word 'morality' as used by his contemporaries has no equivalent expression in biblical or medieval Hebrew or in either classical or *koinē* Greek, or in either classical or high medieval Latin; and if he or any of his contemporaries had taken notice of this linguistic fact, its significance for them would presumably be only that the speakers of such languages had not yet recognized the distinctiveness or the autonomy of morality. Sidgwick's falsifying history thus projected back into the past the conceptual structuring of the author's present and thereby suggested that Plato and Aristotle, Hobbes, Spinoza, and Kant and Sidgwick himself were all offering accounts, albeit rival accounts, of the rational status of one and the same timeless subject matter. And what on this view Adam Gifford was doing was inviting his lecturers to complete the task so far left uncompleted, even after the long history of progress up to this point, by showing how the timeless truths of morality find their place within that whole of which he believed every part of everything whatsoever to be a part, that which Gifford in his will called "the Infinite, the All . . ." A question which neither Sidgwick nor Gifford nor their culture in general was able to frame was whether the tasks of the rational elucidation of the status of moral rules and the rational justification of obedience to them had not been finally carried through, not merely because some present or future philosopher had yet to succeed where Plato, Aristotle, Hobbes, Kant, and Sidgwick had all in some degree failed—and, in thus succeeding, to make the progress of ethics definitive in the same way that Darwin and Clerk Maxwell had made the progress of biology and of physics definitive—but because in fact morality, conceived as that late Victorian culture conceived it, is not in significant and central respects susceptible of rational justification. They were unable, that is to say, to envisage the possibility that both morality and rationality ought to be understood in a way which would make much of what they took to be morality appear as irrational and as arbitrary as the taboo customs of the Polynesians appeared to them.

A second unasked question was closely related. It was whether morality, understood as these late Victorians understood it, might not itself after all be what Tylor termed a survival, or a set of survivals, that is, rules, attitudes, and responses which had once been at home within some larger context in terms of which their intelligibility had been spelled out and their rationality justified but which had become detached from that context. Were it such, its discreteness, its separateness from other social phenomena would be a sign, not of its universality, but of its being a fragment, broken off and thus separated from something else, a connection to which human beings had by the late nineteenth century become blind.

Both the contemporary contending parties of which I spoke earlier treat these two questions as crucial and they would agree in understanding the morality of the culture of Adam Gifford and the Ninth Edition as in important respects an irrational survival, to be understood in terms of a narrative of historical contingency. As to which respects and as to the character of that narrative they would of course be in radical disagreement with each other. Those whose intellectual history derives from *Aeterni Patris* tell a very different tale from those who are the heirs of *Zur Genealogie der Moral*. From the standpoint of *Aeterni Patris* the morality of the Victorian nineteenth century was the outcome of a degeneration from a theory and practice of natural and divine law, an understanding of which had been elaborated within that theological tradition whose definitive statement was by Aquinas. From the standpoint of *Zur Genealogie der Moral* the morality of the Victorian nineteenth century was only the latest version of a reactive, herd morality in which enmity to the biologically vital was masked by the false pretensions of reason. Moreover in the perspective afforded by *Zur Genealogie der Moral* the doctrines of *Aeterni Patris* are only in minor and unimportant respects distinguishable from those of Victorian rationalism. Nietzsche's diagnosis of the sickness afflicting the post-Enlightenment thinkers of his own age was not so different from his diagnosis of the ills of Catholic Christianity, while in the perspective afforded by *Aeterni Patris* Nietzsche's doctrines are one more variant of the characteristic errors of nineteenth-century modernity. Yet the partisans of both documents at least agreed and agree in separating themselves in a decisive way from the morality of Adam Gifford's milieu.

Earlier I had argued that the conception of a science and the corresponding conception of rationality as unitary which are presupposed by Adam Gifford's will are ones which we can no longer share. Now I am adding to that the thesis that it is not only that our conceptions of enquiry and of rationality may be too much at odds with those of Adam Gifford for us to be able to fulfil his intention, but also that that about which we are to enquire is, at least in the case of morality, something which we cannot understand as Adam Gifford understood it. Thus at the very least we are inescapably involved in conducting an enquiry of a kind very different from any which he envisaged into a subject matter understood in a way very different from that which he understood himself to be presenting. And this does put once more in question whether, even had he survived to the present, Adam Gifford could have recognized our enquiries as a version, even a remote version, of what he understood.

Yet at this point it is important to remember one clause from the will: "the lecturers shall be under no restraint whatever in their treatment of their theme." It is the reckless generosity of this clause that makes it clear that after all Adam Gifford was himself prepared to recognize almost any remotely relevant discourse as a Gifford Lecture. And it is only in virtue of this reckless generosity that I am able to proceed to the ensuing lectures in order to enquire in some detail what would have to take the place of Adam Gifford's project if we were to be guided by *Zur Genealogie der Moral,* and what if instead we were to be guided by *Aeterni Patris,* and finally what is at issue between the standpoints which define themselves in terms of these rival texts.

II

Genealogies and Subversions

In the first of these lectures I argued that, if and insofar as we are still able to ask and to answer questions about God and the good which Adam Gifford would have been willing to recognize as legitimate successors of his own, it has to be from some standpoint alien to his and that of his Edinburgh contemporaries precisely in its rejection of their unitary conception of reason as affording a single view of a developing world within which each part of the enquiry contributes to an overall progress and whose supreme achievement is an account of the progress of mankind – or, to rewrite Bagehot's remark about Adam Smith's view, of how man, having been originally and still being in remote colonial parts of the globe a biologically evolved savage, had risen to the height of being a Scottish professor of the 1880s. The canonical books of those who gave their allegiance to this *weltanschauung,* so I suggested, were the volumes of the Ninth Edition of the *Encyclopaedia Britannica.* The encyclopaedia article was the genre whose form perfectly matched that particular content. But it was not the only such genre. Many of the writers of the Ninth Edition were the professors of a university establishment dominant in Scotland, Germany, and those other countries from which the contributors to the Ninth Edition were drawn. And just as in their encyclopaedia articles they gave written form to the type of lecture in which they spoke *ex cathedra,* so their university lectures were spoken encyclopaedia articles. This type of lecture was thus a genre very different either from its medieval predecessors or from what a lecture can be today.

The medieval lecturer shared with his audience a background of beliefs concerning which texts were authoritative. The lecture as interpretative commentary upon such texts appealed to an authority beyond itself and had as its sequel the disputation in which the lecturer's theses were tested dialectically and demonstratively. It was just because both audience and lecturers accepted standards of truth and rationality independent of either that each could summon the other to test any particular thesis in the forum of disputation, the intellectual equivalent of trial by ordeal. In the late nineteenth-century lecture, by contrast, it was the lecturer who himself was the authority upon the standards in constituting himself as the voice of the *weltanschauung;* authority resided in the lecturer himself and in the lecture. The audience came to hear and to learn from authoritative, encyclopaedic pronouncements, not to dispute. Deference on the part of the audience was one of the defining marks of the late nineteenth-century university.

For us in the contemporary university the nineteenth-century lecture is a genre as impossible as the medieval, for we no more share the agreements presupposed by the deference of the nineteenth-century audience than we do the acknowledgment of authoritative texts by the twelfth or thirteenth century. For us in our situation of radical disagreements a lecture can only be an episode in a narrative of conflicts; sometimes it may be a moment of truce or negotiation between contending parties, or even a report from the sidelines by a necessarily less than innocent bystander, but nonetheless it is always a moment of engagement in conflict. And this is why it is not only the intellectual content of Adam Gifford's will which is so alien to us that the implementation of his intentions has become problematic but also the very form of performance which he prescribed for that implementation, the lecture. For content and form were matched perfectly. The lectures were to be, so the will declares, "public and popular, open . . . to the whole community" because they were to convey "real" knowledge of a kind which "lies at the root of all well-being." A summons to the hearing of such a lecture is very different from a summons to participate in a conflict over what the reality of knowledge consists in, if anything.

It is therefore unsurprising that one of the two most notable nineteenth-century rejections of the encyclopaedists' conception of knowledge and of rationality should have been accompanied, indeed preceded by an abandonment of the lecture itself as a genre. Nietzsche's breaking away from the university, his abandonment of both professorial chair and professorial stance, was an integral part of his preparation for the assumption of a new role, that of genealogist.

No one had been more thoroughly educated into the orthodoxies of nineteenth-century academia than had Nietzsche. He was both the pupil and the protegé, first at Bonn and then at Leipzig, of Friedrich Wilhelm Ritschl, who died in 1876, in time for his work to be celebrated in volume 20 of the Ninth Edition by the Cambridge classical scholar James S. Reid. Ritschl's great work on Plautus had played its part in the development of a view of *Altertumswissenschaft* in which the philological study of texts united with the study of ancient institutions and art and archeology to provide a portrait of the ancient world serviceable for the culture of the nineteenth century, a view developed most fully by Nietzsche's younger contemporary at Bonn, Ulrich von Wilamowitz-Moellendorf, who in 1877 was chosen to deliver an address *On the Splendor of the Athenian Empire* to celebrate the birthday of the German emperor. And when Nietzsche was appointed to the chair of classical philology at Basel in 1869 at the age of twenty-four, those who recommended and appointed him clearly had the same expectations that they were to have of Wilamowitz.

Nietzsche's repudiation of the whole ethos of *Altertumswissenschaft* derived from his perception of a very different relationship between classical antiquity and nineteenth-century modernity from that taken for granted by his teachers and contemporaries. Were the classical philologists in fact to understand classical realities, he was to remark, they would recoil horrified. And they would do so in part at least because they would have to acknowledge that their own academic purposes had alienated them from their object of study and concealed it from them. The initial offense which separated Nietzsche from academia was his discovery in archaic Greece of a standard by which to judge the inadequacies and distortions of the present, a discovery expressed in 1872 in *Die Geburt der Tragödie aus dem Geiste der Musik,* a book whose lack of respect for academic boundaries was integral to its judgment upon modernity. The outrage of the scholarly and literary establishment was unambiguous, ranging from Ritschl's public silence—his private comment was "*geistreich Schwiemelei*" ("clever giddiness")—and the rejection of a favorable review by Erwin Rohde by the *Literarisches Zentralblatt* to Hermann Usener's "Anyone who has written a thing like that is finished as a scholar" and the twenty-two-year-old Wilamowitz's savage pamphlet *Zukunftsphilologie!* (See more generally *Nietzsche and the Classical*

Tradition, ed. J. C. O'Flaherty, T. F. Sellner, and R. M. Helm, Chapel Hill, 1976.)

Nietzsche did not finally resign his Basel chair until 1879. But he had previously been absent on sick-leave for part of the time and his departure not only from the university but from *bürgerlich* society into the self-imposed exile of one without any fixed home expressed in his life the thought that much earlier he had uttered in a letter to Erwin Rohde: "No genuinely radical living for truth is possible in a university" (December 15, 1830). Yet it was not long before not only the university but truth itself had to be put in question.

By 1873 he was asking, "What then is truth?" and replying, "A mobile army of metaphors, metonymies, anthropomorphisms, a sum, in short, of human relationships which, rhetorically and poetically intensified, ornamented and transformed, come to be thought of, after long usage by a people, as fixed, binding, and canonical. Truths are illusions which we have forgotten are illusions, worn-out metaphors now impotent to stir the senses, coins which have lost their faces and are considered now as metal rather than currency" (*Über Wahrheit und Lüge im Aussermoralischen Sinn* I). In this short passage there are already to be found four key aspects of Nietzsche's later developed thought, psychological, epistemological, historical, and literary.

Psychologically what is taken to be fixed and binding about truth—and Nietzsche would of course have said the same about knowledge and duty and right—is an unrecognized motivation serving an unacknowledged purpose. To think and speak of truth, knowledge, duty, and right in the late nineteenth-century mode, the mode in fact of the Ninth Edition, is to give evidence of membership in a culture in which lack of self-knowledge has been systematically institutionalized. To be, and not to rebel against being, a member of the professoriate or of its disciples is to be a deformed person, deformed by whatever drive it is whose inhibition and distortion have led to an unacknowledged complicity in a system of suppressions and repressions expressed in a fixation whose signs and symptoms are the treatment of highly abstract moral and epistemic notions as fetishes. That drive turns out to be what Nietzsche was later to characterize as the will-to-power.

Epistemologically what this lack of self-knowledge and the arguments which are assembled in its support sustain is a blindness to the multiplicity of perspectives from which the world can be viewed and to the multiplicity of idioms by means of which it can be characterized; or rather, a blindness to the fact that there is a multiplicity of perspectives and idioms, but no single world which they are of or about. To believe in such a world would be the illusion of supposing that "a world would still remain over after one subtracted the perspective!" (*Der Wille zur Macht*, 567).

Such a passage cries out for commentary and the cry has been more than sufficiently responded to. Nietzsche has surely committed himself, it has been argued, for example, to the thesis that all claims to truth are and can only be made from the standpoint afforded by some particular perspective. There is then no such thing as truth-as-such, but only truth-from-one-or-other-point-of-view. But this is of course itself, so the commentators go on, a universal nonperspectival theory of truth. And such commentators have then gone on further to debate whether Nietzsche's theory of truth is or is not some kind of pragmatic account. But it is not the outcome of such debates at the level of commentary that I wish to examine; it is rather the status of such commentary. Is such commentary no more than a spelling out of Nietzsche's own intentions and presuppositions? If so, it is presumably what Nietzsche himself would have asserted, had he only made those intentions and presuppositions fully explicit.

There are passages in Nietzsche which perhaps lend support to understanding him in this way, especially perhaps in his denials rather than in his affirmations. The denials of truth to Judaism, to Christianity, to Kant's philosophy, and to utilitarianism do seem to have the force of unconditional and universal nonperspectival denials. And insofar as Nietzsche's affirmations are the counterpart of such denials they too may seem to have the same kind of force. So the assertion that there *are* a multiplicity of perspectives as a counterpart to the denial that there is one world, 'the world,' beyond and sustaining all perspectives, may itself perhaps seem to have an ontological, nonperspectival import and status. If this is so, Nietzsche thus understood will have been restored to conventional academic philosophy, an apparent radical at one level but not at all so at another.

Yet if this way of understanding Nietzsche as someone who speaks and writes at two distinct levels, as not only the author of but also implicitly at least the earliest academic commentator upon his own works, predecessor to such as Danto and Stern and Nehamas, can find some apparent support in the texts, it is nonetheless wholly at odds with what Nietzsche himself says about the relationship of any interpreter to any text: "Ultimately, the individual . . . has to interpret in a quite individual way even the words he has inherited. His interpretation of a formula at least is personal, even if he does not create a formula: as an interpreter he is still creative" (*Der Wille zur Macht*, 767). And it is not just that all interpretation is creative, but also that all commentary is interpretation; Nietzsche held of utterances what he held of things: "That things possess a constitution in themselves quite apart from interpretation and subjectivity is a quite idle hypothesis . . ." (560, see also *Die Fröhliche Wissenschaft*, 374).

From this point of view to comment upon Nietzsche's texts is not to move to another level of discourse, one at which covert conventional ontological commitments can be identified; instead it is to rewrite and to extend Nietzsche's texts as texts of one's own. This creative action has two aspects. It is not freed from the constraints required by accuracy in reproducing Nietzsche's or anyone else's words. On this point the classical philologist in Nietzsche survived: "What is incorrect [in a particular text] can be ascertained in innumerable cases" (letter to Claus Fuchs, August 26, 1888), although Nietzsche goes on to insist that even in this respect in many cases lack of evidence ensures the multiplication of interpretations. But within the constraints imposed by such accuracy each interpretation brings to bear its own metaphors. For metaphors are the currency of interpretation just as they are of the texts interpreted. The notion that we can escape from metaphor to some other conceptual mode – especially to the idiom of ontology – is a mistake, although those who apparently commit that mistake may in fact covertly be using their own metaphors in some more-or-less successful attempt to preempt the possibility of rival interpretations.

So it is perhaps with the metaphor of levels of discourse to which I referred earlier; it and kindred metaphors may be read as expressions of an academic attempt to reduce Nietzsche's thoughts to a certain kind of systematic order, metaphors which, rightly understood, reveal the parallel between the way in which analytical philosophers attempt to reduce the hitherto conceptually unsystematic to order and that in which an alien occupying power may reduce to order the hostile inhabitants of a territory which it has attempted to annex. Thus such metaphors express partisanship in a struggle to make Nietzsche safe territory for analytical philosophy. Hence we find in the conflicting texts concerning the interpretation of Nietzsche's texts just that "play of forces" which Gilles Deleuze has taught us to look for in those texts themselves. And each side in this conflict, in which French interpreters such as Deleuze, Jean Granier, and Sarah Kofman are matched against English-speaking analysts, can claim with some justice to be extending Nietzsche's own thought. But this points us towards what is in part ambiguity and in part instability in that thought itself, features that can be illuminated by a comparison with the encyclopaedic mode of utterance so decisively rejected by Nietzsche.

The difference between that mode of utterance and Nietzsche's is not merely a matter of the latter's multiplicity of perspectives and relativization of truth to those perspectives, as against the former's underlying conception of the unity of truth and reason and of the comprehensiveness of the encyclopaedic framework. Nor is it even only a matter of the latter's stress upon the conflict between perspectives and the struggle between rival interpretations as against the former's emphasis upon synthesis and development towards an agreed truth. It is also a matter of the contrast between utterance intended to express what is taken to be a warranted fixity of belief and utterance construed as a moment in the development of one position against others, a moment doubtless to be superseded in the shifting play of forces and use of metaphors. Yet Nietzsche did not entirely deliver himself over to this new or newly revived mode. What he partly withheld was the self as commentator upon and therefore external to both modes, a self who provided the grounds for finding in Nietzsche, as Danto and others have done, anticipations of doctrines advanced within analytic philosophy but who, as those analytic commentators have failed to notice, both comments and, by then further abstracting himself, escapes from his own commentary. It is the movement between this abstracted commenting self and the self whose only voice and view is that of some perspective which is the source of the instability in Nietzsche's writing; it was his failure to demarcate any consistent boundary between those selves which is the source of the ambiguity. But 'failure' may be the wrong word. For it remains to be asked whether such demarcation is in fact possible. That question must however be postponed to a later point in the argument at which its full importance can be made clear. What matters for the moment is to consider the implications of Nietzsche's complex stances for the genres through which he gives expression to those stances.

Nietzsche understood the academic mode of utterance as an expression of merely reactive attitudes and feelings, their negative, repressed, and repressive character disguised behind a mask of fixity and objectivity. It was therefore the perfect form of expression for the fetishistic morality of its culture, a morality which at the level of academic exposition provided the subject matter for debate between Kantians or neo-Kantians and utilitarians of various kinds. Nietzsche in directing his aphorisms against both parties not only undermined their moral and their philosophical theses but also mocked their style and their genre. By contrast the Nietzschean aphorism is active, a place and a play of contrary forces, the medium through which a current of energy passes. "An aphorism," Deleuze has said, "is an amalgam of forces that are always held apart from one another" ('Pensée Nomade' in *Nietzsche aujourd'hui,* Paris, 1973). It is in uttering and responding to aphorisms that we outwit the reactive, academic mode. And what is true of the aphorism is true in another way of the poetic, prophetic mode of *Also Sprach Zarathustra.* But if this is so, then certain other of Nietzsche's works themselves become problematic by reason of their genre and none more so than *Zur Genealogie der Moral,* the book which is, as Deleuze points out, neither a collection of aphorisms nor a poem but "a key for the interpretation of aphorisms and the evaluation of poems" (*Nietzsche et la philosophie,* Paris, 1962, 3, 7). It is in fact, as Nietzsche recognized (Preface viii), an academic treatise. And if Nietzsche was to carry through the task which he had set himself, it had to be. What was that task?

It was to exhibit the historical genesis of the psychological deformation involved in the morality of the late nineteenth century and the philosophy and theology which sustained it, the type of morality, philosophy, and theology shared equally by Nietzsche's teachers and by Adam Gifford and his Edinburgh contemporaries. So the task of the genealogist more generally was to write the history of those social and psychological formations in which the will to power is distorted into and concealed by the will to truth, and the specific task of the genealogist of morality was to trace both socially and conceptually how rancor and resentment on the part of the inferior destroyed the aristocratic nobility of archaic heroes and substituted a priestly set of values in which a concern for purity and impurity provided a disguise for malice and hate.

There have recurred in the course of this history, as Nietzsche recounts it in *Zur Genealogie der Moral,* revivals of the archaic idea: in classical Rome, at the Renaissance, even in debased form in Napoleon, "that synthesis of the brutish with the more than human." But in this conflict between the aristocratic polarity of good against bad and the herd polarity of good against evil it was the latter which had prevailed, embodied most importantly first in Judaism and then in that "new Judaic Rome," the Church. What emerged was the victory of a life-denying ascetic ideal which issues in those conceptions of sin, of duty, of conscience, and of the relationship of virtue to happiness which have perpetuated both resentment and rancor and the denial of life. The ascetic ideal, as Nietzsche understands it, assumes many different forms, among them those of nineteenth-century academic scholarship. That scholarship prided itself on its freedom from those theological and other transcendental illusions which had imprisoned enquiry prior to the Enlightenment. Yet that pride was, according to Nietzsche, a mark of the reestablishment of the ascetic ideal in one more unacknowledged, life-destroying form. What Christianity had once purveyed had become the stock in trade of anti-Christianity.

Among those so indicted were the academic historians. Nietzsche had particularly in mind French and German scholars. But his view of nineteenth-century academic history is recognizably a view of the same terrain as that surveyed by the contributors on historical subjects to the Ninth Edition, although from a very different angle of vision. Where they saw a solid progress which displaced the past's understanding of itself in favor of their own understanding of it as an inadequate precursor of their own institutional, legal, and moral arrangements and views (see, for example, 'History' by J. Cotter Morrison in volume 12), Nietzsche pilloried what he took to be the false claims to objectivity of those who had rejected the teleology of their predecessors and boasted of their own value-neutrality.

Nietzsche thus presents his own narrative in *Zur Genealogie der Moral* as superior to those of the academic historians precisely in that it enabled him to identify limitations and defects in their writing of which they themselves were unable to become aware. But this claim to superiority is easily misunderstood. For it may well be read, and Nietzsche from time to time gives us some reason to read it, as a straightforward claim to have defeated the academic historians, and indeed the philosophers too, in the light of standards of truth and rationality which may not perhaps be those actually appealed to within academic history and philosophy but which differ from them only in being a corrected and improved version of them, standards which provide a neutral court of appeal for Nietzsche, his adversaries, and his readers. And certainly Nietzsche was gratified by the sympathetic reading which he took himself to have received from such orthodox academics as Burckhardt and Taine (letter to Jacob Burckhardt, 14 November 1887), while at the same time voicing again and again in his letters the thought that his views would have to be unpalatable to the vast majority of the reading public. What he never quite brought himself to say, and perhaps never quite brought himself to think, was that, if his views were not in fact almost universally rejected, they could not be vindicated, that on his own account assent by those inhabiting the culture of his age could only be accorded to theories infected by distortion and illusion.

What Nietzsche could not quite bring himself to think about his own views Adam Gifford and his contemporaries would have found completely unintelligible about theirs: that what is in fact the truth about the nature of God and the foundations of morality and about the forces at work in the formation of beliefs concerning those subjects might be such that, were it to be presented in Gifford Lectures to the late nineteenth-century academic and lay public, it could not but appear to them both incredible and offensive. Their inability even to entertain this type of thought was a sign of the depth of their commitment to a belief in the unity of truth and reason which excluded any possibility of the existence of radically incommensurable standards. Yet it is only in the light of such standards that Nietzsche's claim for the superiority of the narrative of *Zur Genealogie der Moral* can be rightly understood.

For Nietzsche all theorizing, all making of claims occurs in the context of activity and it is from the standpoint afforded by and emerging in and from different modes of participation in and response to activity, some reactive and repressive, others open to the biologically vital possibility of activity, that different perspectives upon the variety of subject matters defined within each perspective become available. So it is not by reasoning that at a fundamental level anyone moves from one point of view to another. To believe that reasoning can be thus effective is to express allegiance to that dialectic of which Socrates was the initiator and in so doing to reaffirm one's inability to escape from the inhibiting and repressing reactive formation to which the repressing and reactive habits of activity exhibited in dialectical reasoning bind its adherents. Nietzsche did of course assert that the most skilful dialectical reasoning had in fact failed by its own standards as well as by his, especially in ethics, in theology, and in antitheology. He had nothing but scorn for both Kant and Mill. But in pointing this out Nietzsche was once again mocking the pretensions of dialectic, not turning it against itself in a way which would have made of him only one more dialectician.

So we have matched against each other two antagonistic views. The encyclopaedist's conception is of a single framework within which knowledge is discriminated from mere belief, progress towards knowledge is mapped, and truth is understood as the relationship of *our* knowledge to *the* world, through the application of those methods whose rules are the rules of rationality as such. Nietzsche, as a genealogist, takes there to be a multiplicity of perspectives within each of which truth-from-a-point-of-view may be asserted, but no truth-as-such, an empty notion, about *the* world, an equally empty notion. There are no rules of rationality as such to be appealed to, there are rather strategies of insight and strategies of subversion. Correspondingly in ethics there is on the encyclopaedist's view a set of conceptions of duty, obligation, the right, and the good which have emerged from and can be shown to be superior to—in respect both of title to rational justification and of what is taken to be genuinely moral conduct—their primitive, ancient, and other pre-Enlightenment predecessors. Problems there may indeed still be, even after Spinoza and Kant and Mill, and progress still has to be made; this is one reason why lectureships such as Lord Gifford's need to be established. But these problems are posed from within, and progress is expected from within, the enclosing framework of a unified, encyclopaedic rationality. By contrast a genealogical view requires of us sufficient insight to understand that allegiance to just such a view is always a sign of badness, of inadequately managed rancor and resentment. The conduct of life requires a rupture, a breaking down of such idols, and a breaking up of fixed patterns, so that something radically new will emerge.

Each of these two rival views, the encyclopaedist's and the genealogist's, contains within itself a more or less spelled-out representation of the other, indeed cannot dispense with such a representation as a counterpart to its representation to itself of itself. From the standpoint of the encyclopaedist the genealogist is reproducing familiar irrationalist themes and theses; so the genealogist's perspectivism is characteristically understood as merely one more version of relativism, open to refutation by the arguments used by Socrates against Protagoras. From the standpoint of the genealogist the encyclopaedist is inescapably imprisoned within metaphors unrecognized as metaphors. And from both standpoints any attempt, such as my own in this lecture, to produce a characterization of this antagonism from some external, third vantage point is doomed to failure; there is no idiom neutral between the encyclopaedist's affirmations and distinctions and the genealogist's subversions.

One can indeed, as I have tried to do, learn the idiom of each from within as a new first language, much in the way that an anthropologist constitutes him or herself a linguistic and cultural beginner in some alien culture. In so doing one can come to recognize that the only capacity which the adherents of each standpoint possess for translating the utterances of the other would always result in what some adherent of that other standpoint who had learned the rival language would have to characterize as mistranslation, as misrepresentation. Of course within both conceptual schemes it is possible for each to recognize the concepts of the other as in some ways variants upon his or her own. So those genealogists who speak only of 'true-from-a-point-of-view' recognize in utterances about *the* truth, or what is 'true as such,' a mystifying reified extension of their own concept, while the encyclopaedist understands 'true-from-a-point-of-view' as a diminished, misleading, and self-undermining reworking of 'true as such.' And a similar understanding extends to a whole range of epistemological and practical concepts, so that we have two radically different alternative and rival conceptual schemes, recognizable as such only by those who have learnt the language of each and of both as two first languages and who are able to speak each as those who inhibit that scheme speak it, but necessarily unrecognized by those who insist that to understand the language of the other it must be translatable into their own. But it is just this insistence which the standpoint of the encyclopaedist requires, for a blindness to the possibility of genuine alternative conceptual schemes is a necessary part of the encyclopaedist's point of view, while an openness to that possibility is equally necessary on the part of the genealogist. So here is one more way in which the two are at odds, exemplifying the truth that in philosophical controversies of any depth what divides the contending parties is characteristically in part how to characterize the disagreement.

Yet it is just at this point that the question of genre becomes urgent once again for the genealogist. In assuming the role of genealogist Nietzsche had had to repudiate that of professor and along with it those modes of public utterance which presupposed and expressed the academic establishment's encyclopaedic allegiance. The lecture as understood by that establishment, whether in Germany or in Scotland, the article in the scholarly and increasingly to be professionalized journal, and the magisterial treatise all provided forms which could not contain Nietzsche's content, any more than the Nietzschean aphorism—and along with it the paragraph of commentary—so well adapted to Nietzsche's purposes, could have become the common currency of academic life. And yet it is quite difficult *not* to read *Zur Genealogie der Moral* otherwise than as one more magisterial treatise, better and more stylishly written indeed than the books of Kant or Hermann Cohen, of Ranke or of Harnack (a contributor to the Ninth Edition), but deploying arguments and appealing to sources in the same way, plainly constrained by the same standards of factual accuracy and no more obviously polemical against rival views. Did Nietzsche then simply relapse into being once again a professor, albeit one now without a chair, and could he indeed have done otherwise if he was to elaborate and defend the central positions of *Zur Genealogie der Moral?* If so, then genealogy in the course of defending itself has both relapsed and collapsed into encyclopaedia.

The genealogist's answer is that it may indeed seem to be so, if any one piece of writing is considered in isolation from what precedes and follows, if it is abstracted from that movement through time of which it is a part and in terms of which alone it is rightly to be understood. Every piece of writing, like every spoken word—and in this at least writing and speech have more in common than what distinguishes them—is utterance on the move, in which the utterer is actively responding to what has gone before and actively expecting both others and him or herself either to react or to act in further response, so that he or she may move beyond it to something else. So the genealogical genre is one in which present theses about what has been are presented in a genre open to what is not yet. Such theses cannot have either the type of fixity or the type of finality to which the encyclopaedic mind always aspires and which it sometimes, as recurrently in Adam Gifford's writings and in the Ninth Edition, believes itself to have achieved. But this answer by the genealogist raises a further difficulty.

For the genealogist who has put the academic stance in question by writing and publishing his or her book is addressing whom? Someone presumably to and with whom he not only puts in question the objects of his critique, but to whom he opens up the possibility of in turn putting the genealogist in question, either in respect of particular theses or in respect of his or her overall project. Yet this cannot be done without adopting a fixity of stance, a staying in place, a commitment to defend and to respond and, if necessary, to yield. A piece of writing, whenever it confronts a reader—or indeed a set speech, when it is reuttered to a new hearer—does so at a time which is not only 'now' for that reader or hearer, but becomes the author's coincident 'now,' no matter how long previously the work was written or spoken. In that shared time, exempted in some respects, although not in others from the temporal separation of the 'now' of utterance from the 'now' of reading or hearing, the timelessness extends to the standards of reason-giving, reason-accepting, and reason-rejecting, in the light of which alone the genealogist and his or her reader can put each other to the question. This appeal to impersonal, timeless standards, so often taken for granted in the post-Enlightenment world by those who take themselves to have rejected metaphysics, is itself only to be understood adequately as a piece of metaphysics.

The possibility of such an appeal is inseparable from the possibility of that atemporal 'now' at which writer and reader encounter each other, that 'now' at which both can appeal away from themselves and the particularity of their own claims to *what is* timelessly, logically, ontologically, and evaluatively, and is only thereby and therefore the property of neither writer nor reader. And Nietzsche recognized the force of this objection. "In order to think and infer it is necessary to assume beings: logic handles only formulas for what remains the same," he was to write (*Der Wille zur Macht*, 517), anticipating the need to respond to this point; and he replied that the beings so assumed are fictitious, among them the being of the ego or of other individuals (517–20). But it is nonetheless necessarily presupposed by the act of writing for a particular reader or readers that the ego of writer and that of reader have enough fixity and continuity to enter into those relationships constitutive of the acts of reading-as-one-who-has-been-written-for and of writing-as-one-who-is-to-be-read.

The claim that I am making is a modest, albeit metaphysical one, not to be confused, for example, with Habermas's neo-Kantian thesis that allegiance to one specific set of ideal norms is a necessary condition for acts of communication. All that writer and reader must presuppose is enough of logical, ontological, and evaluative commitment—and the commitments of the one need not be in all respects the same as those of the other—to ensure the continuities and fixed identities and differences without which each cannot by his or her own standards, even if not yet or not at all by those of the other, convict that other of inconsistency, falsity, and failure of reference. Yet even this is enough to engage both parties in the kind of metaphysics which Nietzsche and a variety of post-Nietzscheans have tried to proscribe. It is one sign of the inescapable character of this metaphysics of reading that those who proscribe it so often fail nonetheless in the eyes of their post-Nietzschean colleagues to eliminate all traces of it from their own work. Thus Heidegger has accused Nietzsche of retaining in his thought an unacknowledged metaphysical remnant and so Derrida has in turn similarly accused Heidegger.

It is not of course that some forms of writing and reading cannot occur without this metaphysical dimension; but its absence makes of the encounter of writer and reader one in which each can be no more than and no other than the other's intentional object, cast for whatever role that particular intentional stance requires, victim to the other's victimizer. So perhaps the vigilant suspicion of a completely consistent Nietzschean antimetaphysician, always on the watch for distorted expressions of the will-to-power, would find its self-confirming justifications in a type of situation which it itself had created and sustained. But to all this there is of course a Nietzschean reply, one which in its strongest and most plausible version recognizes, as Nietzsche himself did, that at the moment of writing for a reader and at the moment of a reader confronting that writer in his or her writing, something very like what I have been describing, a now of the present and of at least apparent ontological presencing, must occur and endure for a time: but *only,* so the reply runs, for a time. It is its temporariness which disengages us and which enables us to regard once more as a fiction this apparent momentary metaphysical disregard of the temporality of flux and perspective.

So the genre of the academic treatise is, it may be conceded, the apparent genre of Nietzsche's writing in *Zur Genealogie der Moral,* but only apparent, not real, because it represents no more than a temporary stance, a mask worn only for the purposes of certain particular addressings of certain particular audiences. "Metaphysical theories are masks," said Oscar Wilde, and Nietzsche would have added that our apparently cognitive attitudes towards them are no more than modes of putting on, displaying, and discarding such masks. The problem then for the genealogist is how to combine the fixity of particular stances, exhibited in the use of standard genres of speech and writing, with the mobility of transition from stance to stance, how to assume the contours of a given mask and then to discard it for another, without ever assenting to the metaphysical fiction of a face which has its own finally true and undiscardable representation, whether by Rembrandt or in a shaving-mirror. Can it be done? The research program of the post-Nietzschean enterprise, so prodigally endorsed by Nietzsche for his intellectual heirs, is to find out by trying and either failing or succeeding in a systematic attempt to carry through that program. No such attempt in terms of systematic implementation or erudition or honesty is likely to be more impressive than that to which Michel Foucault devoted so much of his life.

Yet this way of understanding Foucault's project as a continuation of Nietzsche's—and it was for much of the time Foucault's own understanding of that project—requires a response to the objection that Nietzsche's thought was not, and indeed could not have been, as radically alien to conventional modes as Foucault and Deleuze and I, following them, have taken it to be. For certainly Nietzsche not only drew upon, but at times identified himself with positions which found a place within the encyclopaedists' scheme. Karl Jaspers spoke of Nietzsche's engagement with theses from nineteenth-century physics and biology as his positivist phase. Nietzsche wrote history on occasion much as some other nineteenth-century historians wrote it, even while disowning his kinship with them. And he reserved some of his most radical remarks either for unpublished texts or for the characterization of conceptions such as that of the Eternal Recurrence, which he may later have rejected.

So it is possible by excision and reinterpretation and change of emphasis to construct an alternative account of Nietzsche's development in which Nietzsche did indeed attempt to break systematically with conventional modes of thought but failed to do so. Nor on this alternative view could it have been otherwise. The attempt to spell out the consequences of the death of God by moving beyond the constraints of grammar and logic and of all established values was bound to end in tragic failure. For what Nietzsche may have aspired to say moves beyond intelligible speech. Incommensurability with what both the encyclopaedists and their academic heirs have taken to be the necessary features of *any* intelligible thought and discourse, the type of incommensurability with such thought and discourse which I and others have ascribed to Nietzsche, cannot occur. If Nietzsche did envisage it as a possibility, *we,* so it is suggested, know better.

It is indeed from the standpoint of such a 'we' that this objection is advanced, a 'we' who insist that intelligibility is nothing other than translatability into 'our' language and conceptual idiom. So Nietzsche, having been translated into 'our' terms and evaluated by 'our' standards, turns out to be after all not so different from 'us.' The objection fails of course for everyone unwilling to equate intelligibility with translatability into one's own initial language and conceptual idiom. And what its attempt to coopt Nietzsche cannot reckon with is his subordination of the elucidatory academic treatise to the poem and the epigram, a subordination designed to enable us finally to dispense with elucidatory treatises altogether in favor of a mode of discourse and a way of life in which mockery, celebration, and disruptions of sense make use of assertions only in order later to displace them.

Hence the argument that Nietzsche could not have propounded a set of statements which put him at such radical variance with traditional ways of understanding the place of logic and grammar in our discourse, because *any* set of statements *must* presuppose to some large degree just that kind of understanding, misses the point. Nietzsche's final standpoint, that towards rather than from which he speaks, cannot be expressed as a set of statements. Statements are made only to be discarded – and sometimes taken up again – in that movement from utterance to utterance in which what is communicated is the movement. Nietzsche did not advance a new theory against older theories; he proposed an abandonment of theory.

Notice that I am not claiming to be able to refute this type of objection by appeal to Nietzsche's writings. What is at issue between those who understand Nietzsche in the one way and those who understand him in the other is in key part how those writings are to be interpreted and how the development from one text to another is to be construed. Nietzsche's writings do not provide us with a set of neutral data, appeal to which will resolve the disagreement. And this is precisely what we should expect if this disagreement is, as I judge it to be, one in which incommensurable standpoints are at odds.

Notice also that I am not at this point claiming that the Nietzschean project, as I have understood it, has been or can be carried through successfully. All that I am claiming is that it must be understood and judged initially in its own terms and that in these terms it is not evidently and at once self-defeating. Whether it can in fact be carried through successfully is a question posed by the history of Foucault's thought.

Nietzsche's progress was from professor to genealogist, Foucault's from being neither to being both simultaneously. And hence for him the problem of academic presentation as a mask assumed by the genealogist exerted pressures perhaps even more intense than those felt by Nietzsche. He confronted that problem directly in his contribution to the *Festschrift* for Jean Hyppolite ('Nietzsche, la généalogie, l'histoire' in *Hommage à Jean Hyppolite*, Paris, 1971) published within a year of his inaugural lecture at the Collége de France. In that essay he addresses in Nietzschean terms not so much the question of what history is and achieves – that is the question to be answered by the whole Nietzschean research program – but the question of who the historian is and how he or she must be transformed by engagement with history if the work of history is to be informed by genuinely Nietzschean insights. History thus understood turns out to have three uses, all of which sever the connection of history with memory and with memorial veneration of the past by creating a disruptive countermemory.

The first of these uses is to understand official academic history—the history propounded by professors of history—as itself a kind of parody of the past, so that instead of taking the identities of the significant figures of the past as solid, we understand them as masks and ourselves as the producers of a charade, producers whose own illusory self-conception has been put in doubt by this understanding. Secondly, we go on to comprehend them and ourselves, not as persons, as identities, but as complex patterns of elements representative of their various differing cultures. So that the identity of the historian, like that of his or her subjects of study, is dissipated, a dissipation which makes visible the discontinuities concealed by the continuities of academic history. The third of these uses of history is to reveal in the consciousness of the historian a rancorous will to knowledge, shared with other modern enquirers, a will which does not in fact issue in any progress towards truth and reason, but which, because it does not recognize limitation, demands destructive and self-destructive sacrifices.

There is of course for Foucault a self-endangering paradox here: the insights conferred by this post-Nietzschean understanding of the uses of history are themselves liable to subvert the project of understanding the project. Consider in this regard *Les Mots et les choses,* published five years earlier. This is at one level a conventional academic treatise, even if a somewhat radical one. It is a recognizable extension of the thought of Gaston Bachelard in its emphasis upon the place of discontinuities and incommensurabilities in intellectual history and it could be read—has been read, for example, by Ian Hacking—as doing for immature sciences, and notably for the human sciences, something akin to what Thomas Kuhn achieved for our understanding of the mature physical and chemical sciences. But this kind of reading of *Les Mots et les choses* undervalues or ignores two key aspects of that book. The first is emphasized by Foucault himself in his preface.

His interest in the immature sciences, he makes it clear, is not or not only for their own sake; it is because they tend to exemplify a middle area, always of some obscurity and confusion, between the fixed codes of a culture, on the one hand, and the well-ordered enterprises of the mature sciences on the other, an area in which what underlies those determinate orders can be identified, an area in which we can be liberated into a perception of what is anterior to the modes of being of order, an insight into sets of coherences, resemblances, and correspondences, capable of being organized in alternative, incompatible, and incommensurable modes of classification and representation.

A second relevant aspect of *Les Mots and les choses* only seems to have become visible to Foucault later. In *Les Mots et les choses* Foucault distinguished three successive styles of thought, each with its own standards in respect of classification and the use of signs, divided historically by moments of rupture, one in which the Renaissance period is displaced by the Classical at the beginning of the seventeenth century, and another in which the Classical in turn loses its place at the end of the eighteenth. But this book about incommensurable ordered schemes of classification and representation is itself organized as an ordered scheme of classification and representation, a scheme not identified or justified within its own pages except by implication in the recurrent methodological remarks, which have the surface qualities–from the standpoint of genealogy–of all such methodological remarks. It thereby, unlike standard texts in academic history, puts itself in question–notice that it is the text which does this, not the author–requiring us to supplement and perhaps correct, how radically we cannot know in advance, our first-order understanding of *Les Mots et les choses* by a second-order understanding of what underlies and orders the ordering of *Les Mots et les choses*. Foucault's threefold Nietzschean indictment of history has become self-referential.

When I say that it is the text which puts itself in question, and not the author, I do not of course only mean that *Les Mots et les choses* could not but be read as a self-subverting text, whatever Foucault's actual intentions at the time of writing. I mean also, and perhaps more importantly, that as Foucault had argued in 'Qu'est-ce un auteur?' (*Bulletin de la Société Francaise de philosophie* 63, July–September 1969) 'the author' for him names a role or function, not a person, and the use of a particular author's name discharges this function by assigning a certain status to a piece of discourse. Hence any possibility of moving beyond and behind the text to authorized intention is already ruled out by authorized intention. Text-and-author, text-as-authored, this is the self-presenting unit. It was of course in part because Foucault thus concurred in the liquidation of the conventional conception of the author that he was, much to his own annoyance, sometimes described as a structuralist. But if he agreed with some of the structuralists in what he, as a genealogist, denied, he disagreed fundamentally with them over what they affirmed.

Structuralisms have been of different and incompatible kinds, diminishing in intellectual power and interest as they moved further away from their sources in the anthropology of Georges Dumézil and the mathematics of Bourbaki. But what they have all shared is the appeal to some set of elements, structured in this or that way, as fundamental to explanation and understanding, as that in terms of which all else is to be explained. That there are any such fundamental sets or structures Foucault consistently denied. And so when he moved from *Les Mots et les choses* to *L'Archéologie du Savoir* (1969) it was not in order to disclose some single fundamental level of the ordering of sciences, even of immature sciences, for that too would be an order whose underlying principle would need to be identified and itself put in question, but a movement towards the preconceptual, the presystematic, and the prediscursive which itself necessarily cannot but be comprehended in terms that are conceptual, systematic, and discursive. So very different and heterogeneous regularities and levels of discourse are disclosed, through which are generated a variety of incommensurable bodies of claims assigned in their assemblage the status of a science. To the set of relations which in any given time and place unify the discursive practices underlying any one such body of claims Foucault gave the name '*episteme*,' mocking Plato's and Aristotle's uses of that word in so doing.

Sciences then, as conventionally understood in the history of science or by natural scientists themselves, have become secondary phenomena. The ruptures in that history, as identified by Bachelard or Kuhn, moments in which a transition is made from one standardized understanding of what it is to be rational to some other, sometimes incommensurable standardized understanding of rationality, are also secondary phenomena. For they, like the standardized orders which they divide and join, are the outcome of assemblages and confluences in the making of which distributions of power have been at work, in such a way that what appear at the surface level as forms of rationality both are and result from the implementation of a variety of aggressive and defensive strategies, albeit strategies without subjects. Truth and power are thus inseparable. And what appear as projects aimed at the possession of truth are always willful in their exercise of power. In so exposing them Foucault thus discharges the third of the genealogist's tasks as characterized by Nietzsche and re-characterized by Foucault himself. But what now about the discourse in which and through which the genealogist performs his or her tasks? I have described Foucault's development in my terms; but what would it be to describe it in his? Could they be so very different? The question arises once again: how far can the genealogist, first in characterizing and explaining his project, to him or herself as much as to others, and later in evaluating his or her success or failure in the genealogist's own terms, avoid falling back into a nongenealogical, academic mode, difficult to discriminate from that encyclopaedist's or professorial academic mode in the repudiation of which the genealogical project had its genesis and its rationale?

Certainly Foucault himself became a professor of professors, restoring Nietzsche's project to the professoriate from which Nietzsche had rescued it. I do not mean by this only that whereas Nietzsche began as a professor but became a homeless wanderer in the lodging places afforded by Nice and Marienbad and Stresa and Genoa, Foucault began as a transient, moving from Lille to Uppsala to Warsaw and later between Clermont-Ferrand and both Brazil and Tunisia, but ended with nearly fifteen years speaking *ex cathedra* from the Collége de France; but also that this inversion symbolizes Foucault's movement towards and final arrival at the plain academic style of the *Histoire de la sexualité* and the even plainer explanations of his explanations offered in that wearisome multitude of interviews in which the academic deference evident in the questions is never rejected by Foucault in his answers.

This final Foucault was in one aspect at least a twentieth-century Hobbes, replying, when asked by Jacques Alain Miller and Alain Grosrichard in a discussion in 1977 (*Ornicar* 10, July 1977) to identify the subjects who oppose each other in those exercises of power which constitute social, cultural, and intellectual life, that it is "all against all . . . Who fights against whom? We all fight each other. And there is always within each of us something that fights something else." When Miller asked whether the components of the transitory coalitions formed by participants in those struggles would be individuals, Foucault replied, "Yes, individuals, or even sub-individuals." So there is even internalized Hobbesian struggle in this war of each against all. And in the portrayal of this struggle ironic distance, un-

masking, self-unmasking, and all the other features of those essentially temporary stances which mark the genealogist's historical dis-
closures are quite absent. So Foucault regressed into academia. But
did this regression from Nietzsche to Hobbes have to happen? Could
the genealogical enterprise have been sustained in its integrity? The
answers to these questions depend upon those to two others.

I noted earlier that the relationship which *Zur Genealogie der
Moral* requires to hold between reader and text involves a mode of
reading and of argumentative debate in the light of certain impersonal and timeless standards of truth, reference, and rationality, standards enduring allegiance to which would be inconsistent with the
genealogical project. To this however it was possible to reply that this
relationship need only be temporary and provisional, an allegiance
to be sustained not by the genealogist him or herself, but only by
one of his or her potentially many *personae,* masks, and thus one not
committing the genealogist him or herself as that elusive figure moves
from stance to stance. Whether this reply could be sustained, so I
have suggested, depends upon the success or failure of genealogy, not
as a single set of claims in a single text, but as a research program
of the kind undertaken, but in the end almost, if not quite, abandoned by Foucault.

Yet now the question arises as to whether what even Foucault's
partial implementation of that program may not have revealed is
that the successive strategies of the genealogist may not inescapably
after all involve him or her in commitments to standards at odds with
the central theses of the genealogical stance. For in making his or
her sequence of strategies of masking and unmasking intelligible to
him or herself, the genealogist has to ascribe to the genealogical self
a continuity of deliberate purpose and a commitment to that purpose which can only be ascribed to a self not to be dissolved into
masks and moments, a self which cannot but be conceived as more
and other than its disguises and concealments and negotiations, a
self which just insofar as it can adopt alternative perspectives is itself not perspectival, but persistent and substantial. Make of the genealogist's self nothing but what genealogy makes of it, and that self
is dissolved to the point at which there is no longer a continuous
genealogical project. Or so I am suggesting.

Is this indeed so? If we press this question, we find ourselves asking another closely related question. In narrating the systematic development and recurrent reworking of Foucault's strategies, it is not just that we have to ascribe a unity of project to a deliberating, purposeful self with its own unity as agent, if that project is to be intelligible. We also have to recognize the parts played by logic, by the identification, for example, of contradiction, by appeals to evidence, by the practical reasoning exhibited in the actions through which Foucault's enquiries progressed or failed to progress towards a from time to time reformulated *telos,* and by his reevaluations of their success and failure. The standards in the light of which such reevaluations are made and such reasoning conducted are independent of the particular stages and moments of the temporary strategies through which the genealogist moves his or her overall projects forward, and the recognition accorded to them is necessary for the genealogist to find his or her own actions and utterances intelligible, let alone for them to be intelligible to anyone else. Hence once again it seems to be the case that the intelligibility of genealogy requires beliefs and allegiances of a kind precluded by the genealogical stance. Foucault's carrying forward of Nietzsche's enterprise has thus forced upon us two questions: Can the genealogical narrative find any place within itself for the genealogist? And can genealogy, as a systematic project, be made intelligible to the genealogist, as well as others, without some at least tacit recognition being accorded to just those standards and allegiances which it is its avowed aim to disrupt and subvert?

The inadequacy of responses so far to these questions may suggest that the history of genealogy has been, and could not have been other than, one of progressive impoverishment. It is not of course so much that Foucault's later scholarly enterprises suffered from impoverishment but that they avoided it only by drawing less and less covertly upon nongenealogical sources and methods. Yet if genealogy now confronts problems for which it does not at least as yet seem able to devise solutions, a resourcelessness which may of course be only temporary, the surviving adherents of the encyclopaedist's mode of moral enquiry can take no comfort from this for two reasons. First, the particular genealogical diagnoses of the moral, metaphysical, and theological attitudes typified by the Ninth Edition of the *Encyclopaedia Britannica* retain a great deal of cogency independently of the fate of the genealogical project in general. If genealogy has not, or not yet, overcome those difficulties which must be overcome if its claims to sovereignty in the realm of moral enquiry are to be vindicated, it has at least succeeded in impugning the encyclopaedist's form of moral enquiry.

Secondly, any defects in the developed genealogical treatment of the incommensurability of rival fundamental moral, scientific, metaphysical, and theological standpoints do nothing to lessen the existence and the importance of that incommensurability and of the presently unresolvable disagreements and conflicts which stem from it. The transformation of the moral enquirer from a participant in an encyclopaedic enterprise shared by all adequately reflective and informed human beings into an engaged partisan of one such warring standpoint against its rivals is an accomplished fact, any adequate recognition of which results in the dissolution of the encyclopaedist's standpoint, a dissolution evident in the current Fifteenth Edition of the *Encyclopaedia Britannica*. In the Ninth Edition the editor's overall standpoint and scheme was widely, if not quite universally, shared by his contributors, and the structure of particular entries, especially in such key entries as those on 'Ethics' and 'Theology,' was consonant with the structure of the encyclopaedia as a whole. But with the Fifteenth Edition it is quite otherwise. Heterogeneous and divergent contributions, which recognize the diversity and fragmentation of standpoints in central areas, are deeply at odds with the overall scheme, insofar as that scheme presupposes any real unity to the work, rather than merely providing some organization for a massive work of reference. Mortimer J. Adler, chairman of the board of editors of this edition (Chicago, 1974), recognizes this when he allows at the close of his introductory account that what the Encyclopaedia embodies is no more than "faith in the unity of knowledge" (*Propaedia*, p. 446). The encyclopaedic mode of enquiry has become one more fideism and a fideism which increasingly flies in the face of contemporary realities.

Since the presuppositions of the encyclopaedist's standpoint and mode of enquiry are, as I argued earlier, the same presuppositions which underlay the endowment of such distinctively academic institutions as the Gifford Lectures, it may well seem that to continue to appoint Gifford lecturers can itself be no more than a similar act of unwarranted faith. Whether it is so or not depends upon whether there is any third alternative to the encyclopaedic and genealogical modes of moral enquiry. It is therefore towards an investigation of the possibility of just such a third alternative that I shall turn in the next four lectures.

III

Too Many Thomisms?

The standpoint of the encyclopaedist, and more especially of the editors of and contributors to the Ninth Edition, is one in radical conflict with that of the genealogist in respect of their rival conceptions of the nature of moral enquiry. Yet it is all too easy to be blind to the fact that they also share certain fundamental agreements and that those agreements have shaped the course of their disputes in significant ways. What are they? Both contending parties agree first of all to a remarkable extent, if not entirely, in the way in which they conceive of the history of philosophy from Socrates up to the nineteenth century. For the encyclopaedist this history is one of the progress of reason in which the limited conceptions of reasoning and practices of rational enquiry generated by Socrates, Plato, and Aristotle were enlarged by their successors, albeit with new limitations, and then given definitive and indefinitely improvable form by Descartes. "Descartes," wrote William Wallace in volume 7 of the Ninth Edition, "laid down the lines on which modern philosophy and science were to build." So from Socrates through Descartes to Kant and the post-Kantians the line both of moral progress and of rational enquiry runs, exhibiting in its outcome the unity of its history.

For the genealogist this history has a very different character. It is one in which reason, from the dialectic of Socrates through to the post-Kantians, both serves and disguises the interests of the will to power by its unjustified pretensions. Where the encyclopaedist sees a unified history of progress, the genealogist sees a unified history of distorting and repressing function. But both at least agree in ascribing a unified history. Both therefore are at odds with any view which understands the history of philosophy in terms of a fundamental break, so that philosophy has a divided history, a before and an after such that the characterization of the before is a very different task from that of the after.

This was the view of the history of philosophy taken by Joseph Kleutgen in his *Die Philosophie der Vorzeit Verteidigt*, published in four volumes in Munich between 1853 and 1860. Later I shall want to put in question some of the ways in which Kleutgen distinguished between the philosophy of 'der Vorzeit' and the philosophy of modernity, but the fact of the distinction was far more important than his particular ways of characterizing it. What Kleutgen distinguished was that philosophy which ran from Socrates to the High Middle Ages and which took its definitive form in the writings of Aquinas and that which recognized Descartes as its outstanding progenitor. So where both encyclopaedists and genealogists had portrayed continuity, Kleutgen portrayed rupture.

Kleutgen was a Jesuit, at one stage in his career a professor at the German College in Rome and later prefect of studies at the Gregorian University. And that is to say he taught and enquired in a university community governed and defined by just those kinds of tests of religious and moral orthodoxy from which Adam Gifford and his Edinburgh contemporaries were so proud of having emancipated themselves. And in this respect too Kleutgen points us to an important way in which the encyclopaedist and the genealogist agree, while the Thomist is equally at odds with both.

Descartes symbolized for the nineteenth-century encyclopaedist a declaration of independence by reason from the particular bonds of any particular moral and religious community. It is on this view of the essence of rationality that its objectivity is inseparable from its freedom from the partialities of all such communities. It is to allegiance to reason as such, impersonal, impartial, disinterested, uniting, and universal, that the encyclopaedist summons his or her readers and hearers. And it is of course this very same conception of reason as universal and disinterested that the genealogist rejects, so that genealogist and encyclopaedist agree in framing what they take to be both exclusive and exhaustive alternatives: *Either* reason is thus impersonal, universal, and disinterested *or* it is the unwitting representative of particular interests, masking their drive to power by its false pretensions to neutrality and disinterestedness.

What this alternative conceals from view is a third possibility, the possibility that reason can only move towards being genuinely universal and impersonal insofar as it is neither neutral nor disinterested, that membership in a particular type of moral community, one from which fundamental dissent has to be excluded, is a condition for genuinely rational enquiry and more especially for moral and theological enquiry. Yet just this possibility was the one presented by Plato in initiating the philosophical tradition, particularly in the *Gorgias* and in the *Republic*. What emerged from Socrates' confrontation with Callicles in the *Gorgias* was that it is a precondition of engaging in rational enquiry through the method of dialectic that one should already possess and recognize certain moral virtues without which the cooperative progress of dialectic will be impossible, something further acknowledged by Plato in the *Republic* in his identification of those virtues the practice of which must precede initiation into philosophical community and by Aristotle in his account of the inseparability of the moral and the intellectual virtues in both political and philosophical community. Enquiry into the nature of the virtues and of human good more generally is on this Socratic view therefore bound to be sterile if disinterested. A prior commitment is required and the conclusions which emerge as enquiry progresses will of course have been partially and crucially predetermined by the nature of this initial commitment.

Hence of course arose Nietzsche's warning not to allow oneself to be entrapped by the Socratic dialectic. For he perceived correctly that only by breaking with that dialectic at the outset could one hope to escape from arriving at Platonic and Aristotelian conclusions. Hence also derived Nietzsche's wholehearted hostility to Plato and his preference for the sophists. E. R. Dodds argued that we find in the Callicles of the *Gorgias* an anticipation of Nietzsche's response to Plato. But it is important also to notice that the Plato of the *Gorgias* and the *Republic* was equally in conflict with one of the major presuppositions of the encyclopaedic stance, that truth not only is what it is, independent of standpoint, but can be discovered or confirmed by any adequately intelligent person, no matter what his point of view (see on this conception David Wiggins's discussion of remarks by M. H. Abrams in 'What Would Be a Substantial Theory of Truth?' in *Philosophical Subjects: Essays Presented to P. F. Strawson*, ed. Z. van Straaten, Oxford, 1980).

By contrast, from the standpoint of the *Gorgias* and the *Republic* the enquirer has to learn how to make him or herself into a particular kind of person if he or she is to move towards a knowledge of the truth about his or her good and about *the* human good. What kind of a transformation is required? It is that which is involved in making oneself into an apprentice to a craft, the craft in this case of philosophical enquiry. For part of what put the philosophical tradition which runs from Socrates to Aquinas at odds with the philosophical thought of modernity, whether encyclopaedic or genealogical, was both its way of conceiving philosophy as a craft, a *technē*, and its conception of what such a craft in good order is. "Every good," said Aristotle "is the *ergon* of a *technē*" (*NE VII* 1152b 19), and what a particular *technē* produces in those who practice it is some particular capacity (1153a 23), a capacity to be achieved, as are the other end-products of any *technē*, only with true reasoning (*VI* 1160a 20–21), which itself requires both intellectual and moral virtues. Enquiry into the nature of what is the good and the best must be a *science* (*epistēmē*) which is a master-craft (*I*, 1094a 27). And at the opening of the *Metaphysics* it is *technē* which enables us to discern unity in multiplicity and the master-craftsman who is the model of the person with *sophia*.

In holding that to be committed to becoming *philosophos* is to embark on a *technē*, Aristotle of course only restated what he had learned from Socrates and Plato. And when in the middle ages conceptions of craft were used to characterize enquiry (the word '*ars*' as used in '*ars liberalis*' means precisely what '*technē*' means; the liberal arts are the crafts of free persons), it was upon either Plato or Aristotle that authors drew to inform that conception of their practice. Dante, as poet-philosopher, was in virtue of these specific craft skills admitted to membership in one of the *arti* at Florence, that of the apothecaries, the guild for all the crafts of book-learning. What then is it about the structure of a craft and of a craft guild which is important for philosophy? What is it that philosophy as a craft shares with other crafts, such as furniture making or fishing, which it may well not share with philosophy conceived in rival modes, such as those of Descartes or of Nietzsche? Some salient characteristics stand out.

One arises from two key distinctions which apprentices in any craft have to learn to apply; indeed only insofar as they learn to apply them can they learn anything else. The first is the distinction between what in particular situations it really is good to do and what only seems good to do to this particular apprentice but is not in fact so.

That is, the apprentice has to learn, at first from his or her teachers and then in his or her continuing self-education, how to identify mistakes made by him or herself in applying the acknowledged standards, the standards recognized to be the best available so far in the history of that particular craft. A second key distinction is that between what it is good and best for me with my particular level of training and learning in my particular circumstances to do and what is good and best unqualifiedly. That is, the apprentice has to learn to distinguish between the kind of excellence which both others and he or she can expect of him or herself here and now and that ultimate excellence which furnishes both apprentices and master-craftsmen with their *telos*.

What the correct and systematic application of these distinctions both by his or her teacher and by the apprentice him or herself results in initially is the identification of the defects and limitations of this particular person, as he or she is here and now, with respect to the achievement of that *telos:* defects and limitations in habits of judgment and habits of evaluation, rooted in corruptions and inadequacies of desire, taste, habit, and judgment. So the apprentice learns what it is about him or herself that has to be transformed, that is, what vices need to be eradicated, what intellectual and moral virtues need to be cultivated. And this need to identify such virtues and to acquire them in order to learn whatever it is in which, in this particular craft, one needs to be instructed has particularly important consequences when the craft in question is, or includes, moral enquiry.

The virtues of course are required for the practice of any *technē* if that *technē* is to be directed towards a genuine good. For although every good is the *ergon* of some *technē*, the skills of a *technē* may be exercised with the purpose of achieving what is not in fact a good. All rational powers, said Aristotle—and to possess a *technē* is to possess a rational power—can have contrary effects. So that the exercise of a *technē* does not of itself determine to what end that exercise will be directed. Something else is needed—*orexis* or *prohairesis,* felt desire alone or desire guided by reason (*Metaphysics IX* 1048a 1–11). And the judgment of right reason informing such a desire will always refer implicitly or explicitly to that *telos* the achievement of which is the genuine good to be achieved for that particular agent in his or her particular circumstances.

The *telos* of moral enquiry, which is excellence in the achieve-

ment not only of adequate theoretical understanding of the specifically human good, but also of the practical embodiment of that understanding in the life of the particular enquirer, most of all requires
therefore not just a craft but a virtue-guided craft. Moral enquiry,
as understood by Socrates, by Aquinas, and by those who took their
place in the movement to Aquinas from Socrates, thus aspires to answer the question 'What is the good and the best, both for human
beings in general and for this specific kind of human being in these
particular circumstances here and now?' both theoretically and practically. But this question cannot be answered without learning how
to catalogue and to characterize the human excellences, the moral
and intellectual virtues. Thus moral enquiry moves towards arriving
at theoretical and practical conclusions about such virtues. But, as
we have already noted, one cannot learn how to move towards such
conclusions without first having acquired some at least of those same
virtues about which one is enquiring and without therefore having
first been able to identify which virtues they are and, to at least some
minimal extent, what it is about them which makes these particular
habits virtues. So we are threatened by an apparent paradox in the
understanding of moral enquiry as a type of craft: only insofar as we
have already arrived at certain conclusions are we able to become the
sort of person able to engage in such enquiry so as to reach sound
conclusions. How is this threat of paradox—recognizably a version
of that posed at the outset by Plato in the *Meno* about learning in
general—to be circumvented, dissolved, or otherwise met? The answer is in part that suggested by the *Meno:* unless we already have
within ourselves the potentiality for moving towards and achieving
the relevant theoretical and practical conclusions we shall be unable
to learn. But we also need a teacher to enable us to actualize that
potentiality, and we shall have to learn from that teacher and initially
accept on the basis of his or her authority within the community
of a craft precisely what intellectual and moral habits it is which we
must cultivate and acquire if we are to become effective self-moved
participants in such enquiry. Hence there emerges a conception of
rational teaching authority internal to the practice of the craft of
moral enquiry, as indeed such conceptions emerge in such other
crafts as furniture making and fishing, where, just as in moral enquiry, they partially define the relationship of master-craftsman to
apprentice.

Such conceptions are of course deeply at odds both with the ethos of encyclopaedia and with that of genealogy. The encyclopaedists had learned from Kant that to be rational is to think for oneself, to emancipate oneself from the tutelage of authority. Any notion that I can only think adequately by and for myself insofar as I do so in the company of others, to some of whom authority must be accorded, is quite alien to the encyclopaedist, as it is indeed also to the gene-alogist, who cannot but see in such authority the exercise of a sub-jugating power which has to be resisted. Moreover, the exercise of authority is related to temporality in a way that is at odds with both the encyclopaedist's and the genealogist's modes.

The standards of achievement within any craft are justified his-torically. They have emerged from the criticism of their predecessors and they are justified because and insofar as they have remedied the defects and transcended the limitations of those predecessors as guides to excellent achievement within that particular craft. Every craft is informed by some conception of a finally perfected work which serves as the shared *telos* of that craft. And what are actually produced as the best judgments or actions or objects so far are judged so because they stand in some determinate relationship to that *telos,* which furnishes them with their final cause. So it is within forms of intellectual enquiry, whether theoretical or practical, which issue at any particular stage in their history in types of judgment and activity which are rationally justified as the best so far, in the light of those formulations of the relevant standards of achievement which are ra-tionally justified as the best so far. And this is no less true when the *telos* of such an enquiry is a conception of a perfected science or hier-archy of such sciences, in which theoretical or practical truths are deductively ordered by derivation from first principles. Those suc-cessive partial and imperfect versions of that science or sciences, which are elaborated at different stages in the history of the craft, provide frameworks within which claimants to truth succeed or fail by find-ing or failing to find a place in those deductive schemes. But the over-all schemes themselves are justified by their ability to do better than any rival competitors so far, both in organizing the experience of those who have up to this point made the craft what it is and in supplying correction and improvement where some need for these has been identified.

The temporal reference of reasoning within a craft thus differs strikingly from that of either encyclopaedic or genealogical reasoning. The encyclopaedist aims at providing timeless, universal, and objective truths as his or her conclusions, but aspires to do so by reasoning which has from the outset the same properties. From the outset all reasoning must be such as would be compelling to any fully rational person whatsoever. Rationality, like truth, is independent of time, place, and historical circumstances. The editors and contributors to the Ninth Edition may not themselves have been Cartesians, but their avowal of their debt to Descartes accorded recognition to an important truth about themselves. And someone who, like Adam Gifford, drew upon Spinoza rather than Descartes for his conception of rationality, held precisely the same view of reason. What that view entails is an exclusion of tradition as a guide to truth, and in his lecture on 'Law a Schoolmaster' Gifford counterposed what he took to be the truths of morality to the forces of custom and tradition, which are on his view as likely to be or more likely to be obfuscating than illuminating and which, even when they do happen to transmit truths, do so in a way which still requires the scrutiny of tradition-independent rationality for what is transmitted to be justifiably accorded the status of truth.

By contrast, just because at any particular moment the rationality of a craft is justified by its history so far, which has made it what it is in that specific time, place, and set of historical circumstances, such rationality is inseparable from the tradition through which it was achieved. To share in the rationality of a craft requires sharing in the contingencies of its history, understanding its story as one's own, and finding a place for oneself as a character in the enacted dramatic narrative which is that story so far. The participant in a craft is rational *qua* participant insofar as he or she conforms to the best standards of reason discovered so far, and the rationality in which he or she thus shares is always, therefore, unlike the rationality of the encyclopaedic mode, understood as a historically situated rationality, even if one which aims at a timeless formulation of its own standards which would be their final and perfected form through a series of successive reformulations, past and yet to come.

The authority of a master within a craft is both more and other than a matter of exemplifying the best standards so far. It is also and most importantly a matter of knowing how to go further and especially how to direct others towards going further, using what can be learned from the tradition afforded by the past to move towards the *telos* of fully perfected work. It is in thus knowing how to link past and future that those with authority are able to draw upon tradition, to interpret and reinterpret it, so that its directedness towards the *telos* of that particular craft becomes apparent in new and characteristically unexpected ways. And it is by the ability to teach others how to learn this type of knowing how that the power of the master within the community of a craft is legitimated as rational authority.

The genealogist has no way of understanding such authority except as one more form of domination imperfectly disguised by its mask of rationality, a mask necessarily worn with a self-distorting lack of self-knowledge. To treat tradition as a resource is similarly one more way of allowing the past to subjugate the present. And the central symptom of the sickness of this type of social existence, from the genealogical standpoint, is that, despite its recognition of the historical situatedness of all reason-giving and reason-offering, it understands the truth to which it aspires as timeless. Hence the rationality of craft-tradition is as alien and hostile to the genealogical enterprise as is the encyclopaedist's to either.

The conflicts between these three are sharply evident in their contrasting attitudes to Christian theology. The Nietzschean and post-Nietzschean genealogist understands Christianity as having a key place in the genesis and sustaining of the illusions which it is their task to combat. Over time the genealogical tone of voice has changed. Nietzschean savagery—"One has only to read any of the Christian agitators, Saint Augustine for example, to realize, to *smell*, what dirty fellows had therewith come out on top" (*Der Antichrist*, 59) or his characterization of the Middle Ages as combining a "dreadful barbarism of custom" with "an equally dreadful exaggeration of that which constitutes the value of men" (*Der Wille zur Macht*, 871)—has been displaced by the measured evaluations of Foucault in his later writings and by the very different historicizing rhetoric of Deleuze and Guattari. But the fundamental hostility remains and among those features at which it is aimed is not only the moral aberration which, on the genealogical view, Christianity inherited from Judaism, but also the metaphysical realism of Jewish and Christian theism.

For such theism has as its core the view that the world is what it is independently of human thinking and judging and desiring and willing. There is a single true view of the world and of its ordering, and for human judgments to be true and for human desiring and willing to be aimed at what is genuinely good they must be in conformity with that divinely created order. Hence both the perspectivism of the genealogist and the concomitant repudiation of the distinction between the real and the apparent involve the rejection of Christian theology. From that standpoint the encyclopaedist's post-Enlightenment critique of orthodox Christianity is at best half-hearted and fainthearted, exhibiting even at its most negative some of the same symptoms of moral and intellectual sickness as does Christianity itself.

The genealogist's accusation is not merely that the type of rationality professed in the Ninth Edition is still too hospitable to Christianity, as in Robert Flint's article on theology. It is also and more fundamentally that that conception of rationality, indeed the conception of language and its mode of application to the world presupposed by that conception, is itself theological. "I fear," wrote Nietzsche in *Götzendämmerung* "we are not getting rid of God because we still believe in grammar," in a conception of language, that is, as representing an order of things by means of a conceptual scheme and a logic of identity and difference. So the genealogical accusation is not just that theism is in part false because it requires the truth of realism, but that realism is inherently theistic.

It is therefore unsurprising that some theologians of the nineteenth century, whose allegiance required them neither to constrict and constrain their creedal affirmations and their theological understanding of those affirmations within the limits imposed by the post-Kantian framework of the nineteenth century encyclopaedist nor to confront the challenge of the genealogist by a nonrational fideism, should have looked back, as Kleutgen did, to that different type of philosophy which had been elaborated in the terms proper to a tradition-directed understanding of philosophy as a *technē*. This was after all how Aquinas had understood *sapientia,* in Platonic and Aristotelian accounts the virtue specific to philosophical activity, in the opening arguments of the *Summa Contra Gentiles* (I, i), where he reiterated Aristotle's position at the beginning of the *Metaphysics.*

What *sapientia* is is there explained in terms of the hierarchy of crafts. Some are subordinated to others, as the craft of preparing medicinal herbs is ordered to the ends of the craft of medicine. And those master-crafts which deal with important but not universal as-

pects of human life, such as medicine or politics or architecture, en-
title those who practise them to be called *sapientes* in a qualified way.
But *sapientes* as such are only those concerned in their enquiry with
first principles and ultimate causes, not with this or that set of truths,
but with the acquisition of the *scientia* of that *veritas* which is the
origo of all *veritas*. Philosophy is thus the master-craft of master-crafts.

What was it about philosophy so conceived which made it, in
its Platonic and Aristotelian modes, so congenial both to such early
and high medieval philosophers as Augustine and Aquinas and to
some of those nineteenth-century theologians who reacted to and
against the dominant thought of their own epoch? In key part it was
certainly, as the argument so far must have already suggested, the
character of its realism. It is a central feature of all crafts, of furniture
making and fishing and farming, as much as of philosophy, that they
require the minds of those who engage in the craft to come to terms
with and to make themselves adequate to the existence and properties of some set of objects conceived to exist independently of those
minds. The embodied mind, in and through its activity, has to become receptive to forms (*eidē*) of what is other than itself and in being constituted by those formal objects becomes, in the appropriate
way, them. It is therefore not judgments which primarily correspond
or conform to those realities about which they are uttered; it is the
embodied mind which conforms adequately or inadequately to the
objects, the *res*, the subject matter, and which evidences this adequacy
or inadequacy in a number of ways, one of which is the truth or falsity of its judgments. It is in becoming adequate to its objects that
the embodied mind actualizes its potentialities and becomes what
its objects and its own activity conjointly have been able to make it.
And, as I noticed earlier, the person who achieves this adequacy
systematically does so through exhibiting those habits of judgment
and action which are the intellectual and moral virtues. Thus failure
in learning what one should come to know is always rooted in defect
in respect of the virtues.

Here then was a type of realism deeply at variance with post-
Cartesian and post-Kantian philosophy and moreoever one which inverted the relationship of theology to philosophy as the philosophy
of the late nineteenth-century encyclopaedist conceived it. For where
that philosophy subjected theology to the same rational standards

which it imposed elsewhere, rejecting, modifying, and truncating theism until it became a doctrine acceptable within the framework imposed by the encyclopaedist's unitary and ahistorical conception of rationality—'God' is for Robert Flint the name of the ultimate object of rational enquiry—so making of the object only what the mind conceived in post-Kantian terms allowed it to be, the philosophy of craft-tradition presented the mind as inadequate until it had conformed itself to the object which theology presented for its attention. And where the philosophy of the encyclopaedia made epistemology primary —Andrew Seth did so explicitly in the article 'Philosophy'—for the philosophy of craft-tradition, knowledge is a secondary phenomenon to be understood in the light of the objects of knowledge and not vice versa. The whole epistemological turn of philosophy is thus from this point of view the outcome of a mistake, that of supposing that the skeptics' challenge was to be met by some vindication of rationality-in-general in which what was evident to any mind whatsoever could furnish an adequate criterion for truth. And so from the standpoint of the philosophy of craft-tradition the later genealogical subversion of post-Cartesian and post-Kantian philosophy was no more than a discrediting of claims which there had been no good reason to advance in the first place. Where it itself is deeply at odds with the central theses of genealogy is, as I remarked earlier, over the genealogical reading of the history of philosophy in which post-Cartesian and post-Kantian philosophers are treated as if they were the genuine descendants of Socrates, Plato, Aristotle, Augustine, and Aquinas and in which the epistemological concerns of post-Cartesian philosophy are misleadingly projected back on to ancient and medieval thought.

The theologians of the late nineteenth century were not, of course, as yet aware of the genealogical challenge. But they could not but be responsive to the recurrent attempts within every major Christian denomination to reshape and to diminish central Christian doctrine in a way that would make it acceptable to post-Enlightenment culture, the culture of the encyclopaedia. And these recurrent attempts evoked a variety of theological restatements, of which Kierkegaard's and Newman's were among the most notable. In Italy a series of Catholic philosophers and theologians, in the course of responding not only to earlier philosophical attacks upon Christianity, such as that of Condillac, but also to those defenses of it which, by conceding too much of the ground of debate to their opponents, had deformed central Christian positions for apologetic purposes, drew more and more systematically upon the resources afforded by a more thorough-going reading of Aquinas than eighteenth-century theological education had provided. The most important of the Catholic philosophers against whom they directed this rereading of Aquinas was Antonio Rosmini Serbati (1797–1855). Rosmini had been engaged in reviving and defending what he genuinely believed to be Augustinian and sometimes Thomistic positions. But because his central enterprise was to vindicate theology against its Kantian critics, he absorbed into his own system a good deal of Kant and thereby, seemingly unwittingly, distorted those older positions by reworking them in Kantian terms. Rosmini's central thesis was that our knowledge consists in more than an awareness of particulars, because we bring to the understanding of those particulars the *a priori* and universal idea of being. The human subject, in performing those transcendental operations which transform awareness of empirically given particulars into universal, necessary, and objective truths, relies inescapably upon its possession of this *a priori* idea, but the idea of being is itself neither a product of, nor primarily a property of, the knowing subject, empirical or transcendental. All ideas, except for the idea of being, are formed by abstraction, either in reflecting upon sensation or in second-order reflection upon first-order reflection. Only the idea of being is not and cannot have been so formed; it is a given and its givenness is such that it must be referred to the action of God. God as being presents Himself to the mind in that aspect of the mind's activity which is the presentation of the idea of being.

Rosmini's intention was certainly not to reduce God to the status of an idea immanent within those Kantian structures and activities which Rosmini ascribed to the mind. But Kant himself had of course been completely in the right in understanding that there is no place for any true knowledge of God within the cognitive structures of the mind if the mind is characterized in terms of his three *Critiques*. And Rosmini's philosophical claims depended for their warrant upon their claim to an authentically Kantian character; it was only by Kantian reasoning and by the making of the key Kantian distinctions that one could justifiably arrive at Rosmini's conclusions. Hence *either* Rosmini failed philosophically by introducing into his Kantian structures an intuitive apprehension of the God of theism which could have no legitimate place there *or* he failed theologically by giving the name of 'God' to something other than God. It was the latter accusation which was characteristically leveled at Rosmini's theorizing by some of his Thomistic contemporaries, who took his identification of God with the universal being apprehended *a priori* by the mind to be a version of pantheism. And equally characteristically some recent Catholic theologians, perhaps moved by their recognition of the fact that Karl Rahner's theology stands in precisely the same relationship to Heidegger's philosophy as that in which Rosmini's stood to Kant's, have argued strenuously that Rosmini ought to be interpreted in a way that frees him from the imputation of pantheism. But these latter-day sympathizers with Rosmini have missed the crucial point, which is not so much that he was guilty of pantheism but that his central theses about the relationship of God to the human mind are susceptible of more than one interpretation and that insofar as they are interpreted so as to secure his theistic orthodoxy, they render his philosophical position incoherent. Thus Rosmini's attempt to render Catholic theology acceptable to modern thought fails in either case. Insofar as it was made acceptable, it ceased to be Catholic theology, and insofar as it was Catholic theology, it failed to be philosophically acceptable by the standards of Kantian or post-Kantian modernity. And in this respect Rosmini was the forerunner both of much of the Catholic modernism of the early twentieth century and of most fashionable Catholic thought since Vatican II.

It was however Rosmini's respect for these post-Kantian standards which gained him the privilege of a sympathetic account in the Ninth Edition. The articles on 'Aquinas' and on 'Scholasticism' were both written by hostile critics of Thomism, but that on Rosmini (volume 23) in marked contrast was by a Rosminian priest. Rosmini as a kind of Kantian was recognized as sharing the encyclopaedist's synoptic vision of the rational and the real. He thus escaped the charge leveled against Aquinas by T. M. Lindsay in volume 2 of identifying "reason" with "the system of . . . Aristotle" and that brought by Andrew Seth against the Scholastics in volume 17: "They appear to contemplate the universe of nature and men not at first hand with their own eyes but in the glass of Aristotelian formulae." Kleutgen's Rosminian critics and other Catholic critics and opponents would not have disagreed.

It is important to remember that in the first half of the nineteenth century theologians such as Rosmini, Vincenzo Gioberti
(1801–52), and Anton Günther (1783–1863), all of whom were
heavily indebted to post-Kantian idealism, were enormously influential within Catholic ecclesiastical and educational institutions. It was
those who attempted a systematic return to Aquinas who were at
first a small and uninfluential minority and often appeared to exert
a disruptive influence. As late as 1865 a Jesuit provincial could write
of two Thomist Jesuits, "Those two members of the Society, well
known as uncompromising Thomists, suddenly rose in defense of
that commonly rejected doctrine . . . Now their way of feeling and
of thinking implies a condemnation of the whole body of the Society and, which is worse, of the Episcopate . . ." (quoted in Paolo
Dezza *Alle origini del neotomismo,* Milano, 1960, p. 96). Yet by 1865
a marked change had already taken place. Matteo Liberatore (1810–
92), yet another Jesuit, had published the three volumes of his *In-
stitutiones philosophicae* in 1860 and 1861; and a good deal earlier one
of the two Jesuits condemned by his superior for his Thomism, Serafino Sordi, had educated into a Thomistic allegiance Luigi Taparelli
d'Azeglio, who was to become rector of the Roman College and had
also made Thomists out of *his* pupils Vincenzo Gioacchino Pecci
and Giuseppe Pecci, brother of Gioacchino. The latter became arch-
bishop of Perugia in 1846 and the former was appointed professor
in the seminary there in 1851. Serafino Sordi in 1852 became provincial of the Roman province of the Society of Jesus and Taparelli
became one of the editors of the Jesuit periodical *Civiltà Catholica;*
and the influence of this Perugian and Roman Thomism was reinforced by developments elsewhere. So that when Gioacchino Pecci
was elected pope as Leo XIII in 1878, Thomism had been enjoying
a revival for about thirty years. The story of its rise both before and
after 1878 is, as any genealogist would expect, a political as well as
an intellectual story. But the chronology of political development
is never the same as that of intellectual development and the political success of Thomism was in one important way, so I shall argue,
premature. For when Leo XIII issued the encyclical *Aeterni Patris* in
1879, drawing the attention of Catholics to the recognition of the
philosophical and theological preeminence of Aquinas by nine of
Leo's predecessors since the fifteenth century and requiring the faithful to follow the example of those who "when turning their minds

recently to the practical reform of philosophy, aimed and aim at restoring the renowned teaching of St. Thomas Aquinas . . ." his mandate to Catholic scholars was, and in 1879 could not but have been, one obedience to which could only lead in a variety of alternative and conflicting directions. Leo XIII's intention was to complete the work of Liberatore, Sordi, Taparelli, his brother Guiseppe, and so many others in reestablishing Thomism; what he succeeded in generating were a number of different and rival Thomisms. Why?

The single most important influence upon the drafting of *Aeterni Patris* was that of Kleutgen, a fact often emphasized by both friends and enemies of modern Thomism. What has not been noticed is how much the distinctive features of Kleutgen's interpretation of Aquinas are evident in the way that *Aeterni Patris* was read and implemented, rather than in the text itself. Kleutgen was a thinker of outstanding philosophical ability and erudition and it is unsurprising that he and Thomists who shared his attitudes should have created a climate of opinion in which a certain way of reading *Aeterni Patris* was almost taken for granted. What then were these influential features of Kleutgen's view which conditioned that reading?

First of all, although we owe it to Kleutgen more than to anyone else to have identified the large discontinuity in the history of Western philosophy which separated '*der Vorzeit*' from modernity, Kleutgen mislocated the rupture. Instead of understanding it, as we are now able to do, as deriving from the failure of Aquinas's immediate successors to have appreciated and appropriated that in Aquinas's thought which had transcended the limitations of previous Augustinianism and previous Aristotelianism, Kleutgen overrated later Scholasticism's genuine debt to Aquinas. So he placed the breach in the history of philosophy much too late and failed to distinguish adequately the positions of Aquinas and of Suarez, thus doing both an injustice. For Suarez, both in his preoccupations and in his methods, was already a distinctively modern thinker, perhaps more authentically than Descartes the founder of modern philosophy.

For Suarez the notion of working within a tradition had clear relevance in theology but not in what he took to be the timeless studies of the philosopher. And Kleutgen, following Suarez, was lacking in adequate appreciation both of what it meant for Aquinas that he worked within not merely one but two inherited traditions and of what in general it is to do philosophical and theological work within a tradition. Kleutgen understood very well how important and illuminating the conclusions which Aquinas reached and the structure of the reasoning supporting those conclusions were for Catholic theology. He understood much less the nature of the type of enquiry from which those conclusions and that structure had emerged and from which alone they could have emerged. And that is to say, the conceptual context provided for those conclusions and that structure by the conception of a craft-tradition was almost as alien to his style of thought as it was to the thoughts of his philosophical and theological opponents.

Consider, for example, in a preliminary way the difference between Aquinas's account of truth in the successive articles of the first question of the *Quaestiones Disputatae de Veritate* and Kleutgen's treatment of that account. Aquinas is here engaged in describing how the mind moves to the achievement of that truth which completes its act and, in returning to itself, reflects upon and understands the principle informing that movement. The work is one of conceptual clarification, analysis, and description, not at all one of epistemological justification. And one of its aims is to draw upon the resources of, to correct and to modify, and to integrate into Aquinas's own account, the various relevant arguments and considerations advanced by a variety of writers within the Augustinian and the Aristotelian traditions, now understood as contributing to a single ongoing enterprise of enquiry. In so doing Aquinas summarizes the outcome of that enquiry so far, advances it one stage further, and leaves the way open for the proponents of yet further considerations to continue beyond that point.

Kleutgen instead treats Aquinas as presenting a finished system whose indebtedness to earlier writers is no more than an accidental feature of it. And in so doing what he reproduces is Suarez rather than Aquinas. For Suarez the mind in apprehending necessary truths about possible essences apprehends what may, but need not, exist. Its apprehension of the particular individuals which happen to exist is always mediated by those universal concepts which the mind itself elaborates in order to grasp what such individuals have in common with other individuals of the same kind. But this leaves open the question of what it is outside the mind towards which judgments about what is are directed. What relates our apprehension of possibility and universality to actual singular existence? Suarez does indeed allow that the intellect apprehends individual existents without reflection, but the need to make a transition from apprehensions of essence to judgments of particular existence within his system is one which it is all too easy to interpret as requiring Cartesian foundations (it was no accident that Descartes was taught by Jesuits influenced by Suarez).

It was a mark of the unusual philosophical ingenuity of Kleutgen that, having first misidentified Aquinas's central positions with those of Suarez, thus opening up a kind of epistemological question for which there is no place within Aquinas's own scheme of thought, he went on to supply an epistemological answer to that question by reading into texts in *De Veritate* an epistemological argument which is not in fact there. So by this creative multiplication of misinterpretations Aquinas was presented as the author of one more system confronting the questions of Cartesian and post-Cartesian epistemology, advancing, so Kleutgen contended, sounder answers than either Descartes or Kant.

None of this is in fact to be found in *Aeterni Patris* itself. Among later Scholastics it is Cajetan who is cited, not Suarez. Scholasticism is praised insofar as it continued the work of Aquinas. And Aquinas's achievement is understood as the culmination of a tradition, to which both pre-Christian and patristic authors have contributed. Epistemological questions are nowhere adverted to. Yet those who responded to *Aeterni Patris* all too often followed Kleutgen in making epistemological concerns central to their Thomism. And in so doing they doomed Thomism to the fate of all philosophies which give priority to epistemological questions: the indefinite multiplication of disagreement. There are just too many alternative ways to begin.

Giovanni Cornoldi (1822–1892), yet another Thomist Jesuit, had already indicted modern philosophy on just this point in the Introduction to his *Lezioni di filosofia ordinate allo studio di altre scienze* (Florence, 1872), contrasting the unity of Thomist thought, its ability to integrate disparate elements within itself, with the falling apart into contention of those disparate elements in the history of philosophy from Descartes onwards so that unresolvable disagreements were continually multiplied. Cornoldi was unwittingly prophetic. Thomism, by epistemologizing itself after *Aeterni Patris,* proceeded to reenact the disagreements of post-Cartesian philosophy. Thus there were generated in turn a number of systematic Thomisms, each in contention *both* with whatever particular erroneous tendencies in modern secular philosophical thought *that* particular Thomism aspired to confront and overcome *and* with its Thomistic rivals. Often enough these two kinds of contest were closely connected. So Maréchal, the most distinguished philosopher in the Thomistic school founded by Cardinal Mercier at Louvain, made out of Aquinas a rival and a corrector of Kant, the work of interpretation being inseparable from that of philosophical apologetics. So Rousselot in very different fashion responded to the French academic philosophy of his day, producing a correspondingly different view of Aquinas. And so Maritain at a later date would formulate what he mistakenly took to be a Thomistic defense of the doctrine of human rights enshrined in the United Nations Declaration of Human Rights, a quixotic attempt to present Thomism as offering a rival and superior account of the same moral subject matter as do other modern nontheological doctrines of universal rights alleged to attach to individual persons.

What Maritain wished to affirm was a modern version of Aquinas's thesis that every human being has within him or herself a natural knowledge of divine law and hence of what every human being owes to every other human being. The plain prephilosophical person is always a person of sufficient moral capacities. But what Maritain failed to reckon with adequately was the fact that in many cultures and notably in that of modernity plain persons are misled into giving moral expression to those capacities through assent to false philosophical theories. So it has been since the eighteenth century with assent to a conception of rights alien to and absent from Aquinas's thought. For on Aquinas's view the rights which are normative for human relationships are derived from and warranted only by divine law, apprehended by those without the resources afforded by God's self-revelation as the natural law. Law is primary, rights are secondary. But for Enlightenment and post-Enlightenment modernity, human rights provide a standard prior to all law.

For Maritain this was an uncharacteristic lapse. We owe in part to him, as we do also to Maréchal and outstandingly to Rousselot, the development of a kind of understanding of Aquinas which was necessarily unavailable to the Thomists of Kleutgen's generation, and the work which resulted in that understanding would never have been undertaken but for *Aeterni Patris*. Nonetheless the Thomisms which they constructed appeared to be systems of the same order as, making the same type of inadequately supported epistemological claims as, idealisms, materialisms, rationalisms, empiricisms, and positivisms. And if this were the whole story of Thomism it would at least appear as, and perhaps be, a story of defeat. But happily *Aeterni Patris* also generated a quite different set of intellectual enterprises, those which, in retrieving stage by scholarly stage the historical understanding of what Aquinas himself said, wrote, and did, recovered for us an understanding of what is distinctive about the mode of enquiry elaborated in its classical and most adequate form by Aquinas. The greatest names in this line of descent are those of Grabmann, Mandonnet, Gilson, Van Steenberghen, and Weisheipl, a list in which those who appear later have sometimes had to correct as well as to supplement their predecessors' scholarship, but in which a real progress appears, so that while systematic Thomisms apparently multiplied disagreement, the historical scholars of the Thomistic movement challenged them, as well as the characteristically modern modes of moral and theological enquiry, with their emerging account of Aquinas's own enterprise. That account is one in which the developments within Aquinas's own thought throughout his career (about Aquinas as himself a continuously developing thinker, transforming and correcting his own initial positions in a variety of instructive ways, almost nothing was said by the epistemologically oriented Thomists) were the outcome of his own participation in, as well as his continuously more adequate representation of, a mode of enquiry which was a dialectically open-ended continuation of that craft-tradition stemming from Socrates, Plato, and Aristotle as well as from the church fathers, a tradition of which *Aeterni Patris* spoke with great accuracy but the character of which the readers of *Aeterni Patris* had often been unable to comprehend.

It is then crucial, if Aquinas's thought is to be restored and continued so that it may confront what have been the sovereign modes of moral and theological enquiry in the last hundred years, the encyclopaedic and the genealogical modes, that we recognize that it is not in respect of their individual theses, considered item by item, but only in respect of those theses understood in their relationship to each overall specific mode of enquiry, that the true nature of the conflict between Thomism and these modern standpoints can be adequately explored. And if we recognize this, we shall be compelled to recognize yet another dimension of difference and conflict. That dimension is a matter of the form which each standpoint takes to be appropriate and necessary in recounting and enacting narratives of the moral life. And it will turn out, so I shall argue, that it is through contrasting and comparing the different and rival ways in which each understands the structure of such narratives that the issues which divide them can most easily be defined and perhaps even resolved, although it will also turn out that part of what is at issue is the question of what, if anything, could be accounted such a resolution.

The narrative structure of the encyclopaedia is one dictated by belief in the progress of reason. The individual's life acquires a meaningful narrative structure insofar as he or she participates in that progress, and many of the articles in an encyclopaedia such as the Ninth Edition were designed to identify what some particular individual did either by way of a contribution to that progress or by way of obstructing such progress. Articles of a certain length and tone were the encyclopaedist's equivalent of canonization. Such canonized individuals were taken to have advanced our realization that nothing falls outside the bounds imposed by and prescribed by reason; reason does and can know nothing of anything external to itself. So what reason discovers, when it is successful, is always in some sense itself, some instantiation of the coherence of reason. When it is unsuccessful it finds itself confronted by some so far intractable violation of that coherence. This is what Henry Sidgwick had had in the end to report as the outcome of his own enquiries in ethics. Where he had hoped to discover "cosmos," rational order, he had instead found "chaos," independent, not always compatible fundamental principles, whose brute givenness could neither be denied nor transcended. Yet even such an outcome is, as a finding of reason, an advance upon a past whose place in the progress of reason is never more than a stage towards present principles which owe their status as principles to reason and not at all to the past. "Principles will soon be everything, and tradition nothing . . ." as Sidgwick had declared in 1865. So the narrative of the encyclopaedist issues in a denigration of the past and an appeal to principles purportedly timeless.

For the genealogist this appeal to timeless rational principles has, as we have seen, the function of concealing the burden of a past which has not in fact been discarded at all, and the comprehensive and unitary conception of reason in the name of which this appeal is made has the corresponding function of providing an unwarranted privileged status to those who identify their own assertions and arguments with the deliverances of reason thus conceived. So the genealogists' narrative is designed to disclose what its authors take the encyclo-paedists' narrative to conceal. The genealogists' narrative has two strands to it, one a history of that which the genealogists aspire to undermine by such disclosure, the other the history of the genealo-gists' own project and of the evasions and stratagems without which the genealogist would inevitably fall back into just those modes which he or she is concerned to repudiate and to expose.

So the encyclopaedists' narrative reduces the past to a mere pro-logue to the rational present, while the genealogist struggles in the construction of his or her narrative against the past, including that of the past which is perceived as hidden within the alleged rational-ity of the present. The Thomists' narrative, by contrast with both of these, treats the past neither as mere prologue nor as something to be struggled against, but as that from which we have to learn if we are to identify and move towards our *telos* more adequately and that which we have to put to the question if we are to know which questions we ourselves should next formulate and attempt to an-swer, both theoretically and practically. This reappropriation of the past in a way which directs the present towards a particular—and yet eternal—future takes place at two interrelated levels, that of theoreti-cal enquiry and that of the practical embodiment of such enquiry.

Theoretical enquiry is constituted by a sequence of questions, ordered both so that questions are generated in accordance with the direction of enquiry and so that, at each stage, what needs to be pre-supposed or otherwise appealed to in answering the questions of that stage has already been provided. In the posing of each detailed set of questions, the principal answers made available by the various and conflicting traditions which have contributed to the making of this enquiry are set out and evaluated. At every stage what emerges is the outcome of some particular learner's debate with all those distinct pasts. Hence in theoretical enquiry the readers of Aquinas, like his original hearers, both enact the narrative of their own enquiry and make that narrative a continuing part of a larger narrative of enquiry in which they are only the latest actors, who also understand that what they are able to contribute will lead on beyond them. What such enquiry has disclosed is, on the Thomistic view, a set of answers to such questions as: What is the *telos* of human beings? What is right

action directed towards the *telos?* What are the virtues which issue
in right action? What are the laws which order human relationships
so that men and women may possess those virtues? And so on. To
live a practically well-ordered life is to embody the universal concepts
which we comprehend and justify in those enquiries in the particularities of our individual lives. So the moral life is the life of embodied
moral enquiry and those individuals who live out the moral life as
farmers, or fishermen, or furniture makers embody more or less adequately in those lives, devoted in key part to their own crafts, what
may often not be recognized as a theory, the product of the theorist's
very different craft, but which nevertheless is one. And the particularities of such lives in a variety of significant ways embody and continue the traditions, moral, religious, and intellectual, of such communities as those of the family, the city, the clan, and the nation.
Thus political narratives of success or failure in the making and sustaining of such communities are also inescapably narratives of embodied moral enquiry, itself successful or unsuccessful. If from the
Thomistic point of view Aquinas was the philosopher *par excellence*
of theoretical enquiry into the practical life, Dante was the philosopher *par excellence* of the practical life itself. And moral enquiry can
only therefore extend itself by drawing both upon Aquinas and upon
Dante.

Modern moral philosophy has in general been blind to the complementary character of narrative and theory both in moral enquiry
and in the moral life itself. In moral enquiry we are always concerned
with the question: what *type* of enacted narrative would be the embodiment, in the actions and transactions of actual social life, of this
particular theory? For until we have answered this question about
a moral theory we do not know what that theory in fact amounts
to; we do not as yet understand it adequately. And in our moral lives
we are each engaged in enacting our own narrative, so revealing implicitly, and sometimes also explicitly, the not always coherent theoretical stance presupposed by that enactment. Hence differences between rival moral theories are always in key part differences in the
corresponding narrative.

So the encyclopaedic, the genealogical, and the Thomistic
tradition-constituted standpoints confront one another not only as
rival moral theories but also as projects for constructing rival forms
of moral narrative. Is there any way in which one of these rivals might

prevail over the others? One possible answer was supplied by Dante: that narrative prevails over its rivals which is able to include its rivals within it, not only to retell their stories as episodes within its story, but to tell the story of the telling of their stories as such episodes. Yet we cannot hope even to pose the question of how Dante's standard might be fruitfully applied without first elaborating an adequately full account of the Thomistic understanding of moral enquiry.

What then is this kind of tradition-constituted, craft-constituted enquiry? Any worthwhile answer has to begin from noticing that what made Aquinas preeminent in the exercise of his craft-skill as a philosopher was his ability to integrate two quite different traditions, not only distinct but in their first confrontations deeply at odds with one another, and that without this integration none of the distinctive features of Aquinas's standpoint could have appeared. Aquinas's philosophy and theology were a response to conflict and it is from that conflict therefore that all Thomistic argument has to begin, by considering and evaluating the apparently antagonistic claims of Augustinianism, for Aquinas was certainly an Augustinian, and of Aristotelianism, for Aquinas was equally certainly an Aristotelian. What then were these two forms of moral enquiry which Aquinas encountered as warring rivals during his own education?

IV

The Augustinian Conception
of Moral Enquiry

In medieval Augustinian culture the relationship between the key texts of that culture and their reader was twofold. The reader was assigned the task of interpreting the text, but also had to discover, in and through his or her reading of those texts, that they in turn interpret the reader. What the reader, as thus interpreted by the texts, has to learn about him or herself is that it is only the self as transformed through and by the reading of the texts which will be capable of reading the texts aright. So the reader, like any learner within a craft-tradition, encounters apparent paradox at the outset, a Christian version of the paradox of Plato's *Meno:* it seems that only by learning what the texts have to teach can he or she come to read those texts aright, but also that only by reading them aright can he or she learn what the texts have to teach.

The person in this predicament requires two things: a teacher and an obedient trust that what the teacher, interpreting the text, declares to be good reasons for transforming oneself into a different kind of person—and thus a different kind of reader—will turn out to be genuinely good reasons in the light afforded by that understanding of the texts which becomes available only to the transformed self. The intending reader has to have inculcated into him or herself certain attitudes and dispositions, certain virtues, *before* he or she can know why these are to be accounted virtues. So a prerational reordering of the self has to occur before the reader can have an adequate standard by which to judge what is a good reason and what is not. And this reordering requires obedient trust, not only in the authority of this particular teacher, but in that of the whole tradition of interpretative commentary into which that teacher had had earlier him or herself to be initiated through his or her reordering and conversion.

The key texts were of course those of sacred Scripture. Reading was reading aloud and the liturgical recitation of Scripture was an act of reading in which the oral and the written text were one. The reader in his or her own life enacts and reenacts that of which he or she reads in Scripture; the enacted narrative of a single life is made intelligible within the framework of the dramatic history of which Scripture speaks. So the reading of texts is part of the history of which the same texts speak. The reader thus discovers him or herself inside the Scriptures. The paradigmatic record of such a discovery was Augustine's *Confessions* and it was of course Augustine who had formulated in classical form the doctrine of understanding which came to inform the medieval tradition, a Platonic conception to which Augustine gave a Christian form. The recognition of the Platonism which the tradition thus inherited raises at once the question of whether Augustine's doctrine of interpretation extended to nonsacred texts.

Peter Brown has emphasized how far Augustine went in detaching Greco-Roman literature and doctrine from paganism and thus making them available for Christian purposes, either in ways more generally of benefit to mankind or with special reference to specifically Christian needs, as, for example, a knowledge of secular history aids in the understanding of sacred history (*Augustine of Hippo*, Berkeley, 1969, chapter 23; for Augustine's doctrine see *De vera religione* xxiv, 45, *In Ps. cxxxvi*, 10–11, *De doctrina Christiana*). But it is equally important to emphasize how on Augustine's view the powers of discrimination which are required to judge rightly in understanding secular literature can themselves become an expression of peculiarly Christian virtues, something exemplified in Augustine's own evaluation of the evidence provided by Cicero, Vergil, and Sallust about the virtues of republican Rome.

The relationship of reader to both sacred and secular texts is then mediated by a certain kind of teaching and a certain kind of initiation into a tradition of reading and interpretation. But no merely human teacher can by him or herself succeed in the relevant kinds of teaching. Even when the learner's task is to be introduced to that most everyday of classificatory schemes in which common names are affixed to objects, there is something problematic. For if in those ostensive demonstrations in which a child first learns a name by a teacher pointing at an object, nothing was involved except the utterance of the name, the act of pointing, and the presence of the object, learning could not occur; such learning requires an ability to understand both the significance of the act of pointing and the way in which the act of naming an object differs from that of merely uttering some expression in the presence of some object, and those are presupposed in and not supplied by acts of demonstrative ostension. The mind thus has to find within itself that which points it towards a source of intelligibility beyond itself, one which will provide what ostension by itself cannot; guided towards that source it discovers within itself an apprehension of timeless standards, of forms, an apprehension which is itself possible only in the light afforded by a source of intelligibility beyond the mind. So Augustine's epistemology was Platonic, in a version derived from Plotinus, but with this crucial difference. The intellect and the desires do not naturally move towards that good which is at once the foundation for knowledge and that from which lesser goods flow. The will which directs them is initially perverse and needs a kind of redirection which will enable it to trust obediently in a teacher who will guide the mind towards the discovery both of its own resources and of what lies outside the mind, both in nature and in God. Hence faith in authority has to precede rational understanding. And hence the acquisition of that virtue which the will requires to be so guided, humility, is the necessary first step in education or in self-education. In learning therefore we move towards and not from first principles and we discover truth only insofar as we discover the conformity of particulars to the forms in relation to which those particulars become intelligible, a relationship apprehended only by the mind illuminated by God. Rational justification is thus essentially retrospective.

In the reading of texts there is a movement both towards apprehending what the text says and towards apprehending that of which the text speaks. Because obscurities, discrepancies, and inconsistencies were found both within and between texts obstacles to those movements were identified. So the development of a tradition of commentary and interpretation was required, a tradition which took as its models the commentaries on Scripture of Augustine and Jerome. Within that tradition there were elaborated large agreements in interpretation, so that the onus placed upon dissenting interpretation became progressively more difficult to discharge. But there developed also against this background of agreement a set of more or less systematically disputed and debated issues in which problems of perhaps apparent, perhaps real disagreement within the texts commented upon were multiplied by problems of real disagreement between rival commentators and interpreters. So certain issues emerged as *quaestiones,* the formulation and discussion of which became in time incorporated into the methods of formal teaching, supplementing exegetical exposition by affording opportunity for what became increasingly stylized forms of disputation.

Central to this work of interpretative commentary and to the problematic which it engendered was the acknowledgment that any passage in a text might have more than one sense: a plain historical sense, a moral or tropological sense, an allegorical or mystical sense, and, in some writers, a fourth, an anagogical or spiritually educative sense. Different writers articulated this doctrine of the three or four senses in different ways. But the core of the doctrine commanded wide agreement. The historical sense is of the passage taken as an utterance in a particular context in which one or more persons are represented as acting, uttering, interacting, and the like; the passage is construed as an intended representation of what is reported. So the historical sense of the account of the seven days of creation in *Genesis* is that of a representation of seven sequences of events, each the events of one day. But Augustine himself had suggested that the true sense of the passage, the sense in which the passage is true, is not this. There is here an account of acts of divine creation not themselves temporally ordered in this way; underlying the historical sense there is another sense. Notice that in this example, as in this interpretative tradition generally, it is the historical sense which is primary; the other senses ascribed depend upon a certain analogical relationship to the historical sense. When a passage functions allegorically what can be referred to or described in the allegorical senses, or indeed in the moral or anagogical senses, is constrained by the intended sense and reference of the historical sense. And to say this is to make it clear that the sense of 'sense' when medieval writers speak of the four senses is quite other than that of 'sense' as generally used by contemporary writers, whether Fregean or non-Fregean.

Sense, as used by such medieval writers, does not belong to individual expressions in isolation from context, nor to sentences as such, but to units of discourse which can be characterized in terms of literary genres: narratives, proclamations, conversations, edicts. Such units are understood as uttered by someone to an audience which shares with the utterer a stock of fundamental beliefs, a stock of linguistic meanings, articulated in terms of a shared view of the universe, and a stock of proper names, applied to the same persons, places, and objects by means of agreement in the use of a set of definite descriptions. So according to more than one writer, for example, the narrative of the people of Israel crossing the Red Sea has both the historical sense of a narrative of events occurring in a particular time and place and the allegorical sense of a portrayal of Christ's deliverance of his people from death and destruction by his atonement.

It was in key part through reflection on the theory of the senses of Scripture that secular learning came to be better integrated into the Augustinian scheme. Monastic writers throughout the Middle Ages had drawn upon the classical texts preserved by their own scribes, arguing both that such texts had their due, if subordinate, place in the order of creation and that they provided literary forms for Christian use. So when St. Bernard, for example, eulogized his brother Gerard in a funeral sermon, *Super Cantica,* he quoted in addition to Scripture not only Jerome and Ambrose but also Socrates, Plato, and Cicero. And classical texts were often read as possessing more than one sense, sometimes as prophetic allegories of Christian truth. But these appropriations of ancient authors were for long centuries largely unsystematic. It was only with the development of the exegesis of Scripture in the twelfth century that the relationship of secular to sacred study became more clearly defined. Hugh of St. Victor, who taught at the abbey school of that name in Paris from about 1125 until his death in 1141, argued not only for the necessary primacy of the historical sense in the study of Scripture but for the need of a knowledge of secular history and geography if that sense were to be rightly apprehended. The right apprehension of the allegorical or mystical sense requires the study of theological doctrine. And to understand the tropological sense, human beings have to understand what work in the natural world they have to do as well as the structure of the natural world in which they have to perform that work. In this way the doctrine of the multiple senses of Scripture has an essential integrative function in Hugh of St. Victor's overall scheme of enquiry.

Yet the doctrine of the multiplicity of senses also multiplied occasions for interpretative disagreement and controversy, occasions evident in Hugh of St. Victor's writings. One limitation upon the growth of such disagreements was of course the constraints imposed by agreement upon the central dogmas of Catholic Christianity. But the development of doctrinal enquiry in the twelfth century in areas such as the nature of the atonement or that of the sacraments provided further occasion for the multiplication of dissension and difference. In this multiplication two philosophical aspects of twelfth-century thought were important.

In the twelfth century 'philosophia' is not the name of one particular discipline. 'Philosophia' still names enquiry as such and philosophical themes and theses are deployed as parts of different types of enquiry in different types of context. What was remarkable was the number and the heterogeneity of the philosophical standpoints inherited from the ancient world to which appeal was made, implicitly or explicitly. Consider first the variety of types of twelfth-century Platonism to which M. D. Chenu drew our attention thirty years ago (*La Theologie au douziéme siécle*, Paris, 1957, chapter 5): that derived through Augustine, that whose source was Boethius, that which stemmed from the reading of Pseudo-Dionysius, and the Islamic Neoplatonism of the *De Causis*, an Arabic paraphrase of Proclus, falsely attributed to Aristotle. Alongside these was the genuine, if limited, influence of Aristotle through Boethius's translations, some of which – the *Categories* and the *De Interpretatione* – had a more or less continuous history, others of which – the *Prior Analytics, Topics,* and *Sophistici Elenchi* – had been lost but were rediscovered around 1120. It was also to Boethius's work as translator that the Middle Ages owed that understanding of Aristotle's *Categories* which derived from Porphyry's *Isagōgē*.

Alongside these partial appropriations of Plato and Aristotle were to be found versions of atomism, such as that propounded by William of Conches, and of Stoic positions, some of them transmitted through Jerome, some learned from what was known of Seneca. It would have been unsurprising if what had emerged had been a certain unprincipled eclecticism, a mere *mélange* of viewpoints. What saved the twelfth century from such eclecticism was the existence of an overall framework of belief within which the different uses of different parts of ancient philosophy had to be put to work and in terms of which they had in the end to be justified. But the existence of such a framework did not preclude radical disagreement.

So it was also with the other central philosophical aspect of twelfth-century enquiry, the application of dialectic to theological questions. In this application three different and originally independent strands in the intellectual development of the Augustinian tradition came together. The first concerned the use of the *quaestio*. Beginning from Augustine's own formulation of *quaestiones* there had developed by the eleventh century the custom of interpolating *quaestiones* into commentary on Scripture, both spoken and written, and gradually the proportion of space devoted to such *quaestiones* rather than to commentary increased. In the statement of the alternative solutions to a *quaestio* and the arguments *pro* and *contra* for each solution more and more use was made of materials provided by the subordinate liberal arts of grammar and dialectic, and at the same time, especially in the eleventh century, *quaestiones* were posed concerning the truth or falsity of certain theological doctrines and not simply concerning the interpretation of texts. So emerges a conception of enquiry as consisting in the sequential posing of a series of related *quaestiones* through which the problems concerning some particular subject matter were posed in a sequential systematic way.

To this development in the *quaestio* there corresponds a development in the use of dialectic. The master-text for dialectic in the earlier Middle Ages was that provided by Boethius in the *De topicis differentiis*, a work which followed Aristotle's *Topics* closely, and which, like Aristotle's work, deals with what is distinctive in dialectical as contrasted with demonstrative arguments. Certain differences between dialectic and demonstration are crucial. Demonstrative arguments state and order already known truths, vindicating the status of such truths as certain knowledge, as parts of some science. A perfected science exhibits its form as a chain of such arguments, descending from its necessary first principles to its subordinate conclusions. By contrast dialectical argument is exploratory. Dialectic is the instrument of enquiry which is still *in via*. It is through dialectic that we construct demonstrative arguments, and thus while in demonstrative reasoning we argue *from* first principles, in dialectical we argue *to* first principles. Since on the Augustinian conception the movement of enquiry is towards first principles, dialectic is necessarily its argumentative instrument. But since dialectic argues from premises so far agreed, or at least not put in question, to conclusions which are not necessary truths but only the most compelling conclusion to be arrived at so far, the work of dialectic always has an essentially uncompleted and provisional character. A dialectical conclusion is always open to further challenge.

A third strand of intellectual development was the systematic growth in the making of distinctions in types of sense, not only in explicating Scripture but also in understanding secular texts, so that in time there arises a new genre, a set of works characteristically entitled *Distinctiones*. The technique of making such distinctions of sense was enriched by the contributions of grammarians as well as of commentators. And this technique could then become an additional instrument of dialectical argument, which in turn could serve the purposes of systematic enquiry organized as a succession of *quaestiones*. Thus what had been three relatively independent strands of development came together in the newly comprehensive works of the twelfth century.

When the heterogeneity of the philosophical sources inherited from the ancient world and the multiplication of *quaestiones* and *distinctiones* are juxtaposed, the large possibilities of radical intellectual dissension even within the constraints imposed by an Augustinian framework become clear. This possibility became apparent to his contemporaries in the style, methods, and conclusions of Abelard. Modern accounts of Abelard are generally of two kinds, dry as dust and technicolor. The dry as dust congratulate Abelard on having in some ways anticipated Frege; the technicolor celebrate his passion-driven lack of respect for limits in sexuality and in disputation. Such romantic accounts err not so much by inaccuracy as in lack of perspective. Abelard did indeed anticipate in some respects much later accounts of predication and quantification, but he did so in the course of putting twelfth-century Platonism in its due place within an Augustinian framework and so ensuring that the Platonism served the Augustinianism rather than vice versa. And it is also true that Abelard *did* challenge established authority, but yet by his own obedient acceptance of established authority's response he did as much as anyone to clarify the relationship of dialectic to authority. In these two important respects he elaborated the central tenets of the Augustinian tradition beyond his predecessors.

It was in the course of the controversy over universals that Abelard made his contributions to a better understanding of predication. What was at stake for medieval Platonism in that controversy? St. Augustine had transformed Plato's *eidē* into exemplars of created things in the mind of God. To progress in understanding the world of creation as it truly is is to move away from the initial judgments of everyday life, which in both thought and words are entangled in error, towards the formation of a mind whose judgments conform to what things are. And the truth of things lies in their conformity to the exemplars, a conformity not manifest in those particularities of the natural world which present themselves as subject matter for our initial judgments.

Platonism in this as in all its versions is antagonistic to ordinary language; ordinary uses of language always stand in need of correction. But what William of Champeaux had done was to transform Platonism into a theory of meaning for ordinary language. Universals both distinct and separate from particulars are, on his account, what ordinary language nouns refer to, and in virtue of so referring, have the meaning that they have. So the apprehension of the true forms turns out to be something involved in comprehending ordinary meanings, not something that provides a *telos* for a long process of enquiry. Abelard's achievement in exhibiting the absurdities which followed from William's position had the consequence that a clear and viable distinction was made between the *intellectus universalis,* the mind's everyday grasp of properties common to those objects grouped together by a *nomen universale,* and any apprehension of the essential natures of things present to the mind of God. The perfecting of the mind's understanding is a movement *towards* a comprehension of the genuinely universal, but it does not of itself yield a knowledge of true essences.

Abelard himself recognized his conformity to what he knew of Aristotle, and although John of Salisbury misunderstood Abelard's position, ascribing to him a nominalism which he did not in fact hold, he was right in understanding Abelard's views as reconcilable with an Aristotelian position. Indeed there is here an important and influential anticipation of Aquinas's synthesis of a particular version of Augustinian Platonism with Aristotle. It was therefore important for subsequent enquiry that Abelard rescued the controversy over universals from the earlier sterile debates between nominalists and realists from which the theses of William of Champeaux had emerged.

To understand Abelard in this perspective is in no way to denigrate his achievements, either generally in revising what had hitherto been understood concerning the relationships of grammar and logic or more particularly in his accounts of meaning, denotation, and inference; it is only to insist that the context of these achievements was very different from that of those logicians who rediscovered some of Abelard's theses in the late nineteenth and early twentieth centuries, something which becomes plain when we remember that Abelard's aim was by means of his logical discoveries to elucidate the doctrine of the Holy Trinity. It was in so doing that he laid himself open to accusations of heresy by Bernard of Clairvaux.

Abelard does not in fact seem to have held heretical views. It is all the more striking that he obediently accepted his condemnation, agreeing with Bernard in his understanding of the limits imposed upon the life of enquiry by the need for such condemnations. What Bernard and Abelard agreed upon, and no consistent Augustinian could have held otherwise, was that the integrity of the life of enquiry requires such interventions by authority.

Bernard, as a Cistercian, followed the Rule of St. Benedict, whose practical theology presupposes what St. Augustine had affirmed, that it is only through the transformation of the will from a state of pride to one of humility that the intelligence can be rightly directed. Will is more fundamental than intelligence and thinking undirected by a will informed by humility will always be apt to go astray. It was clearly pride of will which Bernard discerned in Abelard and which Abelard acknowledged by his submission that he had discerned in himself. So it is the underlying epistemology of Augustinian enquiry which requires the condemnation of heresy, since heresy is always a sign of pride in choosing to elevate one's own judgment above that of genuine authority.

It was then the exercise of authority and the recognition accorded to authority which prevented the development of dialectical argument from fracturing the unity of enquiry into a multitude of disagreements, even though that enquiry drew upon heterogeneous philosophical sources. But it is important that the conception of authority thus appealed to is itself a necessary feature of the Augustinian scheme of understanding. Authority enters into that scheme at two points. Initially, because rationally unjustified belief has to precede understanding, belief has to be accepted on authority. What authority provides at this point is testimony to the truth on certain matters. Testimony is to be received in a way very different from reports providing *evidence*. Evidence is to be evaluated in the light of what is taken to be the probability of the occurrence of the type of event reported. Belief in testimony is proportioned by contrast to the degree of trust reposed in the person whose testimony it is and often to the person not as such, but as speaking out of some role or as the holder of some office.

So in the Augustinian scheme when I first believe in order that I may go on to understand, I do not evaluate evidence, but put my trust in certain persons as authorized to represent the apostolic testimony, something which I may come to do in many different kinds of way, none of which will be at that preliminary stage good-reason-providing, because I cannot as yet know how in this area to evaluate reasons as good or otherwise. My belief may indeed be a response to something apparently as accidental as my eye falling upon a passage from Paul in a book which I picked up on overhearing a child playing nearby say "*Tolle, lege; Tolle, lege.*" But the apparent arbitrariness of this initial acceptance of authority is itself something that is to be adequately understood only later, and in that later understanding authority is reencountered in a very different way.

By accepting authority, as we saw at the outset, one acquires a teacher who both introduces one to certain texts and educates one into becoming the sort of person capable of reading those texts with understanding, texts in which such a person discovers the story of him or herself, including the story of how he or she was transformed into a reader of these texts. This story of oneself is embedded in the history of the world, an overall narrative within which all other narratives find their place. That history is a movement towards the truth becoming manifest, a movement towards intelligibility. But in the course of discovering the intelligibility of the order of things, we also discover why at different stages greater or lesser degrees of unintelligibility remain. And in learning this we learn that authoritative testimony, to point us forward from where we now are, can never in our present bodily life be dispensed with. So continuous authority receives its justification as indispensable to a continuing progress, the narrative of which we first learned how to recount from that authority and the truth of which is confirmed by our own further progress, including that progress made by means of dialectical enquiry. The practice of specifically Augustinian dialectic and the belief of the Augustinian dialectician that this practice is a movement towards a truth never as yet wholly grasped thus presupposes the guidance of authority. Hence when the very same authority places restrictions upon dialectical enquiry, it would be unreasonable not to submit. Abelard's submission, therefore, unlike Galileo's, was of a piece with his enquiries. The acknowledgment of authority was already an essential element in those enquiries.

This view of the place of authority within enquiry, like other key parts of the Augustinian scheme, presupposes a particular understanding of how texts relate to that of which they speak and of how progress in the reading and understanding of texts changes the relationship of the reader to that of which the texts speak. Or rather, since the reader him or herself is part of the subject matter about which the texts speak, what is changed is the relationship of the reader to other elements of that subject matter.

Some modern writers on texts in general and on narrative more particularly have argued that the form and the ordering of a text are a literary imposition by its author upon a subject matter which, apart from the text and its form and order, would be unformed and unordered. Every text is thus to some degree a creative falsification of that of which it speaks. On this view any enquiry concerned with truth which examines the subject matter of which some particular text speaks independently of that text will discover a lack of correspondence between text and subject matter. So Tolstoy argued in one way, so Sartre in another.

By contrast there are those other modern writers who have argued that we have no access to the peculiar and idiosyncratic subject matter of any text except that afforded by the text itself. The understanding of any text can only be in the terms provided by that text and hence the question of truth or falsity in relation to some genuinely external subject matter cannot arise. This latter type of view has characteristically been formulated as one stage in an argument which aspires to move to some even more radical conclusion: perhaps that each text must be judged in its own terms, perhaps that texts are nothing but what we, the readers, make of them.

What these very different and mutually incompatible ways of thinking about texts agree in is that no sense can be made of the nature of a systematic correspondence between, on the one hand, a text with its meanings, its sequential and other orderings, its boundaries and its references, and, on the other, some external reality not a text and not therefore to be read and interpreted but rather apprehended in some quite other way. The arguments advanced in support of this contention have much in common with those objections which have been cogently urged against any version of the correspondence theory of truth, in which truth consists in some relationship between the elements and ordering of some linguistic items, often a sentence, and some nonlinguistic item, perhaps a fact.

The Augustinian standpoint is not however open to this type of objection. Particular texts do indeed characterize, refer to, stand in different types of relationships of correspondence to something beyond and outside themselves, but that something is always another text. At once it may be objected: surely the texts of Scripture tell us, or at least purport to tell us, about nature and history. But nature, including human nature and human history, is itself on this view a text: "For the whole perceptible world," wrote Hugh of St. Victor, "is indeed as if a book written by the finger of God" (*De tribus diebus* ii), in this following Augustine himself (*Enarratio in Ps. 45, 7*), and Alan of Lille went further in saying that the whole of the created world is for us "as if a book and a picture and a mirror" (*Rythmus alter*). A text is a series of signs; that of which it speaks is a series of corresponding signs. The dramatic narrative of Scripture mirrors the enacted dramatic narrative of scriptural history. God, as author of both, speaks to us in both, and the texts of Scripture themselves speak of this speaking to us in both and of us as hearing or failing to hear. God is thus the authoritative interpreter of his meanings, and the authorities which he has appointed to speak in his place, both ecclesiastical and secular, are therefore authoritative in interpretation and evaluation, not only of nature and history and of Scripture, but of those theological conclusions of dialectical enquiry which draw their premises either from nature and history or from Scripture. The determinacy of meaning of texts requires and receives the exercise of interpretative authority, authority of just the kind to which Abelard submitted.

What then does progress in reading and understanding texts, including the text of nature, consist in? It consists at one level in activities characterizable by an external observer as an identification of discrepancies and incoherences within texts, the formulation of hy-

potheses for overcoming them and a search for evidence to confirm
or disconfirm such hypotheses, the integration of newly discovered
or rediscovered texts into the body of knowledge, and the construction of ever more adequate ways to classify and systematize what has
been learned. In these activities dialectical argument is employed both
to investigate the underlying ontology of the scheme of knowledge
and to elucidate the problematic issues arising in the course of enquiry. But all of these contribute to and are constituted as progress
only insofar as the mind of the enquirer engaged in such activity moves
from an initial stage, in which it does not know either itself or other
finite beings or God as exhibiting the degree and kind of perfection
which belongs to each of these, towards such apprehensions as it is
capable of, of the perfection of each; and in achieving this progress
it also perfects itself.

There were different and rival Augustinian epistemologies which
provided somewhat different characterizations of the initial and final
states of mind and of the transition from one to the other. Hugh
of St. Victor took one view, Alan of Lille another. What such rival
epistemologies share is a conception of the objects to be apprehended
by the human mind as intelligible as such, prior to any particular
human mind apprehending them. The mind comes to be informed
by this intelligibility, but only because of the light afforded it by God.
This analogical use of the concept of light, with its assimilation of
the intelligible to the visible, is essential to the Augustinian epistemology. So God is present to every human mind, albeit often unrecognized, in every act of apprehension and judgment, and present
not only as omnipresent creator but as constituting that act of apprehension and judgment. And in every such act there is an ineliminable
reference to God, albeit often unintended as well as unacknowledged,
insofar as in saying of anything that it is or what it is, we make at
least an indirect reference to its being perfectly or imperfectly what it is.

It is then in the inescapably universal application of the concept of perfection that God is universally acknowledged, an acknowledgment which Anselm transformed into an argument, an argument
that from the assertion of the existence within the mind of that than
which no greater can be conceived it follows that that than which
no greater can be conceived exists also outside the mind. Anselm's
arguments are in no way accidentally in the form of prayer. To understand the required concept adequately the mind must already be di-

rected by faith towards its true perfection. The rational justification of belief in the object of faith is internal to the life of faith.

It was because such intellectual enquiry in the Augustinian mode is conceived as a progress towards perfection through an ever more adequate apprehension of perfection that theoretical enquiry and practical enquiry were so closely interrelated. The disciplines of the monastic life, more especially of those reformations of the monastic life in which the Rule of St. Benedict had been reestablished, provided a religious ideal to which the twelfth-century scholar was both indebted and from which he was all too apt to distinguish his own vocation. But in the life of the canons who followed the rules designed by Augustine for the secular clergy, exemplified at the Abbey of St. Victor, the two types of ideal were held together. It was however in the course of the twelfth century that the question of what Augustinianism involved for the practical life began to assume new dimensions and did so precisely as the Augustinian tradition came under pressure to provide the intellectual foundation and framework for a type of education directed both at those who were not clergy and at new kinds of clergy.

Such pressure was generated from more than one direction. The centralizing administrations of both royal and papal courts needed lawyers; the changing occupational patterns of town life required new forms of literacy; the clergy had new types of demands made upon them. At the same time developments in logic, in grammar, in the relation between these two, and in the other *artes liberales* had raised in various ways questions about the overall structure and purpose of purely secular knowledge. It was in response to this that there appeared a genre of writing which, in providing a more or less comprehensive conspectus of knowledge and enquiry, became the ancestor of the later genre of the encyclopaedia. Notable among these was Hugh of St. Victor's *Didascalion: de Studio Legendi* of which Beryl Smalley wrote that the author's purpose "was to recall rebellious learning back to the scriptural framework of the *De Doctrina Christiana*" (*The Study of Bible in the Middle Ages,* Oxford, 1952, p. 86) in an attempt to do for twelfth-century Paris what Augustine had achieved for Hippo at the end of the fourth century. What Hugh wanted to achieve was the subordination of all learning to the reading of Scripture in order that study might issue in the perfecting of practical life; in trying to impose an order upon studies designed to achieve this end, he defined one key position in what was to become a debate not only about the structure of the curriculum but about academic and educational institution-building. The importance of the outcome of that debate in Paris is best understood by considering the significance of the contrast between what emerged as a university at Paris and what emerged at Bologna.

It is a commonplace to contrast these two in terms of the structures of corporate power and authority: Paris was a university of masters, a university controlled by teachers, while Bologna was a university of students, in which teachers were employed by their pupils. But underlying this difference is another. The teaching at Bologna was designed to serve the purposes of the students, purposes determined prior to and independently of anything learned from that teaching. The teaching at Paris was designed to reeducate students into a more adequate knowledge of ends and purposes, so that the desires with which they came to study might be corrected. Education at Bologna was designed to be useful in terms of a standard of utility established in the realm of political power, whether secular or ecclesiastical. Unsurprisingly the most important academic subject was held to be law. Education at Paris was designed to put in question just such standards of utility by enquiring how the useful ought to be related to the quest for human perfection, conceived in Augustinian terms, a quest the point of which is necessarily invisible to those not already engaged in it. Hence all education at Paris was subordinated to and directed towards the study of theology. And in understanding university life at Paris in these terms I am not taking an idealized view.

Stephen C. Ferruolo has recently reexamined the question of how the University of Paris came to be founded and has argued that, although the corporate interests of masters in securing their autonomy and security from external authority was certainly important at Paris, as it was at Bologna, both the forms of organization of the university at Paris and its curriculum cannot be adequately explained except as the outcome of a debate over educational ideals (*The Origins of the University*, Stanford, 1985). The needed comprehensive ordering and synthesis of old and new knowledge could only now be achieved on a new kind of institutional bases.

Paris was thus in origin an Augustinian university, expressing in its forms of teaching the distinctively Augustinian conceptions of moral enquiry and of rationality. Those conceptions are apt to affront the characteristically modern mind just because they make rationality internal to a system of beliefs and practices in such a way that, without acceptance at some fundamental level of those beliefs and initiation into the form of life defined by those practices, rational encounter with Augustinianism is ruled out, except in the most limited way. It is not that there are not notable points of intellectual contact between particular Augustinian theses and a number of positions which have been advanced in the modern world in very different contexts and with very different purposes. In Descartes we find Augustine's *si fallor, sum* transformed into the *cogito*. In Berkeley the Augustinian conception of nature as a series of signs reappears. Wittgenstein, mistakenly thinking himself to be repudiating Augustine's view of ostensive learning, in fact reproduced part of Augustine's own central thesis. And a certain relationship to the Augustinian standpoint can be discerned even in some of those who reject it most trenchantly.

Nietzsche remarked, as I noted in an earlier lecture: "I fear we are not getting rid of God because we still believe in grammar." What Nietzsche meant by belief in grammar was belief that the structure of language somehow mirrors and presupposes belief in an order of things, in virtue of which one mode of conceptualizing reality can be more adequate to that reality than another. To rid oneself of such a belief would be instead to treat purely linguistic meanings as a set of context-free structures, available for expressing an indefinitely large number of alternative conceptualizations, none more adequate than any other, because there is *no* underlying reality in relation to which adequacy could be measured. It was Nietzsche's insight that so long as reference to such a reality is still presupposed, belief in God is covertly present. And in so asserting Nietzsche simply inverted the Augustinian standpoint: without God there is no genuine objectivity of interpretation or conceptualization.

More recently Umberto Eco (*Semiotics and the Philosophy of Language*, London, 1984, section 2.2) has chided Porphyry for the inadequacy of his semantics. Porphyry's error, according to Eco, is not to have given an account of categorial predication in which the meanings of the predicates were context-independent in such a way as not to presuppose by their application belief in any one particular conceptual and analogical scheme. Porphyry's Neoplatonic commentary on Aristotle was however acceptable to Platonists, Aristotelians, and

Augustinians precisely because it involved a rejection of the kind of linguistics taken to be science by Eco, a semiformal *a priori* linguistics independent of ontology. Porphyry was not trying to be Eco and failing; he was engaged in an alternative and rival enterprise.

It might be supposed that, since Augustinianism is thus committed to a variety of agreements and disagreements with the protagonists of other positions, we could find in the subject matter of those agreements and disagreements grounds for evaluating Augustinianism without having first to enter into and accept Augustinian faith and practice. Is Augustine's treatment of the *cogito* superior or inferior to Descartes's? Is Berkeley's treatment of natural events and objects as signs more compelling than the Augustinian theses? Does Wittgenstein direct us towards a better treatment of the limitations of ostensive definition than Augustine does? Does Nietzsche's inversion of Augustine discredit Augustine? Are the semantics of Eco and J. J. Katz superior to those of Porphyry?

Yet were we to suppose that we could pursue answers to these questions piecemeal and in order and so test certain Augustinian claims, we should already from the Augustinian point of view have begged the question. For each specific Augustinian thesis stands or falls, from the Augustinian standpoint, as part of the overall scheme of belief. Abstract the parts from that whole, treat them as if they are not parts, and you no longer have the Augustinian theses but only a counterfeit version of them. And it is the scheme as a whole which requires that it be believed before it can be understood. So that there seems to be no way to pass a verdict on the Augustinian scheme of theoretical and practical enquiry from any standpoint which is not that of a participant in that enquiry.

It is to this wholeness, this all-or-nothing character of the Augustinian scheme that the form of the university curriculum at Paris was to owe its shape. Each part contributes a necessary element in the movement towards a more adequate understanding of perfection, both the to-be-perfected status of humanity and the timeless perfection of God, a movement which, embodied in a particular human life, is the enquiry of that particular person about his or her own good. The uneducated understand themselves through the images of scriptural narrative which the educated interpret to them. Hence derives one aspect at least of the crucial importance of preaching. And hence derives also the importance for the University of Paris, as an

Augustinian university, that so early in its life the Dominican order, the Order of Preachers, should have begun to play so large a part in that life, both in the provision of professors of theology and in bringing students to Paris.

Yet to point this out can only be to add to the sense of affront produced in modernity by the impact of Augustine's high medieval theological heirs. Modernity asks for arguments. And the Augustinian responds that in this area there can be no shared premises unless and until the word of the scriptural preacher is heard as authoritative. Yet it does not follow that the Augustinian scheme of belief is or was invulnerable, even from the standpoint of its own adherents. It in fact is and was vulnerable in two different ways. First, like all developed traditions of intellectual and practical enquiry, it has its own internal problematic, that set of questions which arise within the tradition and to the provision of answers to which, or at least to progress towards the provision of answers to which, the adherents of that tradition are committed. For the Augustinian tradition three types of problem arise.

The first is one which arises for every type of Platonism. If to understand any particular is to understand it in its relationship to a form or universal in the light of which alone that particular can be made intelligible, what is the nature of that relationship? Plato's own negative conclusions in the *Parmenides,* let alone Aristotle's criticisms, seem to rule out certain types of answer. And the content of William of Champeaux's arguments reinforces the view that Augustinian Platonism confronted problems in this area, problems defined as such by its own standards, for the solution of which it had hitherto been unable to find adequate resources.

A second set of problems concerns the part played by divine illumination in generating knowledge in the created mind. The difficulties here arise from the apparent incompatibility of a variety of statements made by Augustine himself. Augustine had agreed with Plotinus in denying that the human mind possesses within itself, as part of its own nature, an active principle which effects understanding. Hence all understanding requires divine illumination (*De Civitate Dei* x, 2). But Augustine also held that due to the sin deriving from Adam's fall human beings in a state of nature could not see or benefit from that light. Only by the grace afforded by our redemption is illumination restored. Hence it seems to follow that human beings in a state of nature must lack understanding altogether. And plainly they do not, something which Augustine himself recognizes time and again. So that there is an apparent contradiction at the heart of the Augustinian account of knowledge.

Thirdly, Augustine and the Augustinians both present human defection from the good as a matter of the perversity of the will. It is the will which directs and misdirects the intellect. But what the Augustinian doctrine fails to provide is any adequate account of how the intellect is or was related to the good before and apart from its being misled by the will. What would it be for the intellect to be rightly ordered according to its own nature?

These three sets of problems are closely related to each other in a variety of ways. And by the standards of Augustinianism itself, failure to advance enquiry in respect of them could not but raise questions about the rational justification of the Augustinian scheme of belief as a basis for intellectual and practical enquiry. Yet this is not the only way in which that scheme is and was vulnerable to critical questioning. For the Augustinian is also committed to one central negative thesis about all actually or potentially rival positions: that no substantive rationality, independent of faith, will be able to provide an adequate vindication of its claims.

So the Augustinian is committed to holding that neither Cartesian nor empiricist nor Kantian nor Hegelian nor positivist rationality will be able to vindicate its claims, even in its own terms. Each in its own historical development, so the Augustinian must claim, will exhibit its own failure, either by falling into ineradicable incoherence, or by being compelled to acknowledge points at which there is an unavoidable resort to attitudes of unjustified and unjustifiable belief, or both. And among those projects of enquiry whose failure the Augustinian is committed to predicting are of course both that which was to be expounded in Adam Gifford's will and that defended by Nietzsche.

Where Adam Gifford held that the methods of moral and theological enquiry required a starting point in universally available rationally warranted first principles, the Augustinian denies that there can be any such principles. Where Adam Gifford held that moral and theological enquiry require no prior initial and initiating commitment to any particular form of religious belief, the Augustinian claims that it is only through initial commitment to one specific type of

Christian belief that rational enquiry can be developed. And where Adam Gifford held that tradition presents itself to us to be sifted and evaluated by our standards, the Augustinian holds that we have to learn from authoritative tradition how to sift and to evaluate ourselves.

The contrast with and opposition between Augustine and Nietzsche is of course even sharper, if that is possible. What Augustine condemned, Nietzsche praised. Where the one saw a type of personality which manifested the perversity of the fallen will in the arrogance of the vice of pride, the other saw that "nobility of instinct" which Christianity had crushed. And where Augustine saw the virtue of humility, Nietzsche perceived a perverse weakness and sickness (*Der Antichrist* 59), one manifesting itself centuries later in that *ressentiment* of the Augustinian Luther, from which Nietzsche's father's religion had stemmed.

So Augustinianism requires for its fullest rational vindication not only progress in the solution of its own problems but further confirmation by the way in which such rival projects of intellectual and practical enquiry exhibit incoherence or resourcelessness. And correspondingly it itself is put in question by the success of such rival projects. It was therefore of the first importance for the history of Augustinianism that soon after it had been provided with a new and authoritative form of institutional expression, by the founding of the University of Paris, it confronted a challenge of such dimensions that its ability to vindicate itself was put seriously in question. That challenge was posed by the rediscovery of Aristotle's philosophy in all its integrity, and it was a challenge which raised not only questions of the truth of key theological doctrines but also questions about the Augustinian curriculum and the account of knowledge presupposed by that curriculum.

First, it was the claim of the Augustinian scheme, as expounded not only by Hugh of St. Victor but also by other writers on the curriculum, that within that scheme all types of secular knowledge, new or old, could be integrated. The multiplication of texts from the ancient world had already raised questions about that claim; but the recovery of Aristotelian science, as expounded by the Islamic commentators, did more than raise questions. For it provided as part of its corpus a set of natural scientific texts which assigned to the natural sciences both a content and an importance quite alien to Augustinianism as hitherto formulated.

Secondly, Aristotle provided accounts of what a science is, of what enquiry is, and of the *telos* of all enquiry that were notably at odds with Augustine's version of Platonism, more especially in leaving no place and in having no need, in its account of the genesis of knowledge, for divine illumination. So that in certain respects it seemed to be the case that the Augustinian scheme could be true only if the Aristotelian was false, and vice versa.

Hence at once an Augustinian dilemma. Admit the Aristotelian corpus into the scheme of studies and you thereby confront the student with not one, but two claims upon his allegiance, claims which at key points are mutually exclusive. Exclude the Aristotelian corpus from the scheme of studies and you put in question both the universal, integrative claims of Augustinianism and the claims of the university, at least as understood at Paris. It was on the ability of the protagonists of Augustinianism to resolve the issues posed by this dilemma that the fate of their doctrine turned, something which became increasingly more evident in each successive decade of the thirteenth century. But before the story of the Augustinian response can be adequately told, it is necessary to evaluate the dimensions of the Aristotelian challenge.

Bibliographical Note

On the central topics referred to in the text see: on Augustinian epistemologies T. J. Clarke, S.J., *The Background and Implications of Duns Scotus' Theory of Knowing in the Beatific Vision,* Brandeis University Ph.D. dissertation, 1970; on the *quaestio* and the *distinctio* A. M. Landgraf *Einführung in die Geschichte der theologischen Literatur der Fruhscolastik,* Ratisbon, 1948, chapter II, sections 4 and 7; on the exegesis of Scripture, section 3 of the same work, and Henri de Lubac, S.J., *Exégèse Medievale: les Quatre Sens de l' Écriture,* four vols., Paris, 1959, and Beryl Smalley *The Study of the Bible in the Middle Ages,* Oxford, 1952; on the curriculum and the founding of Paris University David L. Wagner, ed., *The Seven Liberal Arts in the Middle Ages,* Bloomington, 1983, J. W. Baldwin *The Scholastic Culture of the Mid-*

dle Ages 1000–1300, Lexington, 1971, and Stephen C. Ferruolo *The Origins of the University,* Stanford, 1985; on monastic culture Jean Leclerq, O.S.B., *L'Amour des lettres et le désir de Dieu,* Paris, 1958; and on the twelfth century generally R. L. Benson and G. Constable, eds., *Renaissance and Renewal in the Twelfth Century,* Cambridge, Mass., 1982, and J. de Ghellinck *Le Mouvement théologique de XII siède,* second edition, Bruges, 1948. The *Didascalion* of Hugh of St. Victor has been translated by Jerome Taylor, New York, 1961.

V

Aristotle and/or/against Augustine: Rival Traditions of Enquiry

The problems of the relationship of Aristotle's doctrines to those of a theism whose doctrines included belief in divine creation of the world and in the immortality of the soul had of course been posed within Islam before they were confronted by the theologians of Western Christianity. And since what such theologians confronted was not only the greatly enlarged body of Aristotelian texts made available to them in the twelfth and thirteenth centuries but also the accompanying Islamic commentary, culminating in that of Abu-I-Walid ibn Rushd (ibn Rushd, Averroës, was to be for Aquinas simply "the commentator" just as Aristotle was "the philosopher"), the encounter of Islam with Aristotle provides the crucial background to thirteenth-century European intellectual history. Since Jewish thinkers too had had to define their positions in relation to both Aristotle and Islam, they also, and more especially Moses Ben Maimon, Maimonides, had presented treatments of those problems which had led to reformulations of the problems. The difficulty which confronted most of the Latin appropriators of Aristotle, the so-called Latin Averroists, was that, while they inherited their problems from their Islamic and Judaic predecessors, they were unable to accept at certain central and crucial points the solutions proposed by those predecessors.

Averroës had contrasted his own situation as a philosopher in twelfth-century Cordoba with that of Plato in fourth-century Athens. Plato had been able to contrast the conclusions of the philosopher with mere popular belief. Truth belongs to the former, whereas the latter cannot be true. But the Islamic philosopher has to share the beliefs of the masses, affirming the truth of those same beliefs pre-

sented in the form of prophetic narrative as well as of his own conclusions; indeed the perfection of the class of the learned and the
achievement by its members of their *telos* in full happiness cannot
be attained except insofar as they understand themselves as a part of
a whole, the whole community of Islam, masses and learned alike.
So the truths of philosophical theory have to be reconciled with those
of the prophetically authorized and authored stories; but the task
of such reconciliation falls of course to the philosopher. That the philosopher remains faithful to Islam and to its law has to be ascertained
by the religious authorities, but those authorities appeal to the Qur'an
and to the law itself in so deciding, not to any philosophical understanding of truth or of rationality.

For Maimonides, as for Averroës, the problems of the relationship of philosophy to the Torah is a problem for the philosopher,
quite distinct from those of talmudic and posttalmudic commentary.
So there is a crucial distinction of genres; the appeal to authority in
the *Mishneh Torah* provides in the mode of commentary a standard
with which nothing written in any other genre can be allowed to be
inconsistent, but the genre of rational enquiry in *The Guide for the
Perplexed* is that in which theoretical questions are pursued. Within
the *Mishneh Torah* questions of internal consistency arise and in the
first four chapters both the philosophical theses required of anyone
who accepts Halakhic authority and the place of philosophical enquiry, of both metaphysics and physics, within the life of the Jewish
sage are discussed. But philosophical enquiry itself and the understanding of truth and rationality involved in such enquiry are reserved for the philosopher, and it is in *The Guide for the Perplexed* that
Maimonides found a distinctive philosophical genre for the discussion of the systematic relationship of philosophy to the acceptance
of Halakhic authority and all that such acceptance entails.

Thus for both Averroës and Maimonides the religious doctrines
and practices with which Aristotelian philosophy and philosophical
enquiry more generally have to be reconciled and integrated might
place constraints upon the activities and conclusions of the philosopher but were not themselves informed by philosophical themes,
theories, and arguments. More particularly they did not contain within
themselves any well-articulated understanding of truth and rationality. For the Latin Averroists it was of course quite otherwise. They
confronted not only the problems of consistency with prophetic nar-

rative and with legal prescription which had already engaged Averroës and Maimonides but also those which arose from the fact that
the dogmatic theology of Latin Christianity was pervasively informed
by philosophical theories and conclusions and carried within it its
own Augustinian understanding of truth and rationality, an understanding apparently irreconcilable with that of Aristotle as presented
by the best commentators and interpretations so far. Philosophy of
one kind thus encountered philosophy of quite another, each with
its own standards for evaluating the truth and rationality of philosophical claims and those two sets of standards apparently incommensurable as well as incompatible.

Radical inconsistencies between the two standpoints emerged
at three different levels. That which most easily and recurrently drew
the attention of ecclesiastical and theological authority concerned central Christian doctrines. Where Aristotle asserted the eternity of the
world, Christianity assigns to it a beginning at the moment of creation; where Aristotle ruled out the separate immaterial existence of
the individual soul, and where Averroës' interpretation of the *De
Anima,* although it left room for the resurrection of the dead, reinforced the denial of any survival of the soul apart from the body, Christianity was committed to belief in such survival. But although such
antitheses, whereby the truth of the Christian religion seemed to be
put in question, were naturally enough the focus of ecclesiastical attention, they may well obscure from us the importance of two other
levels of encounter, types of encounter both made possible in part
and also delayed by the extraordinary degree of tact and prudence
shown in the first half of the thirteenth century by ecclesiastical authority in the various warnings and prohibitions which it issued on
the subject of the reading and teaching of Aristotle. For where we
might perhaps have expected blanket condemnations, we find instead
a variety of restrictions, partial prohibitions, and cautions, leading
to a selective reading, so that Aristotle's works do not at first make
their impact *as a whole,* as a systematic mode of thought challenging
the dominant Augustinianism not only in respect of this or that particular dogma or philosophical or theological thesis but in respect
of style of thought, of the structuring of enquiry, and of fundamental standards. Instead different works were read in independence of
each other and valued for different kinds of reason.

So in an anonymous guide to how a candidate should prepare

for examinations at Paris, written between 1230 and 1240 and discovered by Grabmann at Barcelona in 1927 (Ripoll, 109; see F. Van Steenberghen *Aristotle in the West,* Louvain, 1955, pp. 95–100) we find some works of Aristotle considered at length (for example, the *De Interpretatione* and the *Ethics*), some adverted to so briefly that they were clearly not studied at Paris (the *Metaphysics* and the *Physics*), and some completely unknown to the author (the *Politics,* for example). The latter of course was not yet translated, but what attention was paid to those works which had been translated plainly varied a good deal from work to work. Yet already, as Van Steenberghen points out, a distinction is being made in this guide between how philosophers—as contrasted with theologians—should respond to certain questions raised by Aristotle, as if philosophy and theology could conduct their enquiries in complete independence of one another, and the specific questions are among those to which certain particular philosophical answers were later to be condemned by ecclesiastical authority. So even before 1240 it was beginning to become clear that it was the established organization and structure of enquiry that was being put in question and, more particularly, the relationship of theology to the other disciplines within that organization and structure, and not just this or that particular thesis. This then was a second level at which Augustinianism came to be challenged, increasingly after 1240, by Aristotle and his interpreters.

One difficulty was this. If the Aristotelian corpus as a whole was assigned for teaching and study to the Faculty of Arts, to correct and complement the studies of the *trivium* and the *quadrivium,* then not only would those studies either have been incorporated into or themselves understood as Aristotelian sciences, integrated into the hierarchical structure of those sciences, but in being so incorporated and understood they would have acquired a greater independence of theology. They would have functioned less as mere prologue. Moreover questions which within the Augustinian curriculum had hitherto been part of the exclusive province of theology would have fallen within their competence, notably, a large range of questions in ethics, politics, psychology, and metaphysics. Such a violation of the Augustinian division of intellectual labor in the curriculum seemed to challenge not only the institutional arrangements of the Augustinianism of the University of Paris but the intellectual presuppositions of those arrangements. And hence arose and continued the underlying Augustinian dilemma: to refuse to integrate the Aristotelian corpus and its teaching into the curriculum would have been to seem to abandon the claim that theology can indeed order and direct the other secular sciences and arts; yet it seemed that to accept the Aristotelian corpus into the curriculum would be to produce incoherence in the structures of teaching and knowledge.

Moreover these issues about the organization and structure of knowledge of enquiry were difficult to bring to constructive debate. For as the awareness of the problems created by them increased, it also became clear that the standards of truth and rationality to which appeal had to be made in order to debate them constructively were not the same for Aristotelians and for Augustinians. Each system of thought had its own set of standards internal to it and there was no third set of neutral standards to which appeal could be made.

For Aristotle the intellect discovers itself in the actualization of its potentiality, an actualization moved by and towards those objects of knowledge to which the intellect in actualizing itself makes itself adequate. In comprehending things as they are, the intellect grasps both the first and the derivative principles in terms of which things of particular kinds are to be classified, understood and explained, and the hierarchical ordering of such principles. The intellect thus discovers its *telos* in a conception of perfected understanding, articulated in a conception of the sciences adequate to all enquiry and discovery. The basic concepts of the Aristotelian scheme—form/matter, potency/act, *archē/telos*—deployed in dialectical and demonstrative argument characterize both the mind's appropriation of the realities which it encounters and the nature of those realities. The mind's potential adequacy to all its objects is then a tenet central to this view of how the mind and what it appropriates are parts of the same whole.

Yet for Augustinian theology it is the inadequacy of the mind in the face of what it encounters—primarily God, but also created objects insofar as they are what they were created to be—and the mind's discovery of its inabilities and incapacities which are essential to its progress. Confronted with the paradox of the *Meno* as to how we can come to know what such and such is without already having the capacity to recognize the true answer to this question, that is, without already knowing in some way what such and such is, Aristotle and Augustine had given very different replies, Aristotle responding with a conception of coming to know as the actualization of what is already present in potentiality in the intellect, Augustine appealing to that divine illumination which affords comprehension to a mind otherwise impotent. For Aristotle an adequate characterization of the mind is of the mind as achieving knowledge; for Augustine it is of the mind as by itself incapable of knowledge but for some external source supplying what the mind cannot itself supply. Withdraw divine illumination from the Augustinian scheme and you have the mind in the predicament to be characterized by that late, solipsized Augustinian, Descartes, whereas from the Aristotelian point of view Descartes's questions do not and cannot arise.

A second closely related area of conflict concerns the understanding of truth. For Aristotle it is the relationship of a mind to its objects and the adequacy or otherwise of that mind to those objects in terms of which truth is to be primarily defined and characterized. Those statement-making sentences through which a particular mind gives expression to its thoughts in ascribing predicates to subjects are true or false in a secondary way, in virtue of their giving expression to the adequacy or otherwise of that mind in relation to the relevant object or objects. But for Augustine it is in terms of the relationships neither of statements nor of minds that truth is to be primarily characterized and understood. '*Veritas*,' a noun naming a substance, is a more fundamental expression than '*verum*,' an attribute of things, and the truth or falsity of statements is a tertiary matter. To speak truly is to speak of things as they really and truly are; and things really and truly are in virtue only of their relationship to *veritas*. So where Aristotle locates truth in the relationship of the mind to its objects, Augustine locates it in the source of the relationship of finite objects to that truth which is God.

A third related area concerns the nature of defect and error. For Augustine the will is the most important cause of error. Human intelligence is of course limited and may err in its judgments. But the intellect serves and is not of itself able to command the will. And the perversity of the will uninformed by that charity which springs from grace is always liable to mislead the intellect, something especially so in that practical life in which the perverse will places before us objects designed not only to attract us away from the true perfection which is our *telos* but also to mislead us as to what that perfection consists in. So the Augustinian, especially in theological and moral enquiry, is always apt to suppose that all intellectual error is rooted in moral defect, as Bernard did with Abelard.

For Aristotle, by contrast, the intellect is fully competent to arrive at both theoretical and practical truth, determining both its proximate goods and the good and the best by the appropriate forms of dialectical, demonstrative, and deliberative argument. Adequacy in so determining does indeed require the exercise of the intellectual virtues, the most important of which is *phronēsis* and the possession of *phronēsis* requires moral virtue. But the virtues themselves are the outcome of practical and theoretical education, and the educated person is fully able not only to determine, so far as they can be determined, but also to pursue through all the relevant stages, the goods of the practical and the theoretical life. Aristotle, like every other ancient pre-Christian author, had no concept of the will and there is no conceptual space in his scheme for such an alien notion in the explanations of defect and error.

So the Aristotelian philosopher and the Augustinian theologian appealed to rival and incompatible standards both in evaluation and in explanation. It was easy enough to conclude, as, for example, did the anonymous author of the Paris guide for examination candidates, that philosophy has its specific conception of the happiness which constitutes human perfection, while theology has its own very different conception, a view among those to be condemned in 1277 by the Augustinian bishop of Paris, Stephen Tempier. It is indeed clear from the list of propositions condemned in 1277 that in large areas of enquiry it had begun to appear that rational debate with consistent Aristotelians was no longer considered possible and this is scarcely surprising in the light of the character of the differences dividing Augustinians and Aristotelians.

For each contending party had no standard by which to judge the questions about which it differed from the other which was not itself as much in dispute as anything else. And there was no possible neutral standard, since all three key areas of disagreements are part of a systematically different and incompatible conceptualization of the human intellect in its relationship to its objects, to the passions, to the will, and to the virtues. Indeed the highly abbreviated account of these which I have given could be extended to include perception and imagination. Suppose, then, that someone aspired to adjudicate between Augustinian and Aristotelian claims by appealing away from their theoretical conceptualizations to how things *in fact* are in the human *psyche*. Any such appeal would have to present empirical data. Yet at the level at which such data are characterizable in a way that makes them independent of and neutral between schemes as conceptually rich and organized as the Aristotelian and the Augustinian – the levels at which it is in terms of reflexes and responses to sensory, linguistic, or other stimuli that human patterns of behavior are described – the data are too meager and underdetermine any characterization at the required level. They are no more than matter still to be given form by characterization at that higher, more theoretical level. And if the data are themselves presented as more fully and richly characterized, in a way that makes them relevant to the disputes between Augustinians and Aristotelians, then some conclusion as to where the truth lies in those disputes will already have been presupposed by the way in which the data have been conceptualized.

Hence the conflict between established Augustinians and rising Aristotelians within the University of Paris could not but have appeared to many, perhaps to the overwhelming majority, as not only systematic and pervasive, but as in principle irresolvable, except by theological fiat. An Aristotelian philosopher who also wished to be an obedient and orthodox Christian, such as Siger of Brabant, especially after the condemnation of 1270, could uphold the autonomy of philosophy, that is, of Aristotelianism, only by insisting that, even when the conclusions of philosophy are incompatible with Christian truth, they must be presented as just that, the conclusions of philosophy, but not as truth (*De Anima Intellectiva* VII). And an Augustinian theologian, such as Bonaventure, who condemned the current Aristotelianism of the Paris masters in his Eastertide lectures of 1273, felt no need to offer arguments at the level of philosophy, even though the positions which he criticized were philosophical positions, but only arguments from his own Augustinian theological point of view.

No scholar now follows Mandonnet (*Siger de Brabant et l'Averroisme latin au XIIIe siècle,* 2 vols., Louvain, 1908 and 1911) in ascribing to the Latin Averroists and notably to Siger a doctrine of two truths, according to which what is true in philosophy could be false in theology and vice versa. No consistent Aristotelian *could* have held such a doctrine. Averroës himself clearly did not, and the interpretations on which Mandonnet rested his case have been thoroughly discredited (see F. Van Steenberghen *Thomas Aquinas and Radical Aristotelianism,* Washington, D.C., 1980 pp. 93–95). Nonetheless, underlying Mandonnet's error was a crucial insight: had the issue between Augustinianism and Aristotelianism, as that issue was commonly understood, been forced to its conclusion, then anyone who attempted to assert both doctrines could not but have been forced into something very like the doctrine invented by Mandonnet. To have been so compelled would have been of course to have become in one's own person a *reductio ad absurdum*. And the fact that the condemnations of 1277 extended to theses advanced by Aquinas, as well as by the Latin Averroists, suggests that Aquinas may have been understood by some of his more hostile and powerful Augustinian contemporaries as being at least in danger of occupying some such position. To understand why, it is necessary to provide a fuller account of the kind of situation in which Aquinas found himself.

We have in the central intellectual conflicts of the University of Paris a classic example of the incommensurability of two standpoints, of two rival alternative conceptual schemes. What conditions have to be satisfied in order to recognize and to characterize adequately any such case of systematic incommensurability? It is important to understand first of all that such incommensurability cannot be recognized, let alone characterized adequately, by those who inhabit only one of the two conflicting conceptual schemes. For these latter the problem of understanding the position of the other will appear as a problem of translation: how can we render *their* beliefs, arguments, and theses into *our* terms?

The projects of translation designed to answer this question will be judged to have succeeded or failed by the standards of those who inhabit the particular scheme within which they were formulated. Insofar as it is judged a failure, the contentions of the rival scheme will appear untranslatable and so unintelligible. They will then fail to constitute any kind of challenge. But insofar as the task of translation is thought to have been successfully performed, it can only be because and insofar as the idiom of the alternative scheme has been rewritten into the conceptual idioms native to the translator's own scheme. This will ensure in any case distortion and characteristically distortions which render the competing theses and arguments into a form in which they appear either compatible with or refutable from the standpoint into whose terms they have been thus distortingly rendered. And in being so rendered, they will of course have been made to appear commensurable, except perhaps in marginal respects. Hence not only will the phenomenon of incommensurability appear in this particular case to have been an illusion, but the conclusion may seem to be warranted that there can be no such thing as a pair of alternative rival conceptual schemes and hence perhaps that the very idea of *a* conceptual scheme cannot but lack application. (See Donald Davidson 'On the Very Idea of a Conceptual Scheme' in *Truth and Interpretation*, Oxford, 1984.) This comforting conclusion leaves one secure in the conviction that nothing can fall outside the sphere in which one is—in principle, as they say—competent to pass judgment. It domesticates the intellectually alien intruder before demonstrating to such an intruder the *a priori* impossibility that such an invasion could challenge one's own most fundamental convictions. And just this was the conclusion presupposed by the dominant Augustinian figures in the conflicts and condemnations at Paris in the 1260s and the 1270s.

I do not of course mean to suggest that those Augustinian theologians were in fact premature Davidsonians. There are other than chronological reasons for asserting the impossibility of post-Quinean philosophy in the thirteenth century. But to understand why, if the phenomenon of incommensurability is approached from a standpoint which insists that the translation of the idiom of one rival alternative conceptual scheme into that of another is a precondition for someone who inhabits that scheme to understand the contentions advanced by the proponents of the other, that phenomenon will appear as illusion enables us to ask and answer the question of what conditions must be satisfied if genuine incommensurability is to be recognized and characterized.

It can only be recognized and characterized by someone who inhabits both alternative conceptual schemes, who knows and is able to utter the idiom of each from within, who has become, so to speak, a native speaker of two first languages, each with its own distinctive conceptual idiom. Such a person does not need to perform the tasks of translation in order to understand. Rather it is on the basis of his or her understanding of both conceptual idioms that the respects in which untranslatability presents barriers around or over which no way can be discovered can be acknowledged. Such persons are rarely numerous. They are the inhabitants of boundary situations, generally incurring the suspicion and misunderstanding of members of both of the contending parties. It was just such suspicion and misunderstanding that Aquinas incurred both from some Augustinians and from some Latin Averroist Aristotelians, and he incurred it precisely because he was just such a person.

How had this come to be? Among the scholars of the generation immediately preceding Aquinas, Albertus Magnus had taken upon himself the massive task of making the new Aristotelian learning, including in that a good deal of Islamic commentary and of other related material, available, so far as possible, as a whole in Latin commentary and exposition. Himself an Augustinian theologian, he took unusual care to separate out this work of commentary and exposition from any declaration of his own views. So that although Albertus rejected a variety of Aristotelian doctrines in his theology and quarreled with Aristotle's observations of rational phenomena on the basis of his own scientific investigations, he did not allow these critical stances to undermine the presentation of Aristotle and of Aristotelianism in his and its own terms. It thus became possible for his pupils to understand the Aristotelian standpoint from within in a thoroughgoing way, in a way and to a degree that no other teacher who was not himself an Averroist made possible. Yet at the same time Albertus as a theologian taught, and indeed reformed and revived, what was distinctively Augustinian, including what was Platonic in Augustine, assimilating to that theology only that in Aristotle which the Augustinian framework permitted. So that his pupils also could come to know Augustinianism from within. Most notable among those pupils in the Dominican *studium generale* at Cologne from 1248 to 1252, was Aquinas.

Albertus's other notable pupils, insofar as they became philosophers as well as theologians, developed themes out of his Augustinian theology, often enough Platonic themes. They learned part of what Albertus had to teach, but only part. Only Aquinas seems to have immersed himself in both the Aristotelianism and the Augustinianism so as to make a central problem, not only of his intellectual enquiries, but of his existence, that of how what he took, or at least was to come to take, to be the truth in each could be reconciled with that of the other. Aquinas thus discharged the tasks of teaching and learning at Cologne and after 1252 at Paris in a way that systematically confronted the rival claims of two alternative and apparently incommensurable standpoints. Yet it was not merely with two rival sets of theses and arguments that he had to deal. For the form in which each set of theses and arguments was now presented was the outcome of, and was inseparable from, a history of development such that the later stages in each case both referred back to and justified their development out of the earlier. What Aquinas had to reckon with were two rival, incompatible and apparently incommensurable traditions, each with its own history and its own developed and developing mode of enquiry and each requiring its own institutionalized embodiment in certain highly specific forms.

Every tradition which embodies a distinctive conception of rational enquiry will also exhibit to some significant extent, simply in virtue of being a tradition, certain characteristics relevant to its rationality as a tradition. It will have some contingent historical starting point in some situation in which some set of established beliefs and belief-presupposing practices, perhaps relatively recently established, perhaps of long standing, were put in question, sometimes by being challenged from some alternative point of view, sometimes because of an incoherence identified in the beliefs, sometimes because of a discovered resourcelessness in the face of some theoretical or practical problem, sometimes by some combination of these. So the beliefs will be further articulated, amended, modified, and added to in order that, in a newer, revised form, they may provide some answer to the questions thus raised and in that form transcend the limitations of their earlier version.

From then on a tradition will move through stages, at each of which a justification of the scheme of belief as a whole could be supplied in terms of its rational superiority to the formulations of its predecessor, and that predecessor in turn justified by a further reference backward. But the availability of this type of reference from the present to the past is not by itself sufficient to constitute a tradition of rational enquiry. It is necessary also that a certain continuity of directedness emerge, so that theoretical and practical goals to guide enquiry are formulated and at later stages reformulated. Notice that among the beliefs and belief-presupposing practices which are subject to reformulation as a rationally mature tradition moves through its various stages may be, and characteristically are, both those which concern what it is to evaluate beliefs and practices as more or less rational, what truth is and how rationality and truth are connected, and those which concern the theoretical and practical goals toward which at each stage those participating in that particular tradition are directing themselves.

Yet it is of course on just these matters that different traditions have in fact developed different, incompatible, and in some cases incommensurable views. Hence the question of what constitutes the rationality of a tradition and how particular traditions are to be evaluated as more or less rational, although it can in part be answered in a relatively uncontroversial way, as I have tried to do up to this point, cannot be adequately answered except from some one particular standpoint. So from the standpoint of the encyclopaedist no tradition is rational *qua* tradition; a tradition is and can be in respect of rationality no more than a milieu in which methods and principles are formulated, for it is only methods and principles to which rational appeal can be made. So also from the standpoint of the genealogist no tradition can be rational, but in this case for reasons which equally undermine any claim that particular methods or principles are ever as such rational. Rationality is, and can be at best, no more than one of the provisional masks worn by those engaged in unmasking the pretensions to rationality of others. And so from the standpoint of the Augustinian tradition in the thirteenth century and again from that of the contemporary Aristotelian, the view of what constituted truth and practical and theoretical rationality was in important ways, as we have already noticed, idiosyncratic to each tradition.

It is at this point in the argument that it becomes evident that in characterizing the variety of standpoints with which I have been and will be concerned, I too must have been and will be speaking as a partisan. The neutrality of the academic is itself a fiction of the encyclopaedist, and I reveal my antiencyclopaedic partisanship by calling it a fiction. It is not that the adherent of one particular standpoint cannot on occasion understand some rival point of view both intellectually and imaginatively, in such a way and to such a degree that he or she is able to provide a presentation of it of just the kind that one of its own adherents would give. It is that even in so doing the mode of presentation will inescapably be framed within and directed by the beliefs and purposes of one's own point of view. And in recording the history of a conflict, in particular, how one recounts that history will depend upon what from one's own point of view one takes to have been the outcome. So in presenting the thirteenth-century history of the conflict between Augustinian theology and Aristotelianism, rival views of the outcome will generate rival histories. An Augustinian account, such as a Franciscan pupil of Bonaventure might have given, would be very different from that offered by a persistent and continuing Latin Averroist, and neither of these would coincide with a history from the standpoint of Aquinas.

It is this latter type of history which I shall be attempting to provide. But in order to do so, it is important to begin not so much by asking how Aquinas did in fact, by integrating the Augustinian and Aristotelian modes of understanding into a unified, if complex, synthesis, reconcile what must have appeared to be, up to this point, as it appeared to many in the thirteenth century, irreconcilable, but how this type of reconciliation could even be possible. For unless we first understand this latter, the significance of certain crucial features of Aquinas's thought may not emerge. What is needed at this point is to consider first more generally the way in which the incommensurability involved in certain radical disagreements may be both recognized and rationally overcome within the context of a certain kind of tradition. Remember, for example, how in the history of early modern science what have been treated as paradigmatic cases of incommensurability in disagreement by writers as different as Bachelard, Kuhn, and Paul Feyerabend were resolved in and through the development of the scientific tradition. From the standpoint afforded by the modified Aristotelian physics of late medieval impetus theory, for example, it has appeared that no rational progress could have been made towards and to the physics of Galileo and Newton, precisely because the systematically different and incompatible observation languages, key concepts, and theoretical structures were framed in terms of rival and incompatible standards and there was no shared common measure. And so Feyerabend was able to argue with at least some appearance of plausibility that Galileo secured his victory over his Aristotelian opponents, not by meeting the standards required by some relevant type of rational argument, but by deceptive rhetorical manipulation (*Against Method*, London, 1975, ch. 6–9). And if adequate reasoning from a starting point within one system of thought and practice to conclusions within another, incommensurable to the first, could have no resources but those provided within the first of these systems, Feyerabend would have been right in at least this, that Galileo's reasoning could not have been effective *qua* reasoning but only in some other nonrational rhetorical way. But Feyerabend's assumptions about the rational resources which can be provided in such cases are defective in three ways.

First, although it is true that characteristically one cannot from within and by means only of the resources afforded by some earlier system of thought, such as late medieval impetus theory, argue to conclusions within a second theory both richer than and incommensurable with the first, such as Galilean physics, it is untrue that one cannot, in some types of case at least, argue retrospectively in the other direction. The former type of system will lack the resources to represent the latter adequately, but those who inhabit and indeed have themselves constructed the latter system, perhaps because like Galileo they have themselves been inhabitants and at one time protagonists of the former system, may be able to include within that system an adequate representation of its predecessor. They may perhaps explain the point of their change of intellectual allegiance by showing how the former had become systematically unable to solve its own problems, framed in its own terms, while the latter opened up a new problematic in which the frustrations incurred by the former no longer arose.

Secondly, it may also be the case—with Galileo and more especially Newton it was in fact the case—that retrospectively the transition from the former standpoint to the latter can be rationally justified, not only because the sterility of the former standpoint relative to the latter discredits it, but also because the sterility of the former standpoint can now itself by explained rather than merely appearing as a brute, inexplicable fact. So the physics of Newton can explain precisely why impetus theory *had* to fail in its projects at just the points at which it did indeed fail, something which impetus theory itself lacked the resources to explain. But this retrospective reasoning justifies the prospective reasoning which made it possible to achieve the new standpoint and not just the new standpoint itself. Prospective reasoning in this kind of case cannot but be dialectical, exploratory, inventive, and provisional, formulating hypotheses as it moves towards a new set of first principles and fundamental conceptions. It is only when these have been successfully achieved that one can move backwards from those first principles to justify what was hitherto tentative, exploratory, and hypothetical. This is a type of movement of thought first described by Plato in Book VI of the *Republic* and then more fully characterized by Aristotle but ignored by Feyerabend.

Thirdly, it may seem that since the rational justification of that prospective reasoning which may on occasion be able to carry us from one fundamental standpoint to another incommensurable with it is always retrospective, this reasoning could only be available to those already committed to the later standpoint. But this too is a mistake. First the onset of an epistemological crisis, a systematic breakdown of enquiry in the face of a certain set of intractable problems within a particular scheme of belief, may, if recognized, provide good reasons for seeking out some rationally different alternative; and secondly the possibility of learning to understand the other incommensurable point of view from within imaginatively, before it can be occupied intellectually, can never be ruled out. It is by such uses of the imagination that one can come as if to inhabit another alien culture and in so doing recognize how significant features of one's own culture to which one has hitherto been, and could not but have been, blind can be discovered and characterized from that other culture's point of view. So one can be invited, as the impetus theorists of his time were invited by Galileo, to understand their own system of thought from another standpoint, by an imaginative identification with a process of prospective reasoning to be justified retrospectively and to conclude to the superior adequacy of the new scheme of belief and practice.

It was a precisely similar invitation to both the Augustinians and the Averroists of his time which was issued by Aquinas. That is, he invited them to understand the point of view which he had constructed, one into which both the achievements of Augustinianism and Aristotelianism had been integrated in such a way that what were, or should have been, recognized as the defects and limitations of Augustinianism as judged from an Augustinian standpoint and the defects and limitations of Aristotelianism as judged from an Aristotelian standpoint had both been first more adequately characterized and then corrected or transcended. In so doing, Aquinas achieved what neither Augustinians nor Aristotelians could have achieved in respect of the other, for, as we have already seen, the specific kinds of radical and incommensurable differences which divided them made it impossible for each party to understand itself from the rival, alien point of view. What conceptual resources was Aquinas by contrast able to discover, construct, and deploy in order to achieve this?

Notice first that any standpoint which enables one in this way to judge between the claims of fundamentally different and rival traditions and standpoints rather than only to judge from within one such tradition or standpoint will have to understand truth in a particular way. We have already seen that to those who do in fact judge only from within one such tradition or standpoint, from the point of view of one particular conceptual scheme, and who also when presented with the problems of incommensurability insist on understanding these as problems of translatability into their own language, their own conceptual idiom, the facts of incommensurability will become or remain invisible. They will have rendered themselves unaware of the radical particularities and partialities of their own standpoint. It will also inevitably appear to such persons that when they judge some statement or theory or whatever true, they can be doing no other than appealing to the fundamental criteria by which assertions are warranted within their own scheme. There could in judging of truth be no reference, so it must seem, to anything beyond or falling outside the purview of such criteria, for it can only be these same criteria which determine what can be referred to in judging of truth. Hence it will be immensely plausible, either implicitly or explicitly, to identify truth with warranted assertibility. And it will make no sense from this point of view to conjecture that one's scheme of concepts and beliefs could be in some way *as a whole* in error, both because the very idea of an alternative conceptual scheme makes no sense, and because, since it is only in terms of that scheme that errors are identified, the notion of the scheme itself being in error, the notion of overall error could never find application.

Yet if one is compelled to enquire where the truth lies between alternative, rival, and incommensurable overall points of view, one cannot but entertain the possibility that either or both of these points of view is systematically false, false as a whole in its overall claims (that does not of course mean that *every* particular judgment made from within it is thereby false), just because and insofar as one cannot but recognize that any such overall scheme of concepts and judgments may fall into a state of epistemological crisis. For to claim that such an overall scheme of concepts and beliefs is true is to claim that no fundamental reality could ever be disclosed about which it is impossible to speak truly within that scheme. But recognition of the features of an epistemological crisis within a particular scheme will always suggest what an explanation of that crisis from some other alien standpoint may on occasion confirm that there is some reality, identifiable from within that particular scheme of concepts and beliefs, about which nonetheless it is impossible from within that same scheme to speak coherently and thus truly. Hence in judging of truth and falsity there is always some ineliminable reference beyond the scheme within which those judgments are made and beyond the criteria which provide the warrants for assertibility within that scheme. Truth cannot be identified with, or collapsed into warranted assertibility. And a conception of *what is* which is more and other than a conception of *what appears to be the case in the light of the most fundamental criteria governing assertability within any particular scheme* is correspondingly required, that is, a metaphysics of being, of *esse*, over and above whatever can be said about particular *entia* in the light of particular concepts.

It is then no accident that among the earliest works in which Aquinas began to define his own distinctive point of view were the *De Ente et Essentia*, written even before he became master in theology at Paris in 1256, and the early questions *De Veritate*, disputed when he was first regent in 1256–57. It would of course be grossly anachronistic to portray Aquinas's understanding of his own early development, as he confronted two rival and incommensurable schemes of belief and enquiry, in the terms in which I have used. Aquinas was not responding to Bachelard, Kuhn, Feyerabend, and Davidson. But he was responding to a type of problem which we now understand much better, thanks to those and kindred writers. What then was his response? Both the questions *De Veritate* and the *De Ente et Essentia* are philosophical dictionaries in which in the one case the various uses of 'true' and 'truth' are spelled out and related both to each other and to other key terms, and in the other, similarly, the various uses of 'being' and of 'essence.'

In both works there is an underlying recognition not only that each of these sets of uses is related analogically, but that there is a primary application of each and that it is to God. It is from God as truth, *veritas*, that all other 'truths' and 'trues' flow; it is from God as being, *esse*, that all that is, insofar as it is, derives. But it is from the derivative that *we* have to begin. So in coming to understand the ordering of each being and each truth or true towards that which is first in being and first in truth, we reverse and retrace the causal order by which they were generated. To understand the analogical relationships is also, so it will turn out, to understand both the causal relationships in terms of which the present states and changes of all finite beings are made intelligible and the practical relationships through which and by means of which all finite beings move towards their perfected end. So finite beings are made intelligible, both as moved and as moving, and the structures through which they are made thus intelligible are those which in a variety of aspects relate all beings to their first cause as unmoved mover, itself not further determined or determinable by anything else.

It is these structures which are analyzed and disclosed in the *Quinque Viae* of the *Summa Theologiae* (I, ii, 3), each of which relies on a principle or principles without which the objects of enquiry, theoretical or practical, cannot be rendered intelligible. To reject the *Quinque Viae* would be to reject the conception of enquiry shared by both Aristotelians and Augustinians. It was into the common framework furnished by this conception, thus spelled out analogically, causally, and practically that Aquinas integrated both rival schemes of concepts and beliefs in such a way as both to correct in each that which he took by its own standards could be shown to be defective or unsound and to remove from each, in a way justified by that correction, that which barred them from reconciliation. Retrospectively we can understand him as having rescued both standpoints from imminent, even if unrecognized, epistemological crises.

So an Aristotelian account of nature, both theoretical and practical, was not merely harmonized with an Augustinian supernatural theology but shown to require it for its completion, if the universe is to be intelligible in the way in which parts relate to wholes. And Augustine's account of the relationship of the human being, as natural intelligence and agent, to the objects of enquiry, both theoretical and practical, was rendered in terms of distinctions unfamiliar to the tradition of Augustinian textual interpretation, so that Aristotle's account of the rational world became recognizably the prologue required for an Augustinian theology. Part of the work involved in achieving this integrated account made use of the techniques of interpretation, of the making of *distinctiones* and the posing of *quaestiones*, elaborated within the Augustinian tradition, while part of it involved those interrelated uses of dialectical and demonstrative argument both employed and described by Aristotle and further extended by his commentators.

So in the three major areas in which the Augustinian tradition had confronted its central problems Aquinas developed new positions by both interpretation and argumentative means. Where Aristotle and Augustine had characterized one and the same relationship of particular individuals to those universal concepts by which essence and kind are identified, in two not only different but incompatible ways, Aquinas uses Augustine's Platonic account to characterize one set of relationships—those of particulars to the exemplars in the divine creating mind which are their formal causes—and Aristotle's account to characterize another set of relationships, those involved in the mind's apprehension of the *quidditas rei materialis* which is that mind's initial object of knowledge and enquiry. Where Aristotle's psychology excluded the possibility of accounting for the phenomenon of the will, while Augustine lacked what Aristotle provided in his findings about the mind's powers and their theoretical and practical embodiments in enquiry, Aquinas was able to show how the will, conceived in Augustinian fashion, could both serve and yet mislead the mind, as conceived in Aristotelian fashion. And all this was achieved in a way not merely concordant with but supporting and illuminating the specific Christian dogmas.

Yet Aquinas, in appropriating both traditions, integrating them, and carrying forward what was specific in each, did so by a method which required that his own work should be essentially incomplete. The conjunction of this requirement with the tasks of synthesis and unification produced a new genre for the discourse of enquiry, first in the way in which Aquinas built up systematic sequences in the *Quaestiones Disputatae* and then later more strikingly in the *Summa Theologiae*. For while the conclusions of each particular question are integrated into an overall hierarchical demonstrative structure which represents the point so far reached in the movement towards a finally perfected science, or rather a finally perfected hierarchy of sciences in which theology is at the apex, yet to each question the answer produced by Aquinas as a conclusion is no more than and, given Aquinas's method, cannot but be no more than, the best answer reached so far. And hence derives the essential incompleteness. For what Aquinas does is to summarize on each question the strongest arguments for and against each particular answer which have so far been formulated, drawing upon all the texts and all the strands of developing argument which have informed the traditions which he inherits—earlier patristic, Augustinian, Platonic, Neoplatonic, Aristotelian, the commentaries of Averroës and Avicenna, the contributions of Maimonides, and of course the texts of sacred Scripture.

But when Aquinas has reached his conclusion, the method always leaves open the possibility of a return to that question with some new argument. Except for the finality of Scripture and dogmatic tradition, there is and can be no finality. The narrative of enquiry always points beyond itself with directions drawn from the past, which, so that past itself teaches, will themselves be open to change. And the narrative of enquiry is of course itself embedded in that larger narrative of which enquiry speaks in settting out the intelligibility of the movements of creatures from and to God.

Within Aquinas's scheme of thought, then, particular theses are justified dialectically or demonstratively or both. We move in our intellectual constructions from a beginning in which we are concerned with what is initially evident to us here now towards a projected end in which rational justification will be by demonstration from first principles which are evident *per se*. And within the organized hierarchy of the sciences at any particular moment in their history some sciences will approach this ideal more closely than others. But the overall scheme itself is, as I have already suggested, not to be justified in this way, but by its capacity to remedy the defects, transcend the limitations, and extend the reach of the tradition of which it is so far the best outcome. What then of future challenges, future, that is, relative to Aquinas? The conception of truth embodied in the scheme requires that claims for truth on its behalf and on behalf of the judgments in which it is expressed commit those making them to hold that when that scheme encounters alternative standpoints making alternative and incompatible, even incommensurable, claims, Aquinas's dialectical synthesis will be able to render those standpoints intelligible in a way that cannot be achieved by their own adherents from their own point of view and to distinguish their defects and limitations from their insights and merits in such a way as to explain the occurrence of what they themselves would have to take to be their defects and limitations at points at which their own explanatory capacities are resourceless.

Thomism then confronts both the substantive claims of the late nineteenth-century encyclopaedia and of its twentieth-century heirs and the subversive claims of genealogy with this commitment, one which opens it up to radical judgments of its own success or failure, one by which it exhibits the kinds of intellectual vulnerability which is the mark of all worthwhile theorizing. And since it is with the specifically moral claims of encyclopaedia, of genealogy, and of Thomistic tradition that I am concerned in these lectures, what is now required is first to specify more precisely how both moral enquiry and the form of the moral life are to be understood within the Thomistic scheme and what the relationship of that understanding to the claims of encyclopaedia and genealogy has turned out to be.

VI

Aquinas and the Rationality of Tradition

Two different characterizations of Aquinas as a philosopher have been presented so far: the first as someone who understood philosophical activity as that of a craft and indeed of the chief of crafts, the second as someone who carried forward two hitherto independent traditions of thought, merging them into one in such a way as to provide a direction for still further development of a new unified tradition. But if we are to understand the relevance of these two characterizations to Aquinas's conception of moral enquiry, it is first necessary to show how they relate to each other.

To become adept in a craft, as we noticed earlier, one has to learn how to apply two kinds of distinction, that between what as activity or product merely seems to me good and what really is good, a distinction always applied retrospectively as part of learning from one's earlier mistakes and surpassing one's earlier limitations, and that between what is good and best for me to do here and now given the limitations of my present state of education into the craft and what is good and best as such, unqualifiedly. But the way in which these distinctions are to be applied within some particular craft is rarely fixed once and for all. Every craft has a history and characteristically a history not yet completed. And during that history differences in the materials to which that craft gives form, differences in the means by which form is imposed upon matter, and differences in the conceptions of the forms to be achieved not only require new ways of applying these distinctions but themselves sometimes are the outcome of new ways in which these distinctions are applied. So learning how to make these distinctions adequately involves learning how to go on learning how to apply them. One has to acquire a certain kind of knowing how which enables one to move from the achievements of the past, which depended upon the making of these distinctions in one way, to the possibility of new achievements, which will depend upon making them in what may be some very different way. It is the possession and transmission of this kind of ability to recognize in the past what is and what is not a guide to the future which is at the core of any adequately embodied tradition. A craft in good order has to be embodied in a tradition in good order. And to be adequately initiated into a craft is to be adequately initiated into a tradition.

Secondly, because this is so, someone who has been initiated into a craft and has acquired in some measure this kind of knowing how will have made him or herself part of the history of that craft, and it is in terms of that history that their actions *qua* craftsperson will be intelligible or otherwise. But no one who engages in a craft is only a craftsperson; we come to the practice of a craft with a history *qua* family member, *qua* member of this or that local community, and so on. So the actions of someone who engages in a craft are at the point of intersection of two or more histories, two or more enacted dramatic narratives. The importance of this latter point is evident when we consider that the lives which are thus lived out are themselves the subject matter of the craft of moral philosophy, that is, of philosophical enquiry insofar as it addresses moral questions.

The philosophical theorist has to enquire: What is the good specific to human beings? Each individual has to enquire: What is *my* good as a human being? And while no true answer can be given by the philosophical theorist which is not somehow or other translatable into true answers that can be given to their practical questions by ordinary human individuals, no true answers can be given to their questions by such individuals which do not presuppose some particular type of answer to the philosopher's question. There is then no form of philosophical enquiry—at least as envisaged from an Aristotelian, Augustinian, or Thomistic point of view—which is not practical in its implications, just as there is no practical enquiry which is not philosophical in its presuppositions.

There is, of course, according to Aquinas a form of moral knowledge which is not itself theoretical. The practice of the virtues and the experience of having one's will directed by the virtues yields knowledge by way of what Aquinas calls "connaturality" (*S.T.* IIa-IIae, 45.2); and a great many ordinary agents, educated into that practice within households or local communities, learn to be and are virtuous without ever explicitly raising philosophical questions. But when established moral traditions encounter situations of change in which old virtues have to be embodied in new ways and rules extended to cover new contingencies—and as the two key craft distinctions find new applications—the moral life from time to time inescapably raises theoretical questions. It does so because in such situations we are forced back to a reconsideration of first principles and how they apply to particulars: "the practical intellect . . . has its *principium* in a universal consideration and in this respect is the same in subject as the theoretical intellect, but its consideration reaches its terminus in a particular thing which can be done" (*Commentary on the Ethics* VI, lect. 2).

So theoretical and practical enquiry are intertwined and the enquiries of the philosopher, framed in universal concepts, are always at least in the background—and sometimes in the foreground—when questions of the particularities of their lives and the goods to be pursued in them are raised by ordinary persons. The history of the moral life and the history of moral enquiry are aspects of a single, albeit complex, history. And to be initiated into the moral life is to be initiated into the tradition whose history is that complex history. How is that initiation to be achieved?

For most persons, at least so long as they inhabit a tolerably well-ordered form of social life, it will be in the course of their practical education at the hands of some teacher. But Aquinas held that all education is in an important way self-education: "a teacher leads someone else to the knowledge of what was unknown in the same way that someone leads him or herself to the knowledge of what was unknown in the course of discovery" (*Quaestiones Disputate De Veritate* XI, 1). It follows that the order of good teaching is ideally the same as the order of effective learning and a book which is well designed to teach, perhaps especially a book designed to teach teachers as the *Summa Theologiae* was, will follow the order of exploratory learning, through which the pupil relives the history of enquiry up to the highest point of achievement which it has reached so far, by rescrutinizing those arguments which have sustained the best supported conclusions so far. Hence the *Summa* sets out in its ordering of universal concepts the framework for a type of narrative of moral enquiry to be enacted by individuals who do and will exhibit their rationality by participating in the forms of rationality established by and through a particular tradition and indeed, insofar as moral enquiry is integral to the moral life itself, a framework for a set of narratives of particular lives. The intended reader of the *Summa,* like those who originally heard the lectures and participated in the disputations which went to its making, is in his or her reading engaged in conceptualizing and reconceptualizing his or her own activities in such a way as to answer the fundamental questions of moral enquiry. But here an already familiar type of difficulty reemerges.

To understand why both the virtues and obedience to divine law are required if we are to achieve our good, we have to learn what the *Summa* has to teach on these topics, whether it be from the *Summa* itself or from elsewhere. But we can only learn this, so it turns out, and we can only know how to read the *Summa* rightly if we already to some degree at least and in some way possess certain virtues, intellectual virtues certainly in the first place, but among those intellectual virtues is *prudentia, phronēsis,* that virtue of practical intelligence and judgment which itself cannot be possessed unless the moral virtues are possessed. So we are once again involved in an apparent circularity akin to that of the *Meno.* The key to the resolution of this form of the difficulty is, as in other cases, in the "to some degree . . . and in some way." We have to begin by acquiring enough of the virtues to order our passions aright, so that we are neither distracted nor misled by the multiplicity of the goods which they seem to propose to us and so that we acquire the initial experiences of rule-following and action-guiding from which we can begin to learn both how to understand our precepts and maxims better and how to extend the application of those precepts and maxims to an increasing range of particular situations. It is in so doing that we acquire the kind of knowing how to apply those key craft distinctions of which I spoke earlier, a knowing how which is both a knowing how to act and a knowing how to learn how to act, putting our nascent virtues themselves to the work of acquiring those same virtues in more adequate form. And it is because we have to learn in this way in this sequence that formal systematic moral enquiry, including the reading of the *Summa Theologiae,* has the place that it has in the overall order of intellectual development and training.

The subjects with which to begin, according to Aquinas, are those through which we learn inference and abstraction, logic and mathematics. Next we are to learn how to apply the principles of inference and abstraction to experience. By this time we should have reached the stage in which we have had sufficient practical experience of pursuing and reformulating goals, of following rules and of disciplining the passions to provide a basis for entering upon systematic moral enquiry. And achievement in this will satisfy one more prerequisite, that for entering upon those metaphysical and theological studies which complete all enquiry, in part by making explicit what is presupposed by the intelligibility discovered in all enquiry (*Commentary on the Ethics* VI, lect. 1).

The *Summa Theologiae* was not misnamed; it is itself a work of instruction at this highest stage, comprehending and integrating into itself however that in the other disciplines which theology needs, and providing also the framework within which the other disciplines have to be understood. The autonomy of subordinate disciplines is real but limited and Aquinas's understanding of both that autonomy and those limitations was at odds with the dominant Augustinian curriculum. What was at issue here can be most easily understood by considering once more the curricular dilemma which the substantial restoration of the Aristotelian corpus presented for the thirteenth-century university, a dilemma stemming from some of the unresolved difficulties in the Augustinian account of knowledge.

On the view which had been constructed from Augustine's Platonism all understanding involved a reference to the universal exemplars in the divine mind. So a theological account of the relationship of God to His creation was required by every enquiry which aimed at understanding: the dependence of all other disciplines upon theology seemed thereby to be secured. But just because the nature of the relationship between the particulars studied in those other disciplines, the universal concepts through which those particulars are apprehended by those engaged in those other disciplines, and the exemplars in the divine mind, themselves not directly accessible to finite minds, remained unexplained and obscure, in practice the links between theology and the other disciplines were minimal. So there was an increasing tendency for those disciplines to proceed with a *de facto* autonomy in respect of their relationships both to theology and to each other, so that the curriculum lost any real unity. It was in response to just this tendency in its earlier forms that Hugh of St. Victor has written the *Didascalion* in order to restore genuine sovereignty to scriptural theology within a reunified curriculum. But the *Didascalion* did not and could not have provided a remedy for the situation in which the reception of the Aristotelian *corpus* presented its problems.

At the level of university organization the question was: in which faculty should the works of Aristotle be studied and taught? If the physical and metaphysical works were assigned to the Faculty of Arts, then teachers in that faculty would be entitled to pronounce independently on matters on which theology had been sovereign and, when the original ban on the teaching of those works by the Faculty of Arts came to be disregarded by the late 1240s, earlier Augustinian fears were confirmed by the growth of Averroist teaching in support of heterodox conclusions concerning the mortality of the soul and the eternity of the world. But were Aristotle's physical and metaphysical works instead to be assigned to the Faculty of Theology, theology itself would have to become philosophical in a quite new and, as it was to turn out, generally unacceptable way. It had at first been among the theologians that the new philosophical themes, theses, arguments, and methods had had the most willing and constructive reception: William of Auxerre (d. 1231) had sought to reconcile the Augustinian and Aristotelian theories of knowledge and William of Auvergne (d. 1269) had identified what was centrally at issue between Platonic and Aristotelian theories of knowledge. Yet it was only after Albertus Magnus had set new standards in the presentation of Aristotle's own views that the extent to which theology itself might have to become a philosophical discipline became clear. And this would have involved a break with the conventional Augustinian understanding of theology.

When Aquinas wrote the *Summa* he prepared himself for the task of writing the parts concerned with detailed moral enquiry in the IIa-IIae by writing a commentary on the *Nicomachean Ethics* at the same time as he was also continuing his exposition of St. Paul's epistles. It was the systematic character of Aquinas's insistence upon giving, within the same extended structures of argument, their due both to Pauline doctrine and to Aristotelian theory which resulted in his producing a work whose genre separated it both from the conventional orthodoxies of the thirteenth-century curriculum and from the Averroist program. As metaphysics stands to the other disciplines within the Aristotelian scheme, so a theology which has integrated metaphysical commentary into itself is now to stand, but this theology has to argue with and cannot merely dictate to the subordinate disciplines in a form of active dialectical encounter, which both the Averroist insistence on the autonomy of philosophy and the conventional Augustinian theology found no room for.

The *Summa* therefore constituted an affront to the thirteenth-century Parisian version of those institutional academic boundaries by which both agreements and conflicts are conventionally defined. And once we have perceived this, the question of what the *Summa* is, a text the quite unusual lucidity of whose Latin is apt to conceal the originality of the author's intentions, forces us back upon the question of what kind of persons we will have to be or become, either in the thirteenth century or now, in order to read it aright. The concept of having to be a certain sort of person, morally or theologically, in order to read a book aright—with the implication that perhaps, if one is not that sort of person, then the book should be withheld from one—is alien to the assumption of liberal modernity that every rational adult should be free to and is able to read every book. Yet this liberal assumption consorts uneasily with the idiom of recent literary interpretation. Consider, for example, the role played in Paul de Man's writings by such words as 'blindness,' 'insight,' 'asceticism,' 'irony' and 'bad faith,' words that signal to us moral relationships between author and text and between text and reader which can have the power to disrupt and undermine academic *explications de texte*.

The *Summa* has just this power. Consider in this respect two very different ways of reading questions 90 to 97 of the Ia–IIae, those which concern law, divine, natural, and human. One way is to focus on those questions in relative isolation from other writings of Aquinas, with only the necessary minimum of citation from elsewhere. The effect is to produce a reading whose assumption is that with sufficient scholarly understanding of the particular words of this particular text we could elucidate Aquinas's doctrine on law. Yet those whose reading of Aquinas has tended to approximate to this end of the spectrum of readings have notably disagreed among themselves and have, sometimes at least, done so because they have imported into their interpretation philosophical principles alien to Aquinas. Aquinas, for example, asserts that the *principium* of the natural law is: 'Good is to be done and evil is to be avoided' (94, 2) and that all other precepts of the natural law are based upon this. But how? Eric D'Arcy gives an account of the *principium* as analytic, a tautology, using a post-Kantian conception of analyticity. Germaine Grisez interprets the *principium* in the light of a post-Humean fact-value distinction. Neither refers us to the Platonic and Aristotelian understanding of 'good' and it is perhaps because of this that Grisez can say in the course of distinguishing his account from Maritain's that "Aquinas does not present the natural law as if it were an object known or to be known; rather, he considers the precepts of practical reason themselves to be natural law," the perhaps unintended implication of which is that the precepts of practical reason cannot themselves be objects of knowledge ('The First Principle of Practical Reason' in *Aquinas* ed. A. Kenny, New York, 1969, p. 347).

What these disputes make clear is that questions 90 to 97 are not self-interpreting and that, even if it is a mistake to import alien philosophical concepts, nonetheless Aquinas's discussion has to be understood in terms of some principles or structure beyond what is said in answer to these particular questions. What is insisted upon by an alternative mode of reading is that questions 90 to 97 could only be asked and answered in the way that Aquinas asks and answers them after questions 1 to 89 have been asked and answered. What the discussion of good in question 1 had initially made clear was that when someone identifies a good as being the true good, that is, the end to which by virtue of his or her essential nature moves, he or she, unless hindered or directed in some way, moves towards it. So 'such and such is the good of all human beings by nature' is always a factual judgment, which when recognized as true by someone moves that person toward that good. Evaluative judgments are a species of factual judgment concerning the final and formal causes of activity of members of a particular species.

The concept of good, then, has application only for beings insofar as they are members of some species or kind; Aquinas in question 96 speaks of our good *qua* being, shared with all other beings, our good *qua* animal being, shared with all other animals, and our good *qua* rational being, the common good of rational beings. Our understanding of those goods changes over time and in the course of changing is subject to error, and in the passage from question 1 to questions 90 to 97 we are guided through the arguments which might have entangled us in error, so that when we arrive at questions 90 to 97 we are able to characterize our earliest and most primitive, albeit genuine, understandings of the natural law from the standpoint of the mature understanding which we have now acquired. And in all of this the conclusions of the *Ia pars* are presupposed. What this view of the reading of Aquinas points us towards is the conclusion that the *Summa* can only be read as a whole and can only be evaluated as a whole. The parts clearly each have their own import, but they have their import in their character as parts of that whole. It is thus on this view a good deal more difficult to encounter, let alone to evaluate, Aquinas's thought than either Thomists or their opponents have sometimes supposed. For the abstraction of particular theses and the matching of these against particular theses similarly abstracted from Kant or Hume or whomever deforms the reading of Aquinas's theses. Yet such deformation is inherent in a great many of our contemporary curricular and publishing habits: questions 90 to 97, for example, are most often published separately as the *Treatise on Law* and students often enough are invited to consider this fictitious treatise alongside the *Grundlegung* or the *Rechtsphilosophie,* as though each of them offered rival answers to one and the same set of questions about the nature of law, questions which can be formulated, so it is assumed, without already having committed oneself by the presuppositions of their formulation to speak either from outside or from within that universe of discourse which is the *Summa* taken as a whole.

What then this type of holistic reading of the *Summa* puts in question, in a way that nineteenth- and early twentieth-century Thomism often did not, is how one can be a critic of the *Summa* without first having been a genuine participant in its processes of dialectical enquiry and discovery, through which the themes of the debates so far, and more especially of the debate between Augustinians and Averroists, were and are reformulated and carried forward. Yet if our dominant curricular and interpretative habits make it difficult to come to terms with the *Summa* thus understood, so in their own way, as we have already seen, did the curricular and interpretative habits of the thirteenth century. The *Summa* has proved easy enough to domesticate academically in terms other than its own, but to read it in its own terms from within the tradition which Aquinas reconstituted in the course of writing it is the only way to reckon with it in other than mock and distorting encounter.

To this it may be said, indeed should be said, that Aquinas in the passages to which I have been alluding is speaking of a knowledge of the natural law which human beings have by nature and that, since we are all human beings after all, we can surely all judge equally of what he says, plain persons and philosophers or theologians alike. Consider then Aquinas's portrait of the plain person in relation to the precepts of the natural law. The plain person initially, as plain child, exhibits his or her knowledge of the *principium* of the natural law, which is the *principium* of practical reasoning, in the same way that he or she exhibits his or her knowledge of the principle of non-contradiction, that is to say, not in any ability to formulate the principle explicitly, but by showing a potentiality to do just that, in the way in which the truth of the principle is presupposed in a multiplicity of particular practical judgments. What will be there presupposed will, however, not only be the *principium* of the natural law understood as a single precept, but that *principium* in its application to the various aspects of human nature in terms of which it has to be spelled out. For the *principium* enjoins the pursuit of our good, and the good of human beings has various aspects or parts. So an apprehension of those goods and ends will be implicit in the plain person's particular practical judgments.

Disagreements about how the *principium* is to be formulated and understood at the level of philosophical enquiry are then going to be as apt to occur as similar disagreements about the principle of non-contradiction. And just as such disagreements are only to be resolved or even adequately formulated in the context of an account of a complex of related concepts, so the explicit articulation of the concepts involved in the *principium* also must involve a web of concepts, concepts which can only be spelled out in terms of their range of uses and applications. So that in moving from the earliest and most primitive apprehensions of our good to a mature understanding of it we have to explore the meaning and use of such concepts as those of end (*telos*), happiness, action, passion, and virtue. What is constant in this movement is the core of our initial apprehension, that if we are to achieve an understanding of good in relation to ourselves as being, as animal, and as rational we shall have to engage with other members of the community in which our learning has to go on in such a way as to be teachable learners. And thus we accomplish the first realization of our good by in the most elementary way respecting the good of those others in encounter with whom we have to learn. What we grasp initially in understanding the binding force of the precepts of the natural law are the conditions for entering a community in which we may discover what further specifications our good has to be given.

The movement towards that further specification may take place at a number of very different levels, but it is in important ways one and the same movement, whether articulated in fully adequate philosophical and theological terms as in the *Summa* or in the relatively inarticulate apprehensions of those who learn *per inclinationem,* through the directedness of their lives in living out the virtues. Where does this movement begin? It may begin either from being taught by parents within the household or, if that is unfortunately lacking, within the wider community, learning from that in its laws which exemplifies the natural law. What that teaching points towards is a discrimination of the ends which one may pursue in the light of that ultimate end or good, which is the true good of one's kind. What is that good?

In the first five questions of the Ia-IIae, Aquinas recapitulates those arguments in Book I of the *Nicomachean Ethics* by which Aristotle had shown that wealth, honor, pleasure, and even the virtues, the peculiar excellences of the human soul, cannot be that good. To this list he adds, in a way that Aristotle would certainly not have objected to, power and the goods of the body. But then in a way quite unexpected by any devoted reader of Aristotle up to this point—a reader who had been using, for example, Aquinas's own commentary on Book I—Aquinas turns the criteria for an ultimate good to which Aristotle had appealed against Aristotle and uses them to show, first, that the ultimate good must lie in the relationship of the soul to something outside itself and, secondly, that in no state available in this created world can the type of good in question be found. There are indeed a variety of imperfect happinesses to be found in this world, but neither separately nor in conjunction can they constitute the human end.

So Aristotle was invoked against Aristotle in the interests of Scripture and of Augustine, not because Aquinas was rejecting Aristotelianism, but because he was trying to be a better Aristotelian than Aristotle. But the Aristotelianism which results has something of a tragic character to it. Without some rationally warranted belief in, some genuine knowledge of that perfect goodness in relationship to which alone the soul finds ultimate good—that divine goodness by reference to which alone, in Augustine's Platonic terms, the unity underlying and ordering the range of uses and applications of the concept of good can be discovered—the soul would find itself directed beyond all finite goods, unsatisfiable by those goods, and yet able to find nothing beyond them to satisfy it. Permanent dissatisfaction would be its lot. What would such a soul become, a soul perhaps which having first embraced a materialist version of Averroism, then went on to discover from Aquinas's arguments the radical imperfection of the only happiness to be envisaged from within philosophy thus understood? It would surely become a Hobbesian soul, concluding both that "there is no such *Finis ultimus* (utmost ayme) nor *Summum Bonum* (greatest good) as is spoken of in the Books of the old Morall Philosophers" and that desire could only issue in the successive pursuit of always unsatisfying objects, "a perpetuall and restless desire of Power after power, that ceaseth only in Death." So a Hobbesian shadow is cast by Aquinas's revision of Aristotle, itself a foreshadowing of much else to come.

I remarked earlier that for an Aristotelian, whether Thomist or otherwise, what is good or best for anyone or anything is so in virtue of its being of a certain kind, with its own essential nature and that which peculiarly belongs to the flourishing of beings of that kind. Particularities of circumstance are of course highly relevant to the determination of what is good and best for one here now. But what one brings to each particular situation, if practically well-educated, are dispositions to judge concerning those particularities in the light of truths about the good of one's species. And to be practically well-educated is to have learned to take pleasure in doing and judging rightly in respect of goods and to have learned to be pained by defect and error in the same respect. So the pleasure and pain which are mine *qua* me supervene upon that doing or being or achieving good which is mine *qua* rational animal. Take away the notion of essential nature, take away the corresponding notion of what is good and best for members of a specific kind who share such a nature, and the Aristotelian scheme of the self which is to achieve good, of good, and of pleasure necessarily collapses. There remains only the individual self with its pleasures and pains. So metaphysical nominalism sets constraints upon how the moral life can be conceived. And, conversely, certain types of conceptions of the moral life exclude such nominalism.

Thus inescapably from the Aristotelian point of view an understanding of oneself as having an essential nature and the discovery of what in one belongs to that nature and what is merely *per accidens* enters into the progress of the self, including the self of the plain person, even though that understanding and discovery may take place in a way that presupposes rather than explicitly formulates the philosophical theses and arguments involved. What, more precisely, is it that has to be understood and discovered, and why? What has to be discovered is how to order the passions so that they may serve and not distract reason in its pursuit of the specific end, the good. What has to be understood are the different relationships in which the passions may stand to reason and to the will and to the different dispositions to judge and to act which exhibit a right ordering of the passions. So an antinominalist philosophical psychology provides the basis for an account of those dispositions which, perfectly possessed, are the distinctively human perfections, the virtues.

Rules and virtues are interrelated. To possess the virtue of justice, for example, involves both a will to give to each person what is due to him or her and a knowledge of how to apply the rules which prevent violations of that order in which each receives his or her due. To understand the application of rules as part of the exercise of the virtues is to understand the point of rule-following, just because one cannot understand the exercise of the virtues except in terms of their role in constituting the type of life in which alone the human *telos* is to be achieved. The rules which are the negative precepts of the natural law thus do no more than set limits to that type of life and in so doing only partially define the kind of goodness to be aimed at. Detach them from their place in defining and constituting a whole way of life and they become nothing but a set of arbitrary prohibitions, as they too often became in later periods. To progress in both moral enquiry and the moral life is then to progress in understanding *all* the various aspects of that life, rules, precepts, virtues, passions, actions as parts of a single whole. Central to that progress is the exercise of the virtue of *prudentia*, the virtue of being able in particular situations to bring to bear the relevant universals and to act so that the universal is embodied in the particular. That virtue is acquired through experience, the experience of judging in respect of how and in what ways the universal has been or is to be embodied in the particular and of learning how to learn from these experiences. But there comes a point at which no degree of prudence, or of the other virtues which are required if one is to have and to exercise prudence, will avail to further one's progress towards one's ultimate good.

What one discovers in oneself and in all other human beings is something surd and unaccountable in terms of the rational understanding of human nature: a rooted tendency to disobedience in the will and distraction by passion, which causes obscuring of the reason and on occasion systematic cultural deformation. This type of disruption of the moral life is very different from that which results from a Hobbesian denial of there being any ultimate end. For in this latter type of case the ultimate end is already at least partly in view. What the discovery of wilful evil disrupts, or apparently disrupts, is the intelligible scheme through which the individual is able to understand him or herself as both directed towards and explicable in terms of that end. And just as an Averroist denial of any achievable state beyond those of this present life pointed forward towards a Hobbesian reduction of good and evil to pleasure and pain, so the discovery of human inability and resourcelessness to live by the natural law and to achieve the excellences of the virtues, the discovery of sin, points forward to a kind of existential despair which was completely unknown in the ancient world but which has been a recurrent malady of modernity. Yet for Aquinas, by contrast, it is in fact this discovery of wilful evil which makes the achievement of the human end possible. How so? The acknowledgment by oneself of radical defect is a necessary condition for one's reception of the virtues of faith, hope, and charity.

It is only the kind of knowledge which faith provides, the kind of expectation which hope provides, and the capacity for friendship with other human beings and with God which is the outcome of charity which can provide the other virtues with what they need to become genuine excellences, informing a way of life in and through which the good and the best can be achieved. The self-revelation of God in the events of the scriptural history and the gratuitous grace through which that revelation is appropriated, so that an individual can come to recognize his or her place within that same history, enable such individuals to recognize also that prudence, justice, temperateness, and courage are genuine virtues, that the apprehension of the natural law was not illusory, and that the moral life up to this point requires to be corrected in order to be completed but not displaced. So a Pauline and Augustinian account retrospectively vindicates that in Aristotle which had provided a first understanding of the core of the moral life.

Take away or reject the Aristotelianism in the Thomist account, but leave the despair of moral achievement and the gratuitousness of grace, and what is foreshadowed is Luther. What an adequately corrected Aristotelianism provides for Aquinas, which is notably absent in Luther and in his ideological heirs, is an opportunity for showing how the understanding of prudence, justice, temperateness, and courage in the light afforded by charity, hope, and faith, and more especially charity, which is the form of all the virtues, furnishes a richly detailed account of the moral life. So, in the best accounts of the virtues to be given so far, inadequacies are remedied by using the Bible and Augustine to transcend the limitations not only of Aristotle but also of Plato (for in his account of the cardinal virtues Aquinas is quite as indebted as Plato as to Aristotle) and by using Aristotle as well as Augustine to articulate some of the detail of the moral life in a way that goes beyond anything furnished by Augustine.

Two features of that detailed treatment are of crucial importance. Modern Catholic protagonists of theories of natural law have sometimes claimed that we can fully understand and obey the natural law without any knowledge of God. But according to Aquinas all the moral precepts of the Old Law, the Mosaic Law summed up in the Ten Commandments, belong to the natural law, including those which command us as to how we are to regard God and comport ourselves in relation to Him. A knowledge of God is, on Aquinas's view, available to us from the outset of our moral enquiry and plays a crucial part in our progress in that enquiry. And it would be very surprising if this were not so: the unifying framework within which our understanding of ourselves, of each other, and of our shared environment progresses is one in which that understanding, by tracing the sequences of final, formal, efficient, and material causality, always refers us back to a unified first cause from which flows all that is good and all that is true in what we encounter. So in articulating the natural law itself we understand the peculiar character of our own directedness, and in understanding the natural law better we move initially from what is evident to any plain person's unclouded moral apprehension to what is evident only or at least much more clearly to the *sapientes,* those whom Aquinas saw as masters of the master-craft (I-IIae 100, 1), and to what supernatural revelation discloses. But in so doing we progress or fail to progress, both as members of a community with a particular sacred history, the history of Israel and the church, and as members of communities with secular political histories.

So a second crucial feature of Aquinas's detailed treatment of the moral life is its political dimension. And in part because the histories of sacred and secular communities intersect at key points, in part because of the internal structures of both types of community, the conflicts of the moral life are on occasion bound up with the conflicts of competing jurisdictions: so it was in Aquinas's own time both within the University of Paris and between the university authorities, the episcopal authority, and the royal authority; so it was also between imperial and papal power and in the kingdom of Naples. It was thus through and in a variety of conflicts that the universal truths of, for example, Aquinas's account of what justice is in all its parts and aspects, had to find their highly particularized embodiments. And it was and is in so doing that the craft-skills of philosophy were and are exercised in elaborating the key distinctions of the moral life, itself always, as we have seen, at some level a life of moral enquiry.

In all these respects the individual moral life continues and extends that tradition which provided it with its initial context for reappropriating and extending teachings out of a variety of pasts. So the enquiries of the individual moral life are continuous with those of past tradition and the rationality of that life is the rationality both embodied in and transmitted through tradition. What the *Summa* achieves is a definitive statement at the level of theory of the point reached by its moral and theological tradition so far. What its sequences portray are a set of possibilities awaiting further embodiment in particular persons, circumstances, times, and places.

What then would it be for the sequences of the *Summa*—in which there is a progression from what must be first presupposed about God and human nature in the first part, through the sequences of moral enquiry of the first and second parts of the second part, to the recognition in the third part of the revealed truths which define for us the Kingdom of God—to be mirrored in the enacted dramatic narratives of particular human lives lived out in particular communities? Aquinas himself does not supply an answer to this question, but Dante does. Yet to understand the import of Dante's answers we need first to notice one further aspect of Aquinas's position. The individual human being is a unity in whom the directedness of the different aspects of his spiritual and social existence have to be ordered hierarchically into a unified mode of life. Yet those different aspects each have their own importance: it is the individual *qua* biological unit, the individual *qua* family member, the individual *qua* citizen of this commune or subject of this monarch, the individual *qua* Dominican friar or Benedictine monk who discharges what is due in justice and charity to him or herself and others in these roles. Hence arises a variety of tensions, and the practical problems of the integrity of the self are the counterpart to the practical problems of competing jurisdictions. The virtues which conjointly inform the actions of an integrated self are also the virtues of a well-integrated political community.

Aquinas himself seems to have negotiated these problems with a rare singleness of purpose, with that purity of heart, which as Kierkegaard said, is to will one thing. He had when very young been a student at the University of Naples, the first lay medieval university, founded by the apostate emperor Frederick II; he was a member of a family deeply involved in the Italian conflicts between the papacy and Frederick II, and he moved between teaching at both Paris and Naples and at the papal court at a time when the interests of the French monarchy in the kingdom of Naples added a further dimension to the political complexities in which he could have become entangled. It was therefore notable that he always rejected any political role, refusing earlier the abbacy at Monte Cassino and later the archbishopric of Naples. And this single-minded insistence on the intellectual character of his vocation underlay the quality for which Dante most admired Aquinas, his *discrezione,* his ability to make the right moral and intellectual distinctions.

Some nineteenth-century Thomists paid Dante what they took to be the compliment of reading him as a Thomist. But it is in part because he was not, because he constructed poetically and philosophically from the Augustinian and Aristotelian traditions a synthesis that was genuinely his own, that his agreements with Aquinas are so impressive. So in the imagined universe of the *Commedia* the vices of those who inhabit the *Inferno,* the virtues of those in the *Paradiso,* and the virtues and vices of those engaged in the transformations of the *Purgatorio* do indeed together particularize the accounts of the virtues and vices in the Ia–IIae and IIa–IIae of the *Summa* and need

to be read as its partial counterpart. What that particularization reinforces is both Aquinas's thesis that the badness and failure of any
one part of a self entails the badness of the whole and his thesis that
there is no badness of any part which is not the redeemable corruption or distortion of some good. The modern reader of the *Commedia* is, however, apt to find just these features in Dante, which exhibit his agreement with Aquinas, problematic.

How can Dante, for example, so obviously admire his own
teacher, Brunetto Latini—yet another author of an encyclopaedia—
and nonetheless place him in Hell? If Brunetto Latini was so admirable
in so many ways, as indeed he was, how can he suffer that unqualified condemnation for the sin of sodomy which places him in the
Inferno? The answer is clearly given by Aquinas: the doing of many
good deeds is perfectly compatible with the perverse choosing of
something in oneself which is defect and error and affirming it as what
one intends unalterably to be. And it is this choice which is one's
own choice of exclusion from the community of the perfected. So
hell is persistence in defection from the integrity both of a self and
of its communities.

Among those thus assigned to the *Inferno* was the Emperor
Frederick II, whom Nietzsche was to call "that great free spirit" and
to place among "the finest examples" of "marvellously incomprehen-
sible and inexplicable beings, those enigmatical men, predestined for
conquering and circumventing others" (other examples were Alci-
biades, Caesar, and Leonardo da Vinci). What Nietzsche praised in
each of them was what he perceived as a ruthless affirmation of the
self and its powers; what Dante saw as Frederick's self-condemnation
was, so it seems, the very same affirmation. And conversely what Dante
and Aquinas saw as achievement of the good, Nietzsche saw as emas-
culation and impoverishment. What is at issue here is in part the answer to the questions: in what larger story or stories, if any, is the
story of each individual embedded? And in what still larger story is
that story in turn embedded? And is there then a single history of
the world within which all other stories find their place and from
which the significance of each subordinate story derives? Dante's af-
firmative answer embodies a challenge to his future readers: tell me
your story and I will show you that it only becomes intelligible within
the framework provided by the *Commedia,* or rather within some
framework provided by that scriptural vision which the *Commedia*

allegorizes. For Nietzsche all such stories, so understood, are mis-
uses and abuses of the historical imagination, a misunderstood reifica-
tion of masks.

Yet Nietzsche greatly admired Dante, while viewing with contempt the ecclesiastical antagonists of Frederick II. For he saw in
Dante's writing, as did that oddly neglected Nietzschean, Stefan
George, the very same creative, assertive strength which he also saw
in Frederick II and in Leonardo. So that a Nietzschean reader's retort to Dante—and indirectly to Aquinas—would be: admit that in
telling your stories about Frederick II and Brunetto Latini what you
were in fact affirming was your self as an expression of the will to
power, just as much as Frederick II and Brunetto Latini did, something for which you placed *them* in Hell. So on a Nietzschean reading Dante's text takes on a different antagonistic set of meanings,
one at odds with Dante's avowed moral intentions. And as it is with
Dante, so it would also *mutatis mutandis* be with Aquinas. But what
resources, if any, can Aquinas then provide for a response to this
Nietzschean reading? To answer this question, we need further to
recognize that from a Thomistic standpoint, as I have characterized
it, questions of rational justification may arise at four different levels.

There is first of all that of the genuinely uninstructed plain person, posing the question "What is my good?" in a number of particularized ways, whose teacher has to assist him or her in the actualization of those potentialities which will carry such persons from
their initial bare moral apprehensions to a discovery of the place of
those apprehensions in a larger scheme. There is secondly the person who shares that larger scheme and is already able to articulate
it in the Aristotelian terms which are its most adequate expression,
so that demands for rational justification are framed in terms of a
shared understanding of natural enquiry and a shared conception of
first principles, even if what is at issue is on occasion their precise
formulation. It was from within this kind of agreement that Aquinas
conducted his debate with some rival Islamic, Jewish, and Latin Averroist positions. Such debate is necessarily very different from that between antagonists each of whom systematically rejects to some significant degree the other's first principles and conception of rational
enquiry.

In this third type of debate, characterized by some large degree
of incommensurability, the type of claim which has to be made and

then established or refuted is precisely that which Aquinas advanced to Augustinians in respect of his amended and enlarged Augustinianism and to Averroists in respect of his amended and enlarged Augustinianism. It is, as we noticed earlier, the claim to provide a standpoint which suffers from less incoherence, is more comprehensive and more resourceful, but especially resourceful in one particular way. For among those resources, so it is claimed, is an ability not only to identify as limitations, defects, and errors of the opposing view what are or ought to be taken to be limitations, defects, and errors in the light of the standards of the opposing view itself, but also to explain in precise and detailed terms what it is about the opposing view which engenders just these particular limitations, defects, and errors and also what it is about that view which must deprive it of the resources required for understanding, overcoming, and correcting them. And at the same time it will be claimed that what is cogent, insightful, and true in that opposing view can be incorporated within one's own view, providing on occasion needed corrections of that view.

This then is the kind of claim in terms of which the rational superiority of Aquinas's philosophical and theological synthesis of traditions to previous versions of Augustinianism and Aristotelianism can be retrospectively exhibited. And it is also the kind of claim in terms of which the superiority of Thomism to later challenges, to Cartesian, Humean, Kantian, or Nietzschean critiques would have to be shown. A mistake of much nineteenth- and early twentieth-century Thomism was to suppose that the task of rational justification against their Cartesian, Humean, or Kantian adversaries was of the second, rather than of this third type. That is, they believed that they shared with their philosophical opponents more in the way of first principles and of a conception of rational enquiry than was in fact the case. Yet against Nietzschean opponents it would not be enough to recognize this error. For it may well be the case, and it is in large part to Nietzsche himself that we are indebted for our understanding of this, that a philosophical or theological position may be so organized, both in its intellectual structures and in its institutionalized modes of presentation and enquiry that conversation with an opposing position may reveal that its adherents are systematically unable to recognize in it even those errors, defects, and limitations which ought to be recognized as such in the light of their own and its standards.

When such a situation is encountered, either in the form of a blindness imputed to one's opponents or in the form of a blindness imputed to one by one's opponents, where such blindness is alleged to arise systematically from the way in which either or both points of view are intellectually and socially organized and not merely from the psychological characteristics of particular individuals, then yet another task of a fourth kind is added to the work of rational justification. What has to be supplied is a cogent theoretical explanation of ideological blindness, the kind of theory to which notable contributions have been made by Gramsci in respect of Croce, by Mannheim in respect of different types of Utopianism, and most of all by Nietzsche. What did Aquinas have to say at this fourth level? Can a Thomist hope to construct a genealogy for Nietzsche's genealogizing?

There is one Thomist book on Nietzsche, Frederick Copleston's *Friedrich Nietzsche: Philosopher of Culture* (London, 1942). Copleston was understandably and rightly preoccupied in 1942 with the question of how European culture was to be defended from the Nazis, and his presentation of Nietzsche was of a philosopher deeply opposed to everything that National Socialism stood for, but whose enquiries issued in positions which could not sustain an intellectually or morally effective alternative. It echoes in a curious way Stefan George's final verdict on Nietzsche as a hero who failed. But while Copleston pointed us towards a genealogy for genealogy, he did not actually provide it. Where then would such a genealogy have to begin? The answer is: with what Aquinas says about the roots of intellectual blindness in moral error, with the misdirection of the intellect by the will and with the corruption of the will by the sin of pride, both that pride which is an inordinate desire to be superior and that pride which is an inclination to contempt for God. Where Nietzsche saw the individual will as a fiction, as part of a mistaken psychology which conceals from view the impersonal will to power, the Thomist can elaborate out of materials provided in the *Summa* an account of the will to power as an intellectual fiction disguising the corruption of the will. The activity of unmasking is itself to be understood from the Thomistic standpoint as a mask for pride.

What I have articulated so far is not at all the substance of those arguments by means of which Aquinas or Dante or their Thomistic successors would have to vindicate the positions of the *Summa* and of the *Commedia*. What I have perhaps achieved at least in the barest outline is a statement of what is at issue and what *kinds* of argument would have to be deployed. And in so doing it has become plain that the intellectual issues which divide Nietzschean genealogy from Thomistic tradition and both from the academic stance of the encyclopaedist cannot be dissociated from answers to questions about the moral errors and ideological distortions which enter into moral enquiry.

VII

In the Aftermath of Defeated Tradition

At the beginning of these lectures I noted that Adam Gifford in his will required of his lecturers that they should treat their theological and moral enquiries "as a strictly natural science," "just as astronomy or chemistry is," and that he gives evidence elsewhere of concurring in the view that one of the marks of a science is that it exhibits more or less continuous progress in its enquiries. I also noted that in the Gifford Lectures of the last hundred years no such progress is to be discerned. It is therefore worth asking what the difference is between rational enquiries in which overall progress is made and those from which it is absent. Part of the answer is that enquiry can only be systematic in its progress when its goal is to contribute to the construction of a *system* of thought and practice—including in the notion of construction such activities as those of more or less radical modification, and even partial demolition with a view to reconstruction—by participating in types of rational activity which have their *telos* in achieving for that system a perfected form in the light of the best standards for judging of that perfection so far to emerge. Particular problems are then partially, but in key ways, defined in terms of the constraints imposed by their place within the overall structure, and the significance of solving this or that particular problem derives from that place. It is one of the marks of the flourishing of such a developing system of thought and practice that from time to time its *telos* is reformulated. And those who contribute to the perfecting of such a system can do so only by developing and deploying their own skills in the manner characteristic of a craft and by participating in the activities in which those skills are put to work in the manner characteristic of a tradition. It is then only in contexts in which enquiry is understood by those participating in it in ways characteristic of system, craft, and tradition, whether or not that understanding is made ex-

149

plicit, that the concept of progress in enquiry will have application. So it is in the history of the modern natural sciences; and so it was, I want to claim, in the history of philosophical enquiry in general, including moral and theological enquiry from Socrates to Aquinas, in whose work, as we have seen, two histories culminate and merge, one of which runs through Plato and Augustine, the other through Plato, Aristotle, and the Islamic commentators. But what is at first sight astonishing is that with Aquinas those histories not only merge but to a remarkable degree terminate, that the unity of system, craft, and tradition in philosophy, at its point of highest achievement, largely disappears from view. I do not of course mean that there were not in succeeding generations Thomists, especially among the Dominicans, from whose ranks emerged commentary after commentary, some of them, such as those by Cajetan (1468–1534) and John of St. Thomas (1589–1644) first-rate. But Thomistic commentary became a marginal activity in an increasingly fragmented and intellectually eclectic set of debates and conversations. Enquiry moved in a number of different and competing directions, and although from time to time in the next three hundred years something in the way of a system was thrown up by this or that individual, the conception of enquiry as long-term cooperative activity in the construction of a systematic overall understanding of theory and practice no longer dominated.

To this it will be retorted, and in part rightly, that in understanding the history of philosophy from Socrates to Aquinas as that of a unified and cooperative project, or rather of at least two unified and cooperative projects, I am imposing retrospectively on what was in fact a heterogeneous, shifting, interrupted, and often chaotic set of enterprises a unified pattern which distorts the history of enquiry *wie es eigentlich gewesen*. What this retort ignores is first of all that the history of all successful enquiry is and cannot but be written retrospectively; the history of physics, for example, is the history of what contributed to the making in the end of quantum mechanics, relativistic theory, and modern astrophysics. A tradition of enquiry characteristically bears within itself an always open to revision history of itself in which the past is characterized and recharacterized in terms of developing evaluations of the relationship of the various parts of that past to the achievements of the present. So Aristotle understood his predecessors as providing a prologue to his own enquiries; so Augustine reevaluated and recharacterized key theses and arguments of Plato and Plotinus; so Aquinas provided the resources for integrating into a single history all those scriptural, ancient, patristic, and medieval predecessors upon whose work he drew both constructively and critically.

What follows from this is that how the history of philosophy is written will depend in key part upon what are taken to be its achievements, what its frustrations and failures. And insofar as the adherents of different traditions and more generally of different standpoints evaluate those achievements, frustrations, and failures in not merely different, but incompatible ways, as they do, to that extent there will be rival, incompatible, and sometimes incommensurable histories of philosophy. The notion of a single neutral nonpartisan history is one more illusion engendered by the academic standpoint of the encyclopaedist; it is the illusion that there is the past waiting to be discovered, *wie es eigentlich gewesen,* independent of characterization from some particular standpoint. So the debate is in part between rival histories and the kind of historical claim which I made in asserting that a particular kind of progress in enquiry terminates, not entirely but to a surprising degree, with Aquinas can only be made from the standpoint of one such partisan history. But to adopt that standpoint is not to obscure the fact that my account of Aquinas's work as the culmination and integration of the Augustinian and Aristotelian traditions is not at all how Aquinas was understood by much the greater part of both his contemporaries and his immediate successors. Aquinas was eccentric to, and in variety of ways at odds with, the dominant and orthodox mainstream of institutionalized thirteenth-century enquiries and even more with their fourteenth-century continuations. What is remarkable in this perspective is not the condemnation of 1277, nor the rejection by the most influential writers of the next generation of Aquinas's most characteristic and central theses, but rather the way in which Aquinas was nonetheless repeatedly revived and invoked after that initial rehabilitation which led to his canonization.

What defeated Aquinas was the power of the institutionalized curriculum. Neither theology nor the subordinate *artes liberales* could in the middle or late thirteenth century find room for the Aristotelian system, in the form in which the Islamic commentators had transmitted it, *as a whole,* either in its Averroist version or in Aquinas's.

What then made an impact were particular Aristotelian theses, arguments, and portions of theory detached from the whole of which
they were parts, and this systematically unsystematic reception of and
response to this or that in Aristotle or Averroes or Avicenna resulted
in a series of equally *ad hoc* revisions of Augustinian positions in theology and of the received positions in other disciplines. The progenitor of, as well as the most distinguished contributor to, this late medieval anti-Thomistic mode was Duns Scotus.

Consider in this light the great differences between Aquinas and
Scotus on the relationship between the *telos* of human beings as considered from the standpoint of philosophy and as considered from
the standpoint of theology. One of the issues on which some, at least,
of the Averroists had argued that philosophy had competence, independently of theology, and which in 1277 was included in the 219
theses condemned by Stephen Tempier, bishop of Paris, was: that
happiness is to be had in this life and not in another (Sent. 176).
Aquinas had argued against this very proposition, contending that
all rational beings seek perfect happiness and that it can be shown
rationally that perfect happiness is not to be had in this life but only
in some other. Scotus, by contrast, argues that so far as natural reason is concerned nothing can be known of any life but this, and that
the imperfections in any human happiness to which Aquinas had
pointed may be imperfections from the standpoint of an intelligence
that is pure and disembodied but not for a human being rationally
convinced, as anyone should be without faith in a revelation, of his
or her mortality. So on one issue at least upon which the Aristotelian
Aquinas had challenged the Averroists, the Franciscan and Augustinian Scotus agrees with them. Why?

The context is Scotus's discussion of whether it can be known
by natural reason that there will be a general resurrection of human-
kind (*Opus Oxoniense* IV,43,ii). Scotus had a specific theological interest in endorsing an amended version of the Averroist interpretation of Aristotle's account of the human being, for that account seemed
to show that an essentially embodied mind could not but understand
itself as mortal. It is only the soul independent of the body which
can be thought of as immortal and the doctrine of the resurrection
of the body is of a purely contingent and incidental addendum to
the immortality of the soul. On Scotus's view only theology, drawing upon the resources of revelation, can speak competently about

these topics, and Scotus's conventionally Augustinian theology envisaged the soul as only incidentally related to the body.

To have recognized that this is what is at stake for Scotus in this discussion, that Aristotle has been put to work only in a limited *ad hoc* way that will absolve Augustinianism from coming to terms with Aquinas's much deeper and more sophisticated Aristotelian understanding of the relationship of body and soul is also to be able to recognize the depth of Scotus's disagreement with Aquinas, not only on particular issues, but above all in overall perspective. The relationship of soul to body, indeed the existence of body, had been something of an embarrassment to later Augustinians, even if not to Augustine. And on this specific point Aquinas's integration of Augustinian and Aristotelian views had seemed to his Franciscan Augustinian contemporaries offensive. More particularly, they were concerned with the implications of soul-body relationships for the knowledge of singulars. For Aquinas a human being is not a soul plus a body but a body which has a soul. Human experience is bodily experience, and the soul knows and knows about singulars only on the basis of that experience as mediated by imagination—itself a bodily phenomenon—and structured in terms of form by intellect. The human mind is thus not self-sufficient, on Aquinas's view; it is rather, to use John F. Boler's illuminating phrase, "radically incomplete" ('Intuitive and Abstractive Cognition' in *The Cambridge History of Later Medieval Philosophy,* Cambridge, 1982, p. 475), incomplete without that encounter with the objects of sense from which it moves to the actuality of knowledge. We cannot, that is, first characterize the mind and then ask epistemological questions about what it can know, for it is only in the actuality of empirical knowledge that the mind exists in its completeness, and that is to say that the mind essentially, and not only accidentally, requires the body for its operations.

The Franciscan William de la Mare in 1279 denounced 117 theses in Aquinas's writings in his *Correctorium fratris Thomae,* among them those which give expression to this view of the relationship of soul to body and thus impugn the competence of the soul to know singulars immediately and independently of bodily experience. In 1282 the Franciscan order prohibited the copying of the *Summa* except as accompanied by the *Correctorium,* a book thereafter referred to by some younger Dominicans as the *Corruptorium.* Scotus, then, in his own assertion of the competence of the soul, independent of the body, adopted epistemological positions which protect Augustinianism from any systematic interpenetration of theology and Aristotelian philosophy. And this is his consistent attitude, evident also in his Augustinian account of the primacy assigned to the will over the intelligence.

According to Aquinas will operates independently of intellect, of practical reasoning, only when and insofar as someone is not pursuing his or her genuine good. It is indeed the case, on his view, as on Augustine's that only through charity is the will returned to its true place in the ordered human being, but what the will is returned to is an order in which the primacy belongs to the practical intelligence. The Augustinian tradition however had assigned an unconditional primacy to will and Scotus's rejection of Aristotle's psychology deprived him of the only available alternative way of conceiving the relationship of will to intellect. This had a consequence of the first importance for future history.

On Aristotle's account, as on Plato's, the human being who has acquired the necessary education in the intellectual and moral virtues and who thereby apprehends what his or her true good is acts so as to achieve that good. For Aristotle and Plato, as for other ancient writers, reason is an active goal-setting, goal-achieving power. Aquinas follows them, integrating into an Aristotelian explanation of why on occasion the good is not achieved or even pursued, namely because of some defect in the virtues, an Augustinian account of the part played by the will. Aquinas, like Aristotle, can find no room for any question as to why, given that one recognizes that something is one's true good, one should act so as to achieve it. Neither further reason, nor—for the morally educated, virtue-informed person whose will is rightly ordered by the intellect—further motive, are either necessary or possible. Hence to know that God commands those precepts of the natural law, in obedience to which one's good is to be realized, gives one no further, additional reason for obedience to those precepts, except insofar as our knowledge of God's unqualified goodness and omniscience gives us reasons—as it does—for holding his judgments of our good, as promulgated in the Old and New Laws, to be superior to our own. The 'ought' of 'One ought to obey God' is the same 'ought' as the 'ought' of 'To do so and so is the good of such a one; so such a one ought to do so and so'—the same 'ought,' that is, as the 'ought' of practical reasoning.

For Scotus, however, an Augustinian understanding of the primacy of the will entails that the intellect is inert, the will is free, and the will's being moved by its good is something distinct from the will's being obedient to the command of another. Part of the freedom of the will to defy God would, on Scotus's view, be taken away if merely by pursuing its own good the will was obedient to God. The will therefore can only exhibit its obedience to God by not only obeying the natural law *qua* directive of our good but also *qua* divine commandment. Hence alongside the 'ought' of practical reasoning, which in any case *qua* reasoning cannot move us to action (since the intellect is practically inert), there appears another 'ought,' one unknown to Aristotle and to the ancient world generally, the distinctive 'ought' of moral obligation. But in generating this new, distinctive concept Scotus makes it possible for his successors to generate a new set of problems, problems which were to become in time central to the about to emerge academic discipline of moral philosophy. For once one has identified a moral obligation as an obligation not because of what it enjoins in the doing or achieving of something good, but in virtue of the command of another, questions arise as to why we should obey this command. And if the answer is that the command is God's and that God is wholly good, then the questions arise as to whether, counterfactually, we would still be morally obliged if God had not so commanded and as to whether, if we are in a position to judge that God is good, then we are not also in a position to judge by the same standard by which we judged the goodness of God whether or not we have an obligation, even if God were not so to command. Scotus thus not only made possible but provoked a good deal of later moral philosophy, directly and indirectly, from Occam all the way to Kant.

In a parallel way Scotus's doctrine of the soul's immediate intuitive knowledge of singulars, so that the singular is intelligible— even if only somewhat so—in independence of the universal, both transforms the conception of intelligibility and places constraints upon how the relationship of particular to universal can be understood, in such a way as to generate a new problematic for the about to emerge academic discipline of metaphysics or first philosophy. Paradoxically Scotus, whose philosophical enquiries were at every point controlled by his theological conclusions and whose primary interest was in protecting the autonomy of Augustinian theology from the inroads of either Averroist or Thomistic Aristotelianism, set the scene instead for the emergence of philosophy as an autonomous discipline or set of disciplines, with its own defining problematic. Much else of course had to happen later, both intellectually and in the curriculum. Nonetheless, viewed from a Thomistic perspective, it is at this point that philosophy is redefined as an autonomous academic discipline, whose boundaries are institutional boundaries, and ceases to be itself a tradition of enquiry. Thereafter, however, it is incidentally hospitable in a variety of ways to some of the concerns of a number of warring traditions, even if characteristically with the proviso that they present themselves only in terms acceptable to the academic conventions and genres of the discipline.

In the University of Paris during Aquinas's tenure there, first as *sententiarius* and then in two periods as regent master, the teaching of the faculty of arts was organized in terms of the seven *artes liberales,* the verbal arts of the *trivium* and the mathematical arts of the *quadrivium,* and a significant factor in the dispute as to in which faculties the works of Aristotle should be taught was the fact that the Aristotelian scheme and synthesis of enquiry–to which whole scheme both by Aristotle himself and by his Islamic commentators the name 'philosophy' had been given–simply could not be fitted into the earlier curricular categories either of the faculty of theology or of the faculty of arts. Aquinas in his unfinished commentary on Boethius's *De Trinitate* had pointed out that "The seven liberal arts do not adequately divide theoretical philosophy . . ." (5, 1, ad.3) and Aquinas's own reworking of the Aristotelian scheme violated the academic boundaries of the *status quo*–not only in its scale and architecture but also by the way in which constantly from the commentary on the *Sentences* to the *Summa Theologiae* theological and philosophical enquiry are at key points made inseparable–as radically as did the Averroist version.

The outcome both at Paris and elsewhere was the enlargement of the Arts curriculum. To the seven liberal arts were added the three philosophies: moral philosophy, natural philosophy, and metaphysics. And philosophy thus began a career in which it was gradually to become the dominant academic discipline within the university, while theology as a discipline was to preserve its autonomy only at the price of its eventual isolation and unimportance, a history which in the late nineteenth and twentieth centuries academic philosophy in turn was doomed to reenact. We should at this point recall that

Hugh of St. Victor, for whose ordered classification of the sciences Aquinas shows some respect in his commentary on Boethius, had written the *Didascalion* in the 1120s in the order to combat what he had already seen then as the fragmentation of the curriculum and the growing independence of the disciplines. But the impact of Aristotle in the thirteenth century not only had the effect of restricting the Augustinian synthesis to theology, which is just what Hugh had feared, but also that of preventing *any* synthetic vision from informing the curriculum as a whole.

Each of the liberal arts to a large extent went its own way and the overall effect was one of more and more heterogeneity and variety. Grammar under the influence of the *modistae* moved into new areas; rhetoric, having been subordinated to and in Paris almost merged into dialectic, began to achieve new independence, especially with the fourteenth-century rediscovery of classical rhetoric; and dialectic was transformed into a set of heterogeneous discussions of a disparate collection of logical and conceptual problems, treated in large part for their own sake and not in respect of any function of dialectic within any overall system. Arithmetic, music, and geometry came to serve new purposes in the world outside the universities. And within astronomy there were the first movements towards a recognition of the conflict between what had been inherited from Ptolemy and what had been more recently learned from Aristotle.

It is instructive to compare the way in which such conflict within astronomy and also within natural philosophy functioned so as to produce ultimately a new tradition of enquiry in the physical sciences and the very different way in which conflict and disagreement within metaphysics and moral philosophy functioned. What emerge in the former, gradually and unevenly, but over time increasingly, are a set of agreements: as to what constitutes an unsolved problem, as to the constraints upon acceptable solutions, as to methods of calculation, and as to the relations between different aspects of enquiry. It is because of this history that when at the beginning of the sixteenth century Copernicus, educated into this late medieval tradition at Cracow, and at the end of the sixteenth century Galileo, also educated into it at Pisa, play the greatest parts in displacing this tradition, they simultaneously overturn *and* complete it. For it was this late medieval tradition which presented in its detailed enquiries just that set of insoluble problems which could only be rendered tractable by being recast within new overall conceptual frameworks. Hence fourteenth- and fifteenth-century physics and astronomy were completed in being defeated. We can write of them just that kind of retrospective history which reveals the continuous directedness characteristic of a genuine tradition of enquiry, in which a great many particular theses, arguments, observation, and debates turn out to have been parts of a teleologically ordered whole. And to have understood this is to be able to say how, as well as why, medieval astronomy and physics moved to a point of culminating achievement, albeit in so doing moving to their own replacement.

By contrast, in what did fourteenth- and fifteenth-century medieval moral philosophy and metaphysics issue? The answer is: as a whole, nothing. The story is one of the dissolution of unified enquiry into variety and heterogeneity; or to put the same point in another way, the story is that of the genesis of the institution of academic philosophy as an organized and professionalized university discipline. It is always salutary to remember that most of the history of philosophy has occurred outside the history of that particular professionalized institution. The ancient philosophers gave a quite different sense to the words which we translate by 'philosophy.' Augustine, Anselm, Abelard, and Aquinas all defined their activities in terms of a very different conception of enquiry. And such theorists as Bacon, Hobbes, Descartes, Locke, D'Alembert, Diderot, Rousseau, Bentham, the Mills, and Nietzsche all worked and contended in arenas very different from that of the university. The conception of philosophy as almost exclusively restricted to institutionalized activities within the university is in the modern world a social phenomenon with roots in eighteenth- and nineteenth-century Scotland, Germany, and France which has achieved its fullest embodiment in the contemporary culture of the United States. But it had a distinguished and very similar predecessor in the philosophy of the later Middle Ages. Were the word not already employed in a way that would make it confusing to use it of what these two periods of institutionalized academic history have in common, the name that would suggest itself is: 'scholasticism.'

What are the marks of this type of philosophy? The first is the achievement and sustaining of high levels of professional skill in the elaboration and use of logical and conceptual techniques. This is in part sustained by admitting to the discussion only those who attain some bureaucratically sanctioned standard in the use of such techniques and thereby receive some official license, in part by control of the curriculum and in part by informal agreements on what kind of thesis or argument is to be taken seriously, what disregarded or scorned. Secondly, ascribed achievement is through the exercise of these acknowledged and licensed types of professional skill on particular problems, treated piecemeal. The problems may well arise by abstraction from some system and may even be recognized as such, but the continuities of the discipline reside in successive treatments of what are recognizedly members of the same set of continuing individual problems. The problems persist because they are never, or almost never, definitively solved, although what are from time to time presented as solutions often lead to reformulations of the problems. The problem is the fundamental unit of discourse.

Thirdly and correlatively, certain types of basic disagreement are recurrent and ineliminable. Agreement on method, technique, and the evaluation of skill is often sufficient to ensure further agreements on what is involved in upholding one solution to some particular problem rather than its rivals, in terms of what else one is committed to thereby through entailment, implication, or presupposition, and on what further difficulties are thereby encountered. But there is no or insufficient shared agreement as to how these commitments and consequences are to be evaluated, on what standard it is by which gain in one respect is to be measured against loss in another, and sometimes indeed on what constitutes gain and what is to be accounted loss. And without such a shared standard a large measure of disagreement is bound to be ineliminable. When does this lack arise?

It derives in key part from a fourth characteristic of this type of philosophy. Those who engage in it characteristically, although not always, come to it bringing with them commitments to some extraphilosophical standpoint. In modern philosophy these have been as various as Tolstoyan morality, the aesthetic *weltanschauung* of Bloomsbury, and scientific materialism. In the later Middle Ages they were characteristically theological or political or both. These ideological *weltanschauungen* cannot be provided with support by this type of philosophy and they are permitted to enter into it only insofar as theses abstracted from them can be brought to bear in a piecemeal way on the acknowledged problems of philosophy. But it is they which furnish, to their adherents, what the philosophy itself cannot furnish, a standard of evaluation and of preference whereby the costs and benefits of each particular rival solution to some particular problem can be assessed. And the range of consequent disagreement within philosophy of this kind will then be as great as the range of prephilosophical disagreement in ideological standpoint.

There is consequently no progress in this type of academic philosophy, whether medieval or modern, except in skill, method, and technique in the formulation of problems. Beyond this, philosophical positions merely replace and displace one another without any overall directedness appearing. Hence not even retrospectively is it possible to give a teleological account of its history, for no *telos* emerges. And thus although the concerns and detailed findings of this philosophy are of the highest relevance to a number of types of tradition of rational enquiry, it is not itself such a tradition and is indeed institutionalized in such a way as to exclude the type of claim and argument characteristic of such traditions from its professionalized discourse.

I am not here directly concerned with twentieth-century embodiments of this type of philosophy except in two respects. I remarked in the first lecture upon how the inability of twentieth-century Gifford lecturers to make discernible progress in the enquiries with which Adam Gifford entrusted them was rooted in part in the resourcelessness of this type of academic philosophy. And just why and how this is so may now be a little clearer. Moreover that there is an important way in which twentieth-century analytic philosophy has condemned itself to repeat the history of late medieval Scholastic philosophy, so that each may be used to illuminate the other, receives striking confirmation from the way in which the history of medieval philosophy is written, when written from this modern twentieth-century philosophical point of view. Consider in this respect *The Cambridge History of Later Medieval Philosophy* (ed. N. Kretzmann, A. Kenny, J. Pinborg, E. Stump, Cambridge, 1982).

The book consists of forty-six essays by forty-one authors, one of the latest imitations of the original *Cambridge Modern History* as conceived by that exemplar of the encyclopaedic mind, Lord Acton. It is the mark of encyclopaedia that the present stands in judgment upon the past, assigning to itself a sovereignty which allows it to approve that in the past which can be represented as a precursor of its own standards of judgment. In Acton's case, as Maitland remarked in his obituary notice, the work was done "to the greater glory of truth and right." For the editors of the *Cambridge History of Later Medieval Philosophy* the work was done to the greater glory of contemporary analytic philosophy, which is equated with "recent philosophy." The publisher says correctly that "this volume is organized by those topics in which recent philosophy has made the greatest progress" in order "to end the era in which medieval philosophy has been studied in a philosophical ghetto," presumably that ghetto in which the attempt was being made to understand medieval philosophy in the light of its own standards and presuppositions, in order perhaps also to understand how those standards and presuppositions – themselves very different at different periods and in different writers – not only are challenged by but themselves challenge our own. The editors, foreseeing a charge of "imbalance in the organization of this History" (p. 4) assert from the same standpoint that "the achievements of medieval logicians are historically more distinctive and philosophically more valuable than anything else in medieval thought, with the possible exception of rational theology," having just noted that *their* history "leaves theology out of account . . ."

The very high quality of a number of the individual essays accentuates, even while it compensates for, the difference between the editorial perspective and that of so many medieval thinkers. No one's thought is treated *as a whole* and therefore the relationship of individual theses and arguments as parts to wholes never appears. It is this, even more than the cursory treatment of, for example, moral enquiry, which would make it impossible for anyone relying solely on this history to begin to understand the scale, nature, and structure of Aquinas's enquiries and therefore to engage in dialogue with Aquinas. Yet it is equally striking that a method and a perspective which in relation to the twelfth and thirteenth century are in significant ways distorting and obscurantist become a great deal less so in the fourteenth. The Middle Ages gradually moved towards becoming what the editors of the *Cambridge History* clearly wished that they had always been. And that is to say, the unity of enquiry, so crucial not only to Aquinas but also to both his Franciscan and his Averroist contemporaries, gradually becomes lost to view. So Occam explicitly rejected any notion of a unified science with a specifically unified subject matter as the goal of enquiry (Prologue, *Expositio super viii libros physicorum*). Enquiry itself became irreducibly multiple and heterogeneous in a way that excluded any genuine architectonic of the sciences. Thus the *Cambridge History* to some degree and perhaps quite inadvertently shows us high medieval thought from the standpoint of late medieval thought and in so doing provides evidence for the strong similarity, if not quite identity, of standpoint of modern analytic philosophy and late medieval philosophy.

We should expect, if this were so, that the later Middle Ages too would by reason of the very structuring of its modes of thought and of the academic institutionalization of those structures be unable to appropriate or even to enter into dialogue with Aquinas's thought as a whole and more particularly with the *Summa* as a whole. And just this was in fact the case. Consider how the *Summa* came to be treated in the light of Aquinas's own intentions. Leonard Boyle, O.P., has argued compellingly that it is no coincidence that it was in the period when for the first time Aquinas had an entirely free hand in organizing the form of teaching for his students, namely in 1265 when he set up a Dominican *studium* in Rome, as enjoined by the Chapter of the Roman Province of the Dominican order, that Aquinas began to write the *Summa Theologiae* "for the instruction of beginners" (*The Setting of the Summa Theologiae of St. Thomas*, Toronto, 1982). Underlying this, so Boyle argues, was a dissatisfaction with the current Dominican manuals and teaching on moral questions and an intention to remedy this by setting moral enquiry in its appropriate systematic theological context so that the parts should not misleadingly be studied in abstraction from the whole, as had all too often been the case with his Dominican predecessors.

After Aquinas's death the Dominican order continually reaffirmed its allegiance to Aquinas's teaching even in hostile ecclesiastical environments and a tradition of commentary upon Aquinas had its first notable figures before the end of the thirteenth century, especially the Oxford Dominican, Thomas Sutton (see Frederick J. Roensch *Early Thomistic School*, Dubuque, 1964). But the subsequent history of such commentary, no matter how distinguished, is quite independent of the mainstream of late medieval philosophy. Even in the Dominican priory schools the *Summa* never became part of the curriculum. Moreover, as Boyle points out (p. 23), the parts of the *Summa* were copied separately and circulated separately, so that Aquinas's views on the topics of the *Secunda Secundae*—which was copied more often than any other part—were studied in isolation from the context in which it had been one of his central intentions to place them.

Thus was the *Summa* dismembered as medieval copyists, responding to consumer demand in the academic marketplace, anticipated the editors of the *Cambridge History*. Aquinas had been an eccentric thinker in the thirteenth century. In the later Middle Ages he became as a thinker both eccentric and marginal, until Renaissance Thomism to some extent reestablished his philosophical authority, even if sometimes misunderstanding what he wrote. It is, in the light of all this, surprising that during this period his theological primacy was continually reendorsed by papal authority, something not at all explicable by the intellectual *Zeitgeist,* but only by what is either pure historical contingency or divine providence.

Academic moral philosophy, in the later Middle Ages, was in some respects untouched by controversies in other parts of philosophy. The *Nicomachean Ethics* was a staple text and when, for example, John Buridan produced his commentary, it bore none of the marks of Occam's influence which appear in his other writings. What his commentary does exemplify, however, is a growing divorce between philosophy as concerned with practice and philosophy as theoretical enquiry. Buridan stresses the immediately practical function of moral philosophy and in the University of Vienna in the fifteenth century – and often elsewhere in central Europe – only the first five books of the *Nicomachean Ethics* were read, while commentators there and elsewhere had even earlier begun to restrict themselves to these books, so that the Aristotelian connection between the intellectual virtues and the moral virtues disappeared from view. At the same time moral standpoints more or less independent of and even hostile to that of Aristotle, let alone that of Aquinas, multiplied.

So we get alongside the often partial readings of the *Nicomachean Ethics* the teaching of Occam's theory of the foundation of obligation in divine commands, with its conclusion that "Evil is nothing other than to do something when one is under an obligation to do the opposite" (*Commentary on the Sentences* II, qu. 5H), recurrences of Augustinian objections to philosophical ethics as such, and the emergence among nominalist scholars of quite new theories of natural rights, for which there is no room within either an Aristotelian or a Thomistic framework. Such theories exemplify the way in which the multiplication and growing diversity of standpoints within moral philosophy are partially rooted in the changing form of the conflicts of the political and social world.

Aquinas had argued that in establishing a political order citizens may either vest authority in themselves or may alienate it from themselves, by conferring on a ruler sovereignty and the power of making positive law. But he had also argued that, even in such a case, insofar as a ruler makes positive laws not in accordance with justice, no one is bound to obey, *and* where the laws enjoin what is vicious one is indeed bound not to obey. Similarly, Dante in arguing from a very different political position for the supremacy of the Holy Roman Emperor in all secular matters had done so on the grounds that a single supreme *imperium* would be most likely to ensure justice and would provide a just court of appeal against subordinate princes. Both Aquinas and Dante, as Augustinians and Aristotelians, made the test of good and legitimate government the degree to which it secures justice.

Unsurprisingly as the conflicts between rival jurisdictions and rival forms of rule, within the church, between church and state, between city-states and emperor, between monarchical nation-states, and between orders within states, not only multiply but produce their own theoretical apologetics, this earlier appeal to justice is displaced by the primacy given to appeals to rights. By the very early fourteenth century *ius* has become understood by some at least as a *facultas* whereby every creature is entitled to exert its abilities in certain ways. Human rights thus understood are characteristically claimed *against* someone else. The relationship envisaged between them and shared conceptions of a common good had become sufficiently indirect for them to be deployable without invoking such conceptions in a theoretically substantial rather than a merely rhetorical way.

Yet this kind of use of 'merely' is itself perhaps inappropriate to a period in which moral philosophy acquired a new rival in the form of the revived classical rhetoric of the fourteenth century, for which as a discipline a political relevance lacking in philosophy was claimed from Petrarch onwards. And among the rhetoricians Cicero was no longer subordinated to Aristotle, as he had been by both Aquinas and Dante, but instead he provided an alternative way of thinking about the virtues and about the politics of their embodiment in practical life. At the same time the practice of casuistry took on new dimensions, perhaps especially in the economic order, so that, for example, the prohibition of usury, unconditional in Aquinas and Dante, was modified and eroded in a way that would finally lead to its being discarded.

What largely disappeared from view during this period in which theses, modes of argument, and problems of disparate kinds were thus multiplied was the possibility of any overall synthetic and systematic mode of thought and practice, embodied within the continuities of a tradition, being recognized, let alone securing widespread allegiance. Texts were still appealed to, but radical differences of interpretation often deprived such appeals of authority, except insofar as particular individuals or groups chose to allow them authority. For all these reasons acceptance of the standpoint of the *Summa Theologiae* would have required so radical a repudiation of the presuppositions and terms of later fourteenth-century and fifteenth-century debate both on moral philosophy and in the treatment of concrete moral questions that its lack of influence on those debates seems in retrospect to have been inevitable. Only when the sterility of late medieval thought had become widely recognized by the beginning of the sixteenth century was it possible for new systematic forms of philosophical enquiry to reestablish themselves in that renascence of Scholasticism from Vitoria to Suarez which drew so largely upon materials provided by Aquinas and yet made such an un-Thomistic use of them.

It is then the case, so I have argued, that the thirteenth-century university confrontation between Averroist Aristotelianism and Augustiniansim had two distinct and contrasting outcomes: Aquinas's own constructive correction, reinterpretation, and integration of the contending traditions into a new dialectical synthesis which had the capacity for directing enquiry still further beyond itself, on the one hand, and on the other the ensuing development both of the university curriculum and of the dominant tendencies in intellectual and moral debate, a development which excluded for the most part engagement with Aquinas's thought understood systematically and not just as a set of discrete theses. But there was yet another way in which Aquinas's distinctive positions were repudiated, one as pregnant with future possibility as the conceptual, theoretical, and moral pluralism of late medieval philosophy, but antithetical in its mode. It too had Dominican origins in the thought of another Dominican regent master at Paris at the close of the thirteenth century, Meister Eckhart.

Eckhart may well have believed that he was only carrying certain strands of Aquinas's thought further. When in 1325 he was accused of heresy, he claimed to be a Thomist. But it is precisely because and insofar as he was not that he has exerted such influence on a variety of later non-Thomistic and anti-Thomistic thinkers, most notably on Hegel and Heidegger. Heidegger's rejection of Aquinas is of course at the most fundamental level. Where Aquinas takes it that it is in moving from sense experience to true judgment that the mind first perfects itself and in its use of 'is' to refer to being exhibits its capacity to move towards that apprehension of first conceptions and principles in which the work of understanding of discursive reasoning is completed, Heidegger rejects this whole theoretical stance as one more episode in the history of that Platonic-Aristotelian tradition whose conceptualization of being, on his view, debars it from understanding that which evades all conceptualization. Aquinas, of course, understood very well that there is indeed that which lies beyond concepts, beyond saying, which our analogical ordering of concepts nonetheless points us towards in our speaking of God as truth and goodness, but there is indeed also a mode of speaking about God at the level of philosophy and theology—as contrasted for example with the prophetic images of Scripture—which *is* conceptually ordered through such analogical predications. We cannot think, in this area as in any other, except through conceptualizations which refer us in our judgments to being. And thus Heidegger did not misunderstand Aquinas in rejecting him. But that in Heidegger's thought which involved that rejection was precisely that in which Heidegger was most akin to Eckhart, a kinship fully and gladly acknowledged by Heidegger.

The relevant parts of Eckhart's writings are not his philosophical works, but his sermons. (The philosophical works are an eclectic mix of idioms and themes in which Neoplatonic influences play a key part.) It is in the sermons that we find Eckhart's anticipation of Heidegger's theses that it is not true that we use language in speaking of being, but that instead being speaks to us in language, being which is to be named, or rather which is to deliver itself, only through nonargumentative modes of speech, in which the categorizations, conceptualizations, and genres of systematic enquiry are repudiated as barriers to openness to being. So Eckhart himself carries language to the point at which conceptualization is evaded because sense is violated. He takes, for example, the Godhead to be the negation of all multiplicity, including that of the divine Trinity, while also claiming not to deny that doctrine. Obedience to God involves not conformity of the human will to the divine will, but loss of human will altogether—something which for a Thomist would involve not that repose of the will which has achieved its final good, but its destruction, and with it the destruction of the integral self.

John D. Caputo has argued that "Eckhart's sermons do not belong to the realm of 'objectivistic' theology, theology as a *scientia*. . . . They belong instead to the existential order" (*The Mystical Element in Heidegger's Thought,* New York, 1986, p. 125; I am deeply indebted to Caputo's discussion). But this type of defense of Eckhart could only be made good by supplying a type of theory of genres of discourse which rescued what Caputo calls the existential order from requirements of either consistency with, or analogical ordering in respect of, the predications of *scientia;* but to do this would be to deprive utterances in that order of the possibility either of truth or of falsity, so rendering Eckhart, in his preaching at least, no sort of Thomist. So that this type of apologia for Eckhart is perhaps as fatal to Eckhart's own defense of his preaching as was the kind of straightforward construal of his utterances made by his fourteenth-century accusers. For what Eckhart resorted to in his preaching was a mode of speech unconstrained by logic, by the structures of rational theory and practice, and by analogical ordering in his predications, a mode which he took to express a power higher than those exhibited in sense experience and in rationality, "a noble power of the soul, which is so high and noble that it grasps God in His own naked being," as he calls it in one place, "a power of the soul which touches neither time nor flesh" (quoted by Caputo, pp. 110–11). It was in the light afforded by this power that Eckhart denied that creatures have being but are rather "a pure nothing," one of the claims rightly condemned by Pope John XXII in 1329.

What Eckhart did, in fact, was to disintegrate the Thomist idiom of speech about being, in the interests of a mode of discourse which claims allegiance independently of and, if necessary, in defiance of reason. His sermons represent a radical separation of preaching not only from philosophy but also from rational theology insofar as it is informed by philosophy. And this setting free of preaching from *scientia,* so opposed not only to the whole Dominican ideal as Albertus Magnus and Aquinas had understood it but also to the Augustinian tradition, resulted in a new cultural artifact, a new form of social practice, preaching as a self-sufficient form of activity in which the warrant ostensibly appealed to in the preaching, whether some text of Scripture or some mystical experience, plays a part determined by and internal to a practice of preaching which is governed by no external criterion. Whatever theology is involved becomes no more than a rationalization of the preacher's purposes.

The development of the popular preacher of this kind as a cultural figure was as characteristic of the later Middle Ages as was that of the academic nominalist philosopher. J. Huizinga in *The Waning of the Middle Ages* (London, 1924) long ago provided a classic account of the various forms, disciplined and undisciplined, of the *devotio moderna*, of the cults centered around images and relics, and of the enthusiasm which provided the climate for such preachers. The contrast between the irrationalism of this type of preacher and the often hyperrationalism of the academic philosopher should not be allowed to obscure the fact that these figures are cultural counterparts, playing complementary social roles. How is this so?

A philosopher can stand in two very different types of relationship to the larger society of which he is a part. He can be in certain types of social situation an active participant in the forums of public debate, criticizing the established, socially shared standards of rationality on occasion, but even on these occasions appealing to standards shared by or at least accessible to a generally educated public. And this can be the case even when the philosopher assumes the role of radical critic, as Plato did. But when professionalized academic philosophy makes the rational discussion of questions of fundamental import the prerogative of an academic elite with certified technical skills, using a vocabulary and writing in genres which are unavailable to those outside that elite, the excluded are apt to respond by repudiating the rationality of the philosophers. In the forums of popular life rhetorical effectiveness in persuasion and manipulation prevails against rational argument.

The content of the doctrines propounded by those who place effectiveness in persuasion above rationality of argument is from this point of view less important than their function. That function is to prevent any challenge to the effective rhetorical performer which might make him or her, or seem to make him or her, rationally accountable by appeal to some public standard. So the doctrines of such performers characteristically present some not to be questioned, scrutinized, or argued about fetish or talisman as exempting them from rational accountability. Modern evangelical fundamentalist doctrines of Scripture—in just the ways in which they differ from classical Augustinianism, either in its Catholic or in its Reformed versions—provide one example of such fetishism. Late medieval mysticism and pietism with its fetishistic appeals to a particular kind of experience provide another.

Caputo has emphasized Eckhart's own defense of his apparently heterodox utterances as "emphatic" language aimed at making an impression upon his hearers; but it is just this aspect of Eckhart's defense which exhibits effectiveness as a preacher being prized above rationality of discourse. And this divorce between rhetorical effectiveness and rational argumentation is deeply at odds with the thirteenth-century Dominican ideal, especially as articulated by Aquinas, in which the homily was to be the end-product of an education in philosophy and theology. So it was in Aquinas's own sermons; so it was designed to be in the discourse of those educated for the pulpit and the confessional by the *Summa*. It was thus not only on account of its overall structure and the understanding of enquiry implicit in that structure that the *Summa Theologiae* as a whole was so alien to the mainstream of intellectual development. Its educational presuppositions as a manual of instruction were generally shared neither by the academic nor by the popular mind.

Every culture is characterized in part by what it conceals and obscures from view, by what its habits of mind prevent it from acknowledging and appropriating. We err therefore in so largely, sometimes exclusively writing the history of ideas, of science, of art, of culture in general in terms of positive achievement. Culture is present also in failure and it can in crucial respects blind the educated to what needs to be seen. So it was with the failure to understand the work of Aquinas in the late Middle Ages. So perhaps it may be with us.

VIII

Tradition against Encyclopaedia:
Enlightened Morality as
the Superstition of Modernity

It became inescapably clear, when the issues which divide the adherents of the encyclopaedic mode of moral enquiry from those of Nietzschean genealogy and Thomistic tradition were first posed at the beginning of these lectures, that their radical disagreements extended
beyond the questions of how moral enquiry is to be conducted and
what its conclusions are to that of how those disagreements are themselves to be characterized. For it also at once became clear that what
is at issue is in key part whether and, if so, how far the three antagonistic standpoints must or can agree upon the standards and criteria
by which their respective claims should be evaluated. It was a central
presupposition of the major contributors to the Ninth Edition, and
one sometimes made explicit, that on questions of standards, criteria, and method all rational persons can resolve their disagreements.
And it is an equally central contention of the heirs of Nietzschean
genealogy that this is not so.

Yet, it may be asked, why at this point in time continue to treat
the standpoint of the Ninth Edition as a serious contender in the
debate? After all, as I remarked at the outset, nobody now shares
the standpoint of the Ninth Edition, so that it may seem absurd to
give to it the kind of critical attention which suggests that its claims
to our intellectual and moral allegiance still deserve to be taken seriously. But there are three good reasons for denying that this is in
fact absurd.

The first is that those who in the earlier part of this century
abandoned the beliefs, attitudes, and presuppositions characteristic

of the Ninth Edition left a good deal of unfinished business behind them. Just because they were unable to see the dimensions and the significance of what they were doing in the perspective in which we can now view them – they for the most part saw a series of piecemeal intellectual and moral rejections, revisions, and innovations, where we can identify a general rupture with an overall *weltanschauung* – their work of criticism was partial and incomplete.

Secondly, even now the organized institutions of the academic curriculum and the ways in which both enquiry and teaching are conducted in and through those institutions are structured to a significant degree *as if* we still did believe much of what the major contributors to the Ninth Edition believed. So we often still behave as if there is some overall coherence to and some underlying agreement about the academic project of just the kind in which those contributors believed. The ghosts of the Ninth Edition haunt the contemporary academy. They need to be exorcized.

Thirdly, and more particularly, one key encyclopaedic belief still informs general academic practice, even if in a modified and weakened version. I refer to the belief that every rationally defensible standpoint can engage with every other, the belief that, whatever may be thought about incommensurability in theory, in academic practice it can safely be neglected. So in the construction and implementation of the curriculum in so-called advanced societies the universal translatability of texts from any and every culture into the language of teacher and student is taken for granted. And so is the universality of a capacity to make what was framed in the light of the canons of one culture intelligible to those who inhabit some other quite alien culture, provided only that the latter is our own, or one very like it.

There are of course some contemporary philosophers who are prepared to defend this belief on the basis of arguments derived from Donald Davidson's work. These are important arguments which deserve to be taken with great seriousness even, or perhaps most of all, by those such as myself who reject their conclusions (I have explained my reasons for so doing in *Whose Justice? Which Rationality?* Notre Dame, 1988, chapter XIX; and this rejection was of course presupposed by part of my argument in Lecture V). But the dominant beliefs in our contemporary academic culture concerning the translatability of alien languages and the intelligibility of alien cultures are not a result of the influence of Davidson's or any other arguments.

They are rather a residue, an inherited set of presuppositions which are all the more powerful for being so seldom spelled out, a legacy from successive eighteenth- and nineteenth-century Enlightenments and not least from the culture of the Ninth Edition.

Yet of course, although contemporary academic practice preserves this continuity with its predecessors, it is also marked by a crucial difference. For whereas it was a tenet of Enlightenment cultures that every point of view, whatever its source, could be brought into rational debate with every other, this tenet had as its counterpart a belief that such rational debate could always, if adequately conducted, have a conclusive outcome. The point and purpose of rational debate was to establish truths and only those methods were acceptable which led to the conclusive refutation of error and vindication of truth. The contrast with contemporary academic practice could not be sharper. For with rare exceptions the outcomes of rational debate on fundamental issues are systematically inconclusive, as I noted earlier when discussing recent philosophy. The accepted standards of rationality, insofar as they are generally shared, provide contemporary academic practice with only a weakly conceived rationality, one compatible with the coexistence of widely divergent points of view, each unable, at least by those generally accepted standards, to provide conclusive refutations of its rivals.

We can thus contrast the various Enlightenments' strong conceptions of rationality with this contemporary weak conception. The rationale for this weak conception is clear and is clearly bound up with that which made the standpoint of the Ninth Edition and of its predecessor Enlightenments unacceptable to later academic generations. What would be required, on this contemporary view, for a conclusive termination of rational debate would be appeal to a standard or set of standards such that no adequately rational person could fail to acknowledge its authority. But such a standard or standards, since it would have to provide criteria for the rational acceptability or otherwise of any theoretical or conceptual scheme, would itself have to be formulable and defensible independently of any such scheme. But—and it is here that contemporary academic practice breaks radically with its Enlightenment predecessors—there can be no such standard; any standard adequate to discharge such functions will itself be embedded in, supported by, and articulated in terms of some set of theoretical and conceptual structures. Thus since, so far as large-scale theoretical and conceptual structures are concerned, each rival theoretical standpoint provides from within itself and in its own terms the standards by which, so its adherents claim, it should be evaluated, rivalry between such contending standpoints includes rivalry over standards. There is no theoretically neutral, pre-theoretical ground from which the adjudication of competing claims can proceed.

It is all too easy to conclude further that therefore, when one large-scale theoretical and conceptual standpoint is systematically at odds with another, there can be no rational way of settling the differences between them. And Nietzsche's genealogical heirs do so conclude, for this as well as for other reasons. But the Thomist has only to remind him or herself that it would have been quite as plausible in the thirteenth century to have concluded that, since Augustinianism and the Aristotelianism of the Islamic commentators were systematically at odds in just this way, each having internal to itself its own standards of rational evaluation, no rational way could be found to settle the differences between them. And since Aquinas decisively showed this conclusion to be false, those able to learn from him have every reason to resist it in the present instance. How then ought a Thomist to proceed?

The questions and problems which Aquinas posed about Augustinianism to Augustinians and about Aristotelianism to Aristotelians are each initially framed in terms internal to the system of thought and enquiry which was being put in question. Aquinas's strategy, if I have understood it correctly, was to enable Augustinians to understand how, by their own standards, they confronted problems for the adequate treatment of which, so long as they remained within the confines of their own system, they lacked the necessary resources; and in a parallel way to provide the same kind of understanding for Averroistic Aristotelians. So we also need to proceed by raising critical questions for encyclopaedists and genealogists, not in our terms, but in theirs. Just such a problem is posed for the genealogist, so I shall suggest in the ninth lecture, by his or her conception of personal identity. And in the encyclopaedist's idiom no expression invites such questions more obviously and more insistently than 'morality' itself.

Contemporary moral debate is notoriously inconclusive in its outcomes, perhaps in part because of the extent to which it makes use of the concepts of the encyclopaedists but has abstracted those concepts from the framework within which and in terms of which they were understood by the moralists of the eighteenth- and nineteenth-century Enlightenments. What then did *those* moralists mean by 'morality'?

No conviction, so I suggested in the first of these lectures, is more central to the encyclopaedist's mind than that 'morality' names a distinct subject matter, to be studied and understood in its own terms as well as in its relationships to other areas of human experience, such as law and religion. This conviction had already informed the first great modern encyclopaedia, *L'Encyclopédie* of Diderot and D'Alembert, more than a century before it exerted its influence on the Ninth Edition of the *Encyclopaedia Britannica*. And in the earlier, just as in the later enterprise, it guided the overall plan of the encyclopaedia as well as the writing of individual articles. So while there are few and only incidental references to morality in D'Alembert's 'Discours Preliminaire,' the article 'Encyclopédie' by Diderot in volume IV summarized the aim of the editors as to "inspire a taste for science, a horror of falsehood and vice, and a love of virtue; because everything which does not aim ultimately at happiness and virtue is nothing."

These two aims were thought to harmonize. The cultivation of virtue both produces individual happiness—at least generally and in the longer run—and undergirds the social order. In this Louis, chevalier de Jaucourt, author of the articles on 'Morale' and 'Moralité' in volume X agreed with Diderot. De Jaucourt was an internationally famous physician, educated at Geneva and Cambridge before he studied medicine at Leyden with Boerhaave, author of a life of Leibniz prefaced to an edition of the *Theodicy*, as well as of medical treatises. Recruited originally to contribute medical articles to the *Encyclopédie* de Jaucourt represents the shared beliefs of educated adherents of the Enlightenment rather than the theorizing of its outstanding leaders. In the articles 'Moralité' and 'Morale' four theses are particularly noteworthy. A good or just action is one which "conforms to a law imposing an obligation." Morality is thus primarily a matter of rules, and to be a good or just person, to be virtuous in character, is to be disposed to do what the rules require. Secondly, on the content of what morality requires ordinary human beings in all times and places agree, sharing "general ideas of certain duties without which society could not sustain itself." Difficulties and disagreements arise not over these general ideas, but only over their application in particular circumstances.

Thirdly, morality is treated as a distinct phenomenon throughout de Jaucourt's contributions, but its independence is made explicit in his emphasis upon its independence of religious faith. Morality is not only independent of faith, but faith, while at its best in the gospels upholding true morality, adds nothing to morality. Moreover the truths of morality are more certain than those of faith. And, finally, plain persons do not need the moral theorist to tell them what the requirements of morality are, except insofar as religious or political interests have obfuscated and distorted true morality, sometimes with the aid of false moral theory, which has often enough been the case. The implication is that the central function of enlightened moral theory is to combat the influence of bad moral theory.

It is striking how far other thinkers of the eighteenth-century Enlightenment agree with de Jaucourt. Plain persons are also thought to be well aware of what their duties and obligations require of them by Kant in Germany and not only by Reid and Stewart in Scotland but also earlier, on the basis of a very different theory, by Hume. In England, Butler and Price, themselves theoretically at variance, concurred. The plain person, so conceived, apprehends what morality requires in a way that is compatible with those apprehensions being elicited in the course of his or her psychological development. But what is thus apprehended is independent of social circumstance, is a set of premises rather than a conclusion, and does not require, for example, in order to be adequately understood, the type of moral education or moral self-education so crucial to the theories of Plato, Aristotle, and Aquinas. For them, of course, every moral agent no matter how plain a person is at least an incipient theorist, and the practical knowledge of the mature good person has a crucial theoretical component; it is for this reason that both Aristotle and Aquinas agree that we study philosophical ethics, not only for the sake of theoretical goals, but so as ourselves to become good.

By contrast, for the thinkers of the Enlightenment generally the only role left open for theory is the vindication and clarification of the philosophically uninfected plain person's moral judgments, so as to protect them against false theory. For Reid the single most dangerous false theorist was Hume. But many Enlightenment thinkers gave that place to the tradition stemming from Aristotle. So Kant explicitly condemned central Aristotelian doctrines. And for de Jaucourt Scholastic theory was a *mélange* drawn from various sources "without rule or principle."

When such eighteenth-century writers proclaimed the universality of moral agreement upon fundamentals, they were not unaware of some of the crucial differences between the cultures of modern Europe and those of other times and places. Sometimes indeed, as with Diderot, they perceived, or half-ironically claimed to perceive, in cultures untouched by Western civilization morality as it *really* is, uncontaminated by either superstition or philosophy. Sometimes, as with Dugald Stewart, they saw cultural differences in morality as stemming from the application of one and the same set of moral rules to very different circumstances, just as de Jaucourt had done. But for the majority of Enlightenment theorists, at least as regards moral fundamentals, just because morality secures the same agreement to the same rules and conceptions of duty and obligation in all societies, it has no history. It is incapable of development.

For the editors and writers of the Ninth Edition this is the point at which their partial rejection of the eighteenth-century Enlightenment is most systematic. Biology and anthropology had combined to supply them with a developmental framework within which to organize what both history and anthropology had discovered about alien cultures. In the perspective thus afforded the distinctness of morality appeared not as a timeless, but as an emerging, phenomenon. It was through a process in the course of which moral rules were disengaged from a variety of nonrational, superstitious entanglements both with rules concerning pollution and contagion and with rules prescribing ritual observances that moral progress was taken to have occurred, a progress towards just such an apprehension of moral truths as the eighteenth century had envisaged but one exhibited in full clarity only by the civilized rather than the primitive or savage mind.

Moreover, as one would expect with such a progress, development had been uneven and moral agreement, even among the civilized, was not quite as complete, even over fundamentals, as the overoptimistic eighteenth century had supposed. Moral theory has therefore not merely the task of recording and protecting the judgments of plain persons. Looking back on their eighteenth-century predecessors the late nineteenth-century encyclopaedists could observe some significant measure of disagreement among the protectors and interpreters of the morality of plain persons as to what indeed plain persons did believe and assert, even when secured against the dangers of superstition and bad philosophy. And plain persons themselves, protected and unprotected, continued to disagree. To the moral philosopher therefore there falls a constructive task, that of organizing and harmonizing the moral beliefs of plain persons in the manner best calculated to secure rational assent from the largest possible number of such persons, independently of their conflicting views upon other matters.

The moral philosopher's aim then is or ought to be that of articulating a rational consensus out of the pretheoretical beliefs and judgments of plain persons. But not all such beliefs and judgments are equally to be taken into account. It depends in part on where they are to be placed in the developmental scheme. So Henry Sidgwick, whose *Outlines of the History of Ethics* (London, 1886) was developed – for the benefit, in the first instance, of the Church of Scotland's theological students – out of the article on 'Ethics' which he contributed to the Ninth Edition, was to write that "the current civilised morality of the present age" is "a stage in a long process of development" in which "We do not find merely change . . . we see progress" (*Lectures on the Ethics of T. H. Green, H. Spencer and J. Martineau,* London, 1902, pp. 351–52). It is out of the beliefs and judgments only of the civilized that rational consensus is to be constructed.

Sidgwick understood his own findings about morality as the outcome of a long history of enquiry in which, just as in morality itself, progress had been made. Not only had morality become and been perceived as a distinct phenomenon but moral philosophy had similarly made itself independent of external ties when after the Reformation "reflective persons" were "led to seek for an ethical method that – relying solely on the common reason and common moral experience of mankind – might claim universal acceptance from all sects" (*Outlines,* p. 157). Sidgwick's own version of that method he was happy to call "ethical science," aiming to exhibit in its pursuit "the same disinterested curiosity to which we chiefly owe the great discoveries of physics" (*The Methods of Ethics,* Preface to the first edition). The resemblance of Sidgwick's aims to those of Adam Gifford is unmistakable. What, then, according to Sidgwick, did that method disclose?

It disclosed first of all the distinctive moral 'ought,' the 'ought' of duty and obligation, not reducible to, nor paraphrasable in terms of, any nonmoral concept, an "elementary notion" ('The Establishment of Ethical First Principles,' *Mind* IV, no. 13 [1879], p. 107), and so also from the outset the distinctness of morality. The progress of moral philosophy and of morality itself thus coincide. Moreover there can be rational consensus in large areas, those in which the civilized agree as to what constitutes justice, prudence, and benevolence on the basis of principles not to be denied by any rational person, principles which make explicit the requirements of the moral 'ought.' What is not supplied is any reason whatsoever for giving to this distinctive 'ought' a central place in our practical lives. That it ought to be accorded such a place is something which Sidgwick, like the vast majority of his educated contemporaries, took for granted. It was presupposed as a surd fact of their social existence. But the propositions in and through which this surd fact was presented were represented as the theses of any adequately rational and reflective mind, so contrasting those propositions with the practices and beliefs of the allegedly primitive and the allegedly savage, as characterized by Frazer in the article on 'Taboo' in the Ninth Edition. The Seventh and Eighth Editions had dealt with taboo in two sentences; the editors of the Ninth allowed three and a half pages to the first extended treatment of the subject ever to be published. And central to the encyclopaedist's point of view, and more especially to that of the contributors to the Ninth Edition, was the claim that the late nineteenth century's conceptions of duties and obligations are both morally and rationally superior to the conceptions of taboo which inform alien 'primitive' and 'savage' cultures.

Franz Steiner remarked that although Frazer began by defining 'taboo' as 'a system of religious prohibitions' the notion of system at once disappears from view (*Taboo*, London, 1956) and with it any possible understanding of the place of taboo rules in some overall system of precepts, prohibitions, and practices. Indeed the various customs observed by Frazer under the rubric 'taboo' are for the most part abstracted and studied in isolation from the systems of thought and practice in which they were or are embedded. Margaret Mead was later to complain with some justice that anthropologists—and Frazer was largely responsible—had allowed what she called "special Polynesian ways" to distort their interpretations (*Encyclopaedia of the*

Social Sciences, New York, 1937). But even in the Polynesian cases from which Frazer began, he did not place taboo rules sufficiently in social context. So the category of 'taboo' as used by Frazer turns out to have been one which to a significant degree he imposed upon his subject matter. And it is worth enquiring whether the type of irrationality which Frazer perceived in taboo practices may not in fact derive from the way in which he had abstracted the concept of taboo and its applications from the contexts to which in actual social life they were and are inseparably tied.

That William Robertson Smith, successor to Baynes as editor of and contributor of the articles 'Angel,' 'Bible,' and 'Hebrew Language and Literature' to the Ninth Edition, did not so enquire is scarcely surprising. For he used much the same concept of taboo as Frazer did – spelled out in an appendix to his *Religion of the Semites* (Edinburgh, 1894) – in distinguishing between primitive survivals (a concept drawn from Tylor, another contributor to the Ninth Edition) of the taboo mentality, "the lowest form of superstition" in the Hebrew Bible, and those other elements in the Hebrew Bible which were precursors of what he took to be enlightened and civilized theological and moral attitudes. So Robertson Smith understood the imposition of taboos, concerning for example uncleanness and pollution, to be the responses of "the savage" to "sources of mysterious danger," and, he goes on, "when the rules of uncleanness are made to rest on the will of the gods, they appear altogether arbitrary and meaningless."

Two aspects of Robertson Smith's extended discussion of taboo stand out. One is his general insistence not only upon treating the writers of the Hebrew Bible just like any other source of evidence but also upon categorizing and conceptualizing their material in the terms of what he took to be enlightened modernity rather than in their own terms, so that the Bible is judged by the standards of that modernity in a way which effectively prevents it from standing in judgment upon that modernity. The other aspect is his blindness to the wholes of which taboo rules, prescribed rituals, social relationships embodied in those rituals, and the physical and metaphysical dangers to whose threats such rules are a response are all parts. It was in fact because of this blindness that the connection between the divine and the rules about uncleanness appeared arbitrary. For Robertson Smith does not seem to have understood that those rules could not, according to the beliefs of the Hebrew writers, protect against physical and metaphysical danger except insofar as they defined and prescribed the mode of relationship to the One God, nor to have given due weight to the fact that all systematic relationships of human to human or of human to divine are and cannot but be ritualized and routinized by means of contingent materials whose use is always arbitrary relative to the nature of those materials themselves. Thus the allocation of the rules of ritual uncleanness to one category and those pertaining to genuine holiness and moral insight to another reflected Robertson Smith's late nineteenth-century moral attitudes, something projected into and not drawn out of the subject matter of his enquiries.

One further consequence of this, shared by Robertson Smith and his contemporaries, was an inadequate grasp of the relationship of the negative aspect of taboo rules to their positive aspect, of the prohibiting to the enabling. This inadequacy is not uncharacteristic of European and North American representations of alien cultures, particularly those which Robertson Smith would have classified as 'primitive' or 'savage.' Rodney Needham has argued powerfully ('Remarks on the Analysis of Kinship and Marriage' in *Remarks and Inventions*, London, 1974, pp. 61–68) that the assimilation of a large number of what are in fact very different rules into what has then been taken to be '*the* incest taboo,' as though it was a single universal or near universal phenomenon, largely invariant between cultures, also resulted in part at least from too exclusive an attention to negative prescriptions, distortingly detached from their enabling counterparts. And so once again this focus upon taboo rules as negative prohibitions ought to remind us of Franz Steiner's thesis that in that categorizing and conceptualizing of alien cultures as different from each other as those of ancient Israel and of eighteenth- and nineteenth-century Polynesia, in which contributors to the Ninth Edition were engaged, observation and explanation were structured in terms of the moral beliefs of those who observed and explained.

It is illuminating to contrast the attitude of the contributors to the Ninth Edition towards the theories and practices of those whom they characterized as savage and primitive with the very different conception of rational superiority implicit and sometimes explicit in the Aristotelian-Thomistic tradition. Just as a later stage within that tradition is held superior to an earlier stage only if and insofar as it is

able to transcend the limitations and failures of that earlier stage, limitations and failures by the standards of rationality of that earlier stage
itself, so the rational superiority of that tradition to rival traditions
is held to reside in its capacity not only for identifying and characterizing the limitations and failures of that rival tradition as judged by
that rival tradition's own standards, limitations and failures which
that rival tradition itself lacks the resources to explain or understand,
but also for explaining and understanding those limitations and failures in some tolerably precise way. Moreover it must be the case that
the rival tradition lacks the capacity similarly to identify, characterize, and explain limitations and failures of the Aristotelian-Thomistic
tradition.

Two features of this conception of rational superiority are importantly different from that characteristically exhibited by the contributors to the Ninth Edition. First it has application only if and
when the two rival bodies of theory and practice have first of all each
been characterized and categorized in its own terms and the limitations and failures of each identified in the light afforded by its own
standards of rationality. By contrast Robertson Smith, Frazer, and
Tylor, and by implication Sidgwick, assert the rational superiority of
their encyclopaedist's stance, its more advanced place in Sidgwick's
"long progress of development," over the stance of the 'primitive' and
the 'savage' by invoking their own standards and not the standards
of the 'primitive' and the 'savage' and by identifying as its failures
and limitations what are failures and limitations in their terms, not
in its.

Secondly, no claim to rational superiority, on the view which
I am ascribing to the Aristotelian-Thomistic tradition, can be made
good except on the basis of a rationally justifiable rejection of the
strongest claim to be made out from the opposing point of view, that
it is able to afford at least as adequate and perhaps a more adequate
account and explanation of the failures and limitations of one's own
standpoint than that standpoint itself can provide. For one view to
have emerged from its encounter with another with its claim to superiority vindicated it must first have rendered itself maximally vulnerable to the strongest arguments which that other and rival view
can bring to bear against it. This is why Aquinas systematically begins
by setting out on any particular issue the strongest arguments yet
advanced from any rival point of view against his own positions.

By contrast it never even occurred to the contributors to the Ninth Edition to enter imaginatively into the standpoint of those allegedly primitive and savage peoples whom they were studying, let alone to enquire how they and their moral and religious theory and practice might be understood from the point of view of those alien cultures. So their minds were closed to the possibility that, for example, a Polynesian view of Europeans might be rationally superior to a European view of Europeans. In this respect of course the contributors to the Ninth Edition were no different from those explorers, traders, and missionaries who had first encountered the idiom and practice of taboo rules.

Captain James Cook made the first European reference to the word in its various Tongan, Tahitian, and Hawaiian versions in the journal of his third voyage across the Pacific in 1778–79, although he had noticed the practices involving its use on his first voyage. He wrote of the word as being "of mysterious significance" and so indeed it must have been to anyone unable to locate its uses within the overall structures of Polynesian beliefs and observances. We owe our understanding of it to the work of successive students of taboo, especially in Hawaii, culminating in the extraordinary recent works of Marshall Sahlins (*Islands of History*, Chicago, 1985) and Valerio Valeri (*Kingship and Sacrifice*, Chicago, 1985). But as Valeri notes in his initial discussion of Hawaiian sources, even our best information comes from a period in which the system of ritual practices in Hawaii was already modified and weakened (pp. xvii–xviii) and approaching its abolition in 1819. And it may well be, as I have surmised elsewhere, that as the system was weakened and modified, those who inhabited it would have found it more and more difficult to make the notion which we call *taboo* intelligible to themselves (*After Virtue* second edition, Notre Dame, 1984, pp. 111–12), let alone to others. But, whether this was so or not, and it is certainly true that the Hawaiian word for *taboo*, 'kapu,' did undergo gradual but crucial changes in meaning and use until it reached its nadir in its contemporary everyday Hawaiian use as meaning merely 'out of bounds,' much as 'taboo' does or did among upperclass English vulgarians, is not my present concern.

What I want rather to enquire is what a nineteenth-century native Hawaiian observer, educated in the moral and theological beliefs of his or her own culture, who had observed through participation in just those decades in the history of that culture which provided the material upon which contemporary and later European observers – including the contributors to the Ninth Edition – drew in formulating their beliefs about *taboo,* would have made of the moral beliefs of those same Europeans. What light can a traditional Hawaiian standpoint throw upon late nineteenth-century Europe? What happens if we make, so to speak, anthropologists out of our Hawaiians and view from the standpoint of their own earlier civilization the alien *haole* culture of the milieu of the nineteenth-century encyclopaedia? To answer these questions we have to begin by summarizing the social and cultural experience through which such a Hawaiian would have been educated.

The whole within which the taboo rules of the older traditional Hawaiian culture, as reconstructed by Valeri, found their function as parts was a ritual enactment and reenactment through which, at sacred places and times and as a result of sacrifice, especially human sacrifice, the gods were reestablished in their actions, transactions, and relationships to human beings, so that the specifically Hawaiian conception of humanity was represented and re-presented and the hierarchical human order of kingship, kinship, and relationships to land was exhibited in its cyclical complexity. What is *kapu* within this system is marked out as standing in some special relation to what is divine or closely related to the divine. Just because hierarchical superiors are closer to divinity *kapu* marks them out to their inferiors, so that what is dangerous in relating to them is focussed and guarded against by being *kapu.* To make something *kapu* is to bind; to release it from being *kapu* is to untie. Of course all this is much too general: it is in highly specific contexts where often enough death and life are at stake that *kapu* rules have their force. Compliance with the rules and infliction of the penalties for their violation sustains a whole structure. The rules are not to be thought of in Hawaiian terms as serving some independently definable interests of this or that individual or group occupying this or that social role; for it is only in and through the structure sustained by compliance with the rules that what is good for whom, when, where, and how receives its definition. What is to someone's interest – and the concept of 'interest' would itself have to be replaced by the appropriate Hawaiian terms – what will yield the goods possible for someone of their role and status, that is, derives from what the rules are, not vice versa. And what the rules are is defined by the part which they play in the total representation.

In the next stage in Hawaiian society, that of the forty years after the Hawaiians first discovered Europeans, three closely related developments transformed the use and meaning of *kapu* rules. First such rules became gradually separated from their older and original function within the total representation that had been Hawaiian culture. And in being thus detached the use of *kapu* rules and of similar *taboo* prohibitions began to take on the appearance of a distinct phenomenon, available as a discrete object of study. Moreover to the extent that such detachment takes place the concept of *kapu* is less and less to be made intelligible by reference to the larger scheme, for it less and less has its character as part of a whole. So its use becomes less and less explicable except as a surd fact of social existence. '*Kapu*' begins to appear as an elementary notion, not to be reduced to or paraphrased into other terms.

Moreover Sahlins has described how the chiefs "began to use tabus for the regulation of European trade, an extension from ritual to practical purposes" not without precedent in Hawaiian history (p. 142 *Islands of History* and *Historical Metaphors and Mythical Realities,* Ann Arbor, 1981) but in this case radically disruptive in its effects. For the invocation of *kapu* was now used to serve the sectional interests of the aristocracy in acquisition and consumption of new kinds of goods at the expense of the interests of commoners. Where '*kapu*' had formerly been used as a sign of what was tied down by reason of its relationship to some god, it was now invoked in contexts of an emerging economic class. So a type of question about the relationship of *kapu* rules to interests could be posed for which there was no conceptual space within the older Hawaiian scheme of beliefs and practices.

A third subsequent but closely linked development was the appearance of uses of '*kapu*' to claim rights for individuals considered apart from their role and status in the older Hawaiian scheme. "Tabu progressively became," Sahlins has remarked, "the sign of a material and proprietary right" (p. 142). The arrival upon the social scene of conceptions of right, attaching to and exercised by individuals, as a fundamental moral quasilegal concept, whether in the European later Middle Ages or seventeenth century, or in nineteenth-century Polynesia, always signals some measure of loss of or repudiation of some previous social solidarity. Rights are claimed *against* some other person or persons; they are invoked when and insofar as those others appear as threats. Hence in this third respect too the use of '*kapu*' changes and from a traditional Hawaiian point of view degenerates.

So it might have appeared to a socially educated Hawaiian, conscious of his or her own history, that the ease with which the *kapu* rules and interdictions were finally abolished by Kamehameha II in 1819 reflected a widespread, even if largely unarticulated, consciousness of the growing degeneration into irrationality of the *kapu* system. But were such a Hawaiian then to reflect upon the corresponding features of the modern European culture which he or she encountered as it displaced the older Hawaiian modes, it would surely have struck him or her that a precisely similar degeneration seemed to have taken place in that culture but with this astonishing difference, that what he or she could perceive as degeneration was precisely what such Europeans as the contributors to the Ninth Edition accounted moral progress. The detachment of European moral rules from their place within an overall theological moral scheme, embodying and representing a highly specific conception of human nature, corresponds to the similar detachment of taboo rules. The appearance of the concept of *kapu* as an "elementary notion," not to be reduced to or paraphrased into other terms, parallels the identification of the European distinctively moral 'ought' as just such an irreducible, surd notion. And the emergence in European societies of morality as a distinct phenomenon of such a kind that questions of the relationships of duty and obligation to independently defined interests became central questions, and this in a social context in which conceptions of rights take on both new import and new importance, strengthens the case for holding that the moral rules of the culture inhabited and defended by the contributors to the Ninth Edition were no more and no less than the taboo rules of that particular culture. The taboos stigmatized by the contributors to the Ninth Edition as belonging to the primitive and the savage were only seen as alien because of the incapacity for cultural self-recognition and self-knowledge which was such a marked characteristic of the society which they inhabited. The authors of the great canonical encyclopaedias just because they insisted upon seeing and judging everything from their own point of view turned out to have had no way of making themselves visible to themselves.

I have, of course, in pointing to this parallel between late Victorian and Polynesian cultures, been drawing upon and extending Franz Steiner's thesis that the preoccupation of late Victorian thinkers with the problem of taboo stemmed in part from this parallel. But I have gone beyond Steiner in suggesting that what this parallel reveals in both cultures is a moment of degeneration and irrationality. It is this latter claim which I wish to support further by considering Sidgwick's various conclusions about morality and the tensions between them. And it will be important in so doing first to remind ourselves that Sidgwick held that a central aim of the moral philosopher is to establish a rational moral consensus. Disagreement among moral philosophers is to be resolved by a convergence of views which, though it may be hindered by "a danger that every energetic teacher will want to write his own book and make it as unlike other people's books as he can," (*Henry Sidgwick: A Memoir*, London, 1906, p. 547) will underpin a similar convergence of views in morality itself.

What then, according to Sidgwick, are the relevant key features of morality which emerge from that history of progress "from Socrates to myself" (*op. cit.*, p. 334) which Sidgwick had chronicled in the Ninth Edition? The source for an answer is *The Methods of Ethics*, the first edition of which he published in 1876, four years before his *Britannica* article, and which he continued to revise in subsequent editions until the sixth, published in 1901, the year after Sidgwick's death. To a reader with our imaginary Hawaiian's view of European morality in mind, three aspects of morality as conceived by Sidgwick stand out, one of them fully recognized by Sidgwick himself, the other two related to the first but important by reason of their absence from Sidgwick's pages.

Sidgwick had argued that the only ultimate good to be sought rationally by human beings consists in happiness, that is, in the pleasant states of individual persons. Each one of us however confronts the requirements imposed by two final ends, not one: that Universal Happiness by reference to which utilitarianism enjoins us to understand our duties and obligations and that Egoistic Happiness whose imperatives none of us are able wholly to set aside. There is available, on Sidgwick's view, a compelling rational justification for judging and acting in accordance with the requirements of either. But on occasions upon which the two sets of requirements conflict, there is no rational way of deciding between them. On such occasions our practical reason is divided against itself.

It had been one of Kant's key insights that the rigorous formulation and determinateness of moral rules depended upon individuals not being permitted to make exceptions in their own favor or in favor of those whom they peculiarly favor, and, when younger, Sidgwick had agreed with him (*Memoir,* p. 113). One of Kant's central failures – not by the standards of his own system, of course – had been the failure to provide a psychology which could explain how this complete setting aside of one's own particular goals and interests was possible. Sidgwick, breaking with Kant's implausible psychology, although attempting, in accordance with his pursuit of consensus, to accept into his own system as much else of Kant's views as possible, produced the very outcome which Kant had rightly judged to be fatal to morality both theoretically and practically. For if with Sidgwick one holds, and once one has conceded Sidgwick's premises and methods it would be rationally impossible not to hold, that whenever the requirements of Universal Happiness conflict with those of Egoistic Happiness the choice as to what and how much to grant to each has to be understood as an arbitrary preference, then every rule as held by each individual has a prospective indeterminacy of indefinite range, for each rule is vulnerable to whatever range of exceptions each particular individual may make in his or her own favor. And it was no idiosyncracy of Sidgwick's position to have arrived at conclusions with this further consequence. For the pattern of argument whereby appeals to what duty (understood in terms of an impersonal devotion to the general happiness) requires and to what the particular happiness of me and mine requires are both recognized as legitimate, while the weight accorded to each is a matter left to individual preference, was surely the dominant pattern of the entire encyclopaedist culture for which Sidgwick aspired to be a rational spokesman, as it also still remains in our own late twentieth-century culture.

Two other features of Sidgwick's position are relevant to understanding the full implications of his acknowledgment of this division within practical reason. The first is Sidgwick's conviction that the cases in which this division becomes operative, "cases of a recognized conflict between self-interest and duty" (*Methods,* seventh edition, p. 508), are relatively rare. To which it must be retorted that how rare they are depends upon the degree to which respect for duty, understood as Sidgwick understood it, continues to be widely shared and generally inculcated. Sidgwick's evaluation of the relative unimportance of the division within practical reason, understood in his own terms, presupposed a degree and kind of social and moral homogeneity which has rarely, if ever, been the case in later modern societies. And to the degree that Sidgwick overestimated that homogeneity, he underestimated the extent to which indeterminacy would systematically infect the shared moral rules of modern societies. What has in fact emerged is a high degree of indeterminacy so that the standard form of shared, public moral rule now runs as follows, in the case of, for example, the rule concerning truth-telling: "One *ought* [the distinctively moral 'ought'] never to lie [this part of the rule is pronounced especially to children with a good deal of emphasis] except when . . ." and there follows a list of types of exception, characteristically concluding with an "etc." Of the making of exceptions in someone's favor, often one's own, there appears to be no end.

So our imagined Hawaiian commentator would be able to note that the distinctively moral 'ought' had changed its use and correspondingly its meaning, just because of its vulnerability to the effects of self-interested utterance, in a way analogous to that in which '*kapu*' changed. Detachment from earlier contexts in theological and moral systems of belief and practice had in both cases led to conceptual transformation and to a weakening of those moral ties which are partially defined through determinate moral rules. But there is a third feature of Sidgwick's thought, equally important for its evaluation, which can only be accorded its full weight in the retrospect afforded by the intervening hundred years. Sidgwick aspired to achieve, indeed himself to be the voice of, a certain kind of consensus, as did characteristically, if not universally, the other contributors to and editors of the Ninth Edition. Sidgwick recognized—what contributor to an encyclopaedia could fail to acknowledge?—the authority of experts. But that authority derived, so he affirmed from "the unconstrained agreement" ('Authority, Scientific and Theological,' Appendix I, *Memoir,* p. 609) of individuals, and he saw the antagonism between theology and the natural sciences as rooted in what he took to be the fact that while unconstrained consensus is the mark of such sciences, in theology agreement arises only in communities constrained by enforced religious tests. And this belief that consensus without either formal or informal tests is always a mark of rationality was clearly presupposed by the major contributors to the Ninth Edition.

Yet if this is so, Sidgwick's thought, and with it the moral stance underlying the Ninth Edition, becomes problematic in yet another way. For the subsequent history of moral philosophy has been a history of ramifying disagreement in which all of Sidgwick's attempted reconciliations of hitherto warring post-Enlightenment points of view into a synthesis—which was itself intended to foreshadow a coming convergence of an even more complete kind—have been dissolved into new and multifarious conflicts. Universalizability theorists, utilitarians, existentialists, contractarians, those who assert the possibility of deriving morality from rational self-interest and those who deny it, those who uphold the overriding character of an impersonal standpoint and those who insist upon the prerogatives of the self, disagree not only with each other but among themselves, and the certitude of those who maintain each point of view is matched only by their inability to produce rational arguments capable of securing agreement from their adversaries. Thus post-Sidgwickian moral philosophy, judged by the standards of the Ninth Edition and of Sidgwick himself, has turned out to be a dubious type of activity, self-discrediting in just the way that Sidgwick held that the theology of the late nineteenth century was self-discrediting.

So there is further confirmation of what had already emerged from our imagined Hawaiian's critique, that the fundamental contrast between the civilized and the superstitious, between what took and takes itself to be enlightened modernity and the allegedly savage and primitive, a contrast central to the overall encyclopaedic framework and one in terms of which its distinctive concepts of human progress and moral development were defined, cannot be sustained. Judged by its own standards and in its own terms, the project of the major contributors of the Ninth Edition failed; and in the failure of those contributors and their readers to break out of their own self-protective academic rhetoric in a way that would have enabled them to perceive the emerging defects of their enterprise, they failed twice over.

To characterize these failures of the encyclopaedists in any more fundamental way we need to supply a type of characterization which does not suffer from the limitations of the encyclopaedists' own standpoint, so that we can understand more precisely *what* happened and *how* and *why* it happened. To these problems adherents of the Aristotelian-Thomistic tradition on the one hand and post-Nietzschean genealogists on the other would have to advance very different and incompatible types of answer.

The genealogist's critique would focus upon two features of the

encyclopaedist's stance. The first is the pretension involved in the unwitting elevation of the culturally and morally particular to the status
of what is rationally universal. So, for example, the nature of that
cultural artifact of the seventeenth and eighteenth centuries, "the individual," whose social and moral relationships were held to be merely
contingent and incidental to his rational being and who has within
him or herself (although usually *him*self) the resources to criticize
those relationships in the name of utility or of rights, was systematically confused with human nature as such. "Man," wrote Nietzsche,
"does *not* pursue happiness; only the Englishman does that" ('Maxims and Arrows,' No. 12, *Götzendämmerung*). But this type of pretension is, after all, on the genealogist's view, characteristic of the
whole history of morality.

Hence the genealogist's second accusation would emphasize
how the attempt to contrast the morality of enlightened, civilized
modernity with its unenlightened, uncivilized predecessors functions
so as to conceal the continuity of the moral enterprise. The lack of
legitimacy of the morality of the late Victorians is and was no more
and no less than the lack of legitimacy of all those invocations of
good and evil by means of which the *ressentiment* of the repressed and
the repressing, the distorted and the distorting, has expressed itself.
At different periods the will to power takes on different forms, and
there are times at which it is more difficult and times at which it is
easier to understand the surface manifestations of the will to power
as just that, surface manifestations. So it was that Nietzsche himself
in diagnosing the sickness of the contemporary German equivalent
of late Victorian morality identified a peculiarly self-revealing stage
in the genealogical transmission of morality. But it is what that stage
shares with its moral predecessors rather than what divides them
which is important.

In one respect encyclopaedist and genealogist, Sidgwick and
Nietzsche agree. There is on both their views such a thing as *the* history of morality and correspondingly such a thing as *the* history of
ethics, a history with a single subject matter and genuine continuity.
As to the character of that continuity there is radical disagreement,
but that one and the same history begins with Socrates and runs to
the late nineteenth century is not a point of contention. Yet from
the Aristotelian and Thomistic standpoint it is just this that needs
to be put in question. There is indeed from this latter standpoint

a history of moral thought in and through which moral apprehensions are articulated and moral practice provided with its theory, a history initially generated by Socrates. But this history was interrupted in the most radical way, and it was in and through its interruption and disruption that morality as understood by post-Enlightenment modernity was generated. If by 'morality' and by 'ethics' we mean roughly what Sidgwick and the other contributors to the Ninth Edition meant, then 'morality' is, on this Aristotelian and Thomistic view, a distinctively modern phenomenon.

Notice that there is no word correctly translatable by our modern word 'morality' in any ancient or medieval language. And this lack of a word is a symptom of the different ways in which different forms and aspects of social life were classified in the societies in which those languages were spoken and written. Consider such related facts as that there is also no word correctly translatable by our word 'art' (as contrasted with 'craft') in such languages and that religion was characteristically not a separate segregable aspect of life in such societies but was rather the mode in which every aspect of life was related to the divine. So when Sidgwick or later modern historians of ethics (including myself) have extracted from the writings of ancient or medieval authors that which, according to the modern conception, belongs to ethics, we have too often projected back on to the past categories alien to that past with two highly misleading results. The first is that we detach with a certain arbitrariness parts from those wholes from relationship to which they derived important aspects of their character. Ethics, in both Greek practice and Aristotelian thought, was part of politics; the understanding of the moral and intellectual virtues, in both medieval practice and Thomistic thought, was part of theology. To abstract the ethics from its place in either is already to distort.

A second damaging consequence is that the nature of the rupture, of that extended moment in which morality became a distinct and largely autonomous category of thought and practice, is obscured. Notice also, of course, that how we describe this moment will depend upon our point of view. Sidgwick laid great emphasis upon this break as a moment in which ethics was emancipated from obfuscating entanglements. For a genealogist the adherents of the encyclopaedic stance, because they have a false view of emancipation, misunderstand and exaggerate the importance of the break. For a

Thomist the later history of ethics is the essentially quixotic enterprise of attempting to render intelligible a part of human practice and a corresponding part of theory, the genuine intelligibility of which does and can only derive from their relationship to those wholes from which they were in the later Middle Ages and successive centuries distortingly abstracted. There is, it once again becomes clear, no theory-neutral way of writing the history of ethics and no theory-neutral way of characterizing those events which Thomists understand, or ought to understand, as a moment of fundamental moral and historical disruption.

The Thomistic claim, then, is that the central conceptions of distinctively modern morality, the morality of Diderot, D'Alembert, and de Jaucourt, the morality of Robertson Smith and of Sidgwick, are best understood as a set of fragmentary survivals posing problems which cannot fail to be insoluble so long as they are not restored to their places in those wholes from which they took their character as parts. On this view, modern moral philosophy is a form of enquiry whose defeat has been from the outset predetermined by the terms in which the enquiry has been framed. Consider two examples.

Central to much and perhaps in some way to all modern moral philosophy is Sidgwick's problem of how to reconcile the impersonal requirements of moral rules with the attachments and interests of the self. What the rules demand seems to be one thing; what the self wants and aspires to seems to be another, often an incompatible thing. Cooperation with and consideration for others is to be understood alternatively as either a means to the satisfaction of one's own desires or as required by the rules in disregard of one's own desires. The problem is thus to fit together a certain conception of the self and its interests, on the one hand, and a certain conception of moral rules and their mandatoriness, on the other. But the conception of the self underlying this formulation is, from the standpoint of Thomism, of a self already misleadingly and distortingly abstracted— both in philosophical theory and in institutional practice—from its place as a member of a set of hierarchically ordered communities within which goods are so ordered and understood that the self cannot achieve its own good except in and through achieving the good of others and vice versa.

Within such communities the moral rules are or were apprehended as the laws constitutive of community as such, constitutive and enabling in their function rather than the negative taboos which they later became when divorced from that function. So from the standpoint of such communities we do not have to find it problematic that the self should have the kind of regard for others enjoined by the natural law; the self for which such regard is problematic could only be a self which had become isolated from and deprived of any community within which it could systematically enquire what its good was and achieve that good. What for the kind of ancient and medieval moral enquiry and practice which Thomism embodied was the exceptional condition of the deprived and isolated individual became for modernity the condition of the human being as such.

A second, closely related example concerns the genesis of the distinctively moral 'ought.' The variety of words translatable as 'ought' in ancient and medieval languages never have a sense which allows them a mandatory force independently of the reasons given for uttering the statements which are expressed by means of them. And such reasons always refer us to some good of some specific type. An 'ought' may indeed then have categorical force, but only in virtue of its place in a statement of the form "If and since to do so and so is best for such-and-such a specific type of person in these particular circumstances and you are just such a person, then you ought to do so and so." Shared moral precepts or rules using this type of 'ought' depend therefore for their authority upon there being a set of shared beliefs as to what is good and best for different types of human beings, just that kind of shared belief which is the mark of those communities of moral enquiry and practice within which alone, on the Thomistic view, human goods can be adequately identified and pursued.

Destroy or marginalize such forms of community and replace them with the social order of modern individualism; replace earlier shared forms of belief with the pluralism of indefinite and growing disagreement as to what the goods of human beings are and how or whether they are to be hierarchically ordered but retain as a shared possession most, if not all, of the inherited moral precepts and rules. Such rules will be consequents, deprived of their "if and since" antecedents. In their new independence of circumstance they will assume the impersonal and unconditional form "One ought to do such-and-such." A new and distinctive 'ought' will have appeared, one not reducible to or paraphrasable into other terms. The distinctively moral 'ought,' Sidgwick's elementary notion, will have been generated — something which seems first to happen in the fourteenth century — and the problem of how moral rules are to be related to the interests of the individual self will have been provided with the idiom needed for its statement.

The Thomist therefore agrees with our imagined Hawaiian in seeing the moral rules of European modernity as what Tylor called, and taught Robertson Smith to call, "survivals," unintelligible residues from a lost past. But the Thomist, unlike the Hawaiian, also discerns in the continuous reappropriation of the rules, and in the recurring resistance to discarding them, evidence of the work of *synderesis*, of that fundamental initial grasp of the primary precepts of the natural law, to which cultural degeneration can partially or temporarily blind us but which can never be obliterated. So the Thomist claims to be able to render intelligible the history of both modern morality and modern moral philosophy in a way which is not available to those who themselves inhabit the conceptual frameworks peculiar to modernity. They cannot hope to understand themselves in the only terms which they and their institutions allow themselves for understanding. And their own theories, the theories of those imprisoned within modernity, can thus provide only ideological rationalizations, the rationalizations of modern deontology, modern consequentialism, and modern contractarianism.

The Thomist is therefore committed to the writing of a type of history as yet never more than sketched in outline. Embodied in that history would be the claim that, as a result of that disruption through which morality became distinct and largely autonomous, morality was rendered vulnerable to the genealogical critique. But, nonetheless, what that genealogical critique successfully impugns belongs to the same distinctively modern modes of thought and practice as does genealogy itself. And the Thomist is thereby committed to resisting the view that the same type of genealogical critique can be applied to the thought and practice of Socrates, Plato, Aristotle, Augustine, and Aquinas as that which Nietzsche and his heirs have successfully deployed against Kant and the utilitarians.

Both genealogist and Thomist therefore seek to subvert and to displace the encyclopaedist's narrative of progress by some very different type of history. But genealogist and Thomist are of course deeply at odds over what type of narrative it is through which the encyclo-paedist's errors are to be disclosed. What, then, is at stake in this con-flict between those who have learned from Nietzsche and those who have learned from Aquinas?

IX

Tradition against Genealogy:
Who Speaks to Whom?

Who in the debates between the heirs of encyclopaedia, the adherents of post-Nietzschean genealogy, and those who give their allegiance to the traditions unified by Aquinas speaks to whom? And how? Texts are always moments in conversations and are to be interpreted from the standpoint of the participants in those conversations, each of whom is apt to bring to his or her participation a different history and with it a different point of entry into that conversation and sometimes, as in the present case, a different understanding of what is involved in having such a conversation. And from those facts stem both conflict and misunderstanding.

Conversations are extended in time. At later points someone may always refer back to some earlier point with a variety of purposes: to evaluate what has only emerged cumulatively, to examine the consistency or inconsistency of what has been said, to put an old point in a new light or vice versa. Crucial to polemical conversations therefore is how the different and disagreeing participants understand the identity and continuity of those with whom they speak, of how each stands in relation to his or her past and future utterances in what he or she says or writes now. Underlying the conflicts of polemical conversations are the rival participants' presuppositions about continuing personal identity through time.

For anyone whose point of view is defined in terms of some synthesis of the Aristotelian and Augustinian traditions the concept of personal identity must have three central dimensions. Because, as Aquinas put it, I *am* and do not merely have a body, albeit a soul-informed body, part of being one and the same person throughout this bodily life is having one and the same body. Secondly, I as a member of more than one community engage in transactions extended through time with others, and because I within my community undertake projects extended through time, it must be possible throughout this bodily life to impute continuing accountability for agency. So my identity as one and the same person requires me on occasion to make intelligible to myself and to others within my communities what it was that I was doing in behaving as I did on some particular occasion and to be prepared at any future time to reevaluate my actions in the light of the judgments proposed by others. So part of being one and the same person throughout this bodily life is being continuously liable to account for my actions, attitudes, and beliefs to others within my communities.

Thirdly, because my life is to be understood as a teleologically ordered unity, a whole the nature of which and the good of which I have to learn how to discover, my life has the continuity and unity of a quest, a quest whose object is to discover that truth about my life as a whole which is an indispensable part of the good of that life. So on this view my life has the unity of a story with a beginning, a middle, and an end, beginning with birth and ending, so far as concerns the final judgment to be passed on it – in respect of the achievement of my good – with death. And this third aspect of the unity and continuity of a human life is inseparable from the other two, as they are from each other and from it. Bodies only have the significance that they have as the bodies of accountable agents, able to understand their own lives as wholes. Accountability for particular actions and projects cannot be entirely independent of accountability for one's life as a whole, since the adequate characterization of some actions and projects, and these not the least important, depends in part upon how the whole life is to be understood and characterized. And every particular life as a whole exists in its particular parts, in that range of particular actions, transactions, and projects which *are* the enacted narrative of that life, and as the life of that one particular body.

About this complex and metaphysical account of the identity and continuity of human beings four points need to be made. First, although this is a Thomistic account, or rather perhaps an account in terms of that which Dante and Aquinas share, even if I have intentionally framed it in terms which use as little of a specifically Thomistic idiom as possible, it is not an account invented primarily by philosophical theorists. For this is how the identity and continuity of human lives are or were understood in a great many, perhaps in all traditional societies, societies as various as those of the many American Indian peoples or of the ancient and medieval peoples speaking the Celtic languages or of the many African tribes. And it is found later on in urban political societies with a shared religion which sometimes grow out of and replace their older traditional predecessors, societies such as those of the Greek *polis,* of the Islamic caliphates, and of the Mayan empire. This conception of personal identity and continuity was then embodied in practice long before it was articulated as theory.

Secondly, although it ascribes a unity to each human life and often, perhaps characteristically, understands that unity as the unity of a single *psyche,* its ascriptions depend upon the contingent coincidence of a variety of features of human beings: the uninterrupted existence of human bodies from conception to death, the relative, although far from complete continuity and reliability of memory, the relative stability of certain character traits, the stability and endurance of recognition abilities, and the fact of a variety of communally shared understandings and beliefs. We can easily imagine universes different from our own in which one or more of these features has been abolished or has never existed and in which, to the extent that this is so, this account of personal identity and continuity ceases to have application. Some recent philosophers have thought that by asking what judgments about identity we would make in such an imagined world, we shall throw light upon the standards of judgment explicit in or presupposed by those that we do make in this actual universe. And their own autobiographical reports about what they would say if, for example, we inhabited a world in which sometimes one person might wake up with what we now think of as another person's memories, are strong evidence that such persons do indeed have beliefs about personal identity which commit them to the truth of certain bizarre counterfactuals. So when W. V. Quine warned that "To seek what is 'logically required' for sameness of person under unprecedented circumstances is to suggest that words have some logical force beyond what our past needs have invested them with" (*Journal of Philosophy,* 1972), Derek Parfit was able to respond that "these cases arouse in most of us strong beliefs. And these are beliefs, not about our words but about ourselves" (*Reasons and Persons,* Oxford, 1984, p. 200). To this it can only be retorted in turn that the appeal to "most of us" depends for its strength upon who "we" are. The ability to have philosophical beliefs which extend to the universes of science-fiction is, I strongly suspect, the ability only of the inhabitants of one particular type of culture or subculture. And for those of us with a sufficiently different cultural formation, as for example those educated in or into communities presupposing the complex metaphysical view which I have described, the only true answer to the question: "What would you say about personal identity if the contingent facts underlying the application of your concept were to be bizarrely otherwise?" is in the first place "I do not know; I should be baffled," and perhaps, if the imagined alteration were sufficiently strange: "You have imagined a universe which excludes the application of the concept of personal identity as *we* understand it."

Thirdly, it is important to notice that this complex metaphysical conception is not proposed as a solution to what philosophers have thought of as 'the problem of personal identity,' a problem to which rival answers have been given from Locke and Butler to Flew and Parfit. That problem is only generated, and perhaps it can only be generated, in the aftermath of some tradition, when the shared beliefs which formerly underpinned the complex metaphysical conception of personal identity and continuity, such beliefs as that in life-long accountability and in the teleological ordering of each life, are no longer widely held, but there still remains as part of the common stock of shared concepts some residual conception of a personal identity which is more and other than that of either bodily continuity or psychological continuity, such as that of memory. The concept of *same person,* detached as it has been from the context of belief in which it was at home, then poses a problem with rival solutions: those impressed by the failure of attempts to reduce personal identity to physical or psychological continuity may insist that there must be what Parfit has called some Further Fact (p. 210); those who recognize that there is no such Further Fact may, like Parfit, conclude that "Personal identity is not what matters" (p. 217), that what matters is a certain kind of psychological connectedness between more or less related stages, episodes, and events in a person's life. From the traditional point of view this dissolution of a whole into its parts is precisely what should be expected in a society in which the background beliefs which made it possible to identify and understand that whole are no longer shared.

What then must those beliefs which underpin any socially shared conception of the complex metaphysical unity of the self include? What else must be shared by way of belief if such beliefs as those in life-long accountability and in each life as a unitary life-long enquiry are to be the beliefs of an enduring community? In making the nature of my own life and the good of that life the objects of my enquiry, I clearly presuppose that there is a truth to be discovered about that life and its good, which may, of course, evade discovery; so I must ask: through what form of social engagement and learning can the errors which may obstruct such discovery be brought to light? The first and basic answers to these questions are those proposed by Socrates. It is only insofar as someone satisfies the conditions for rendering him or herself vulnerable to dialectical refutation that that person can come to know whether and what he or she knows. It is only by belonging to a community systematically engaged in a dialectical enterprise in which the standards are sovereign over the contending parties that one can begin to learn the truth, by first learning the truth about one's own error, not error from this or that point of view but error as such, the shadow cast by truth as such: contradiction in respect of utterance about the virtues.

Full accountability for one's whole life takes many later institutionalized forms: with Plato in the Academy in the disciplines of enquiry towards the light afforded by the Form of the Good, with Augustine in reordering his presentation of himself as bishop to and within the Church in the disciplines of the *Confessions* and the *Retractationes,* with Aquinas in living out within the Dominican order as well as in thinking through the dialectical enterprise of the *Summa.* What they all have in common is at least fourfold: a conception of a truth beyond and ordering all particular truths; a conception of a range of senses in the light of which utterances to be judged true or false and so placed within that ordering are to be construed; a conception of a range of genres of utterance, dramatic, lyrical, historical, and the like, by reference to which utterances may be classified so that we may then proceed to identify their true sense; and a contrast between those uses of genres in which in one way or another truth is at stake and those governed instead only by standards of rhetorical effectiveness. It is only within a community in which to some large degree shared beliefs embodying this fourfold scheme are presupposed in everyday practice—whether or not they are made explicit at the level of theory—that the concept of systematic accountability for one's utterances and one's actions can also inform the shared life of a community. Consider some further aspects of such a scheme of shared belief.

To be accountable in and for enquiry is to be open to having to give an account of what one has either said or done, and then to having to amplify, explain, defend, and, if necessary, either modify or abandon that account, and in this latter case to begin the work of supplying a new one. Socrates, Plato, and Aristotle invented and perfected a dialectical mode of accountability, the Bible and Augustine a confessional mode. Anselm moved from confession to dialectic, Aquinas both from confession to dialectic and from dialectic to confession. Within this tradition philosophical interrogations and accusations of heresy are both summonses to accountability; both refuse to separate the person from the thesis or argument or doctrine uttered by the person. No thesis or argument or doctrine is better than the best grounds proposed for it by those who adhere to it; every thesis, argument, and doctrine is somebody's thesis, argument, or doctrine, playing its part in public belief or debate as the expression of the commitment of one or more persons. Yet, when accountability in enquiry is understood and practiced aright, how the person fares is a matter of how the thesis, argument, or doctrine fares and not vice versa. We flourish or fail to flourish, live or die, as our theses, arguments, and doctrines live or die. And in asserting them we assert that it is they which are *true* or *sound* and so attempt to establish and succeed or fail in establishing the adequacy of our minds as judged by a measure which we did not make. Truth as the measure of our warrants cannot be collapsed into warranted assertibility.

In a community which shares this conception of accountability in enquiry, education is first of all an initiation into the practices within which dialectical and confessional interrogation and self-interrogation are institutionalized. And that initiation has to take the form of a reappropriation by each individual of the history of the formation and transformations of belief through those practices, so that the history of thought and practice is reenacted and the novice learns from that reenactment not only what the best theses, arguments, and doctrines to emerge so far have been, but also how to rescrutinize them so that they become genuinely his or hers and how to extend them further in ways which will expose him or her further to those interrogations through which accountability is realized. There is then an acknowledgment of truth as a measure independent of the tradition which aspires to measure itself by truth, but there is nonetheless no thesis, argument, or doctrine to be so measured which is not presented as the thesis of this particular historically successive set of tradition-informed and tradition-directed individuals and groups in whose lives the dialectical and confessional interrogation have gone on. It is no trivial matter that all claims to knowledge are the claims of some particular person, developed out of the claims of other particular persons. Knowledge is possessed only in and through participation in a history of dialectical encounters.

Such encounters require, as I noticed earlier, shared understandings of meanings and shared discriminations of genres. Why so? And what is involved in these? If I affirm a thesis, argument, or doctrine and am challenged by interrogation, whether Socratic or Augustinian, I may always respond by distinguishing between different senses in which what I have affirmed may be construed, affirming in one sense and denying in another. Thirteenth-century formalized disputations proceeded through just such a systematic process of distinction making. But the making of such distinctions in such a forum presupposes shared standards for discriminating senses, for recognizing new senses, and for judging whether disambiguation has in fact been achieved.

Moreover such discriminations of senses can only be carried out when it has already been established to what genre a particular utterance or set of utterances is to be allocated. So that a necessary condition for the possession of shared standards for discriminating senses is the possession of shared standards for identifying and understanding genres. When a quotation from a poet is responded to by a dialectical argument or when such an argument is in turn responded to by an anecdote and the whole is then reinterpreted in the form of a dramatic narrative, within which a variety of other types of drama are identified, culminating in the telling of a myth—I am of course referring to the structure of the *Republic*—grasping the senses of the author's assertions is inseparable from an understanding of the genres of epic, of drama, of myth, and of dialectical enquiry. And since the use of genres is never static, there have to be shared ways of understanding generic innovation, the kind of innovation involved in moving from the distinct genres of tragedy and farce, for example, to the writing of a work which is both farcical and tragic.

Hence from this tradition-informed Thomistic point of view

every claim has to be understood in its context as the work of someone who has made him or herself accountable by his or her utterance in some community whose history has produced a highly determinate shared set of capacities for understanding, evaluating, and responding to that utterance. Knowing not just what was said, but by whom and to whom in the course of what history of developing argument, institutionalized within what community, is a precondition of adequate response from within this kind of tradition, something itself characteristically presupposed rather than stated.

Consider how different in this respect is the encyclopaedist. For the encyclopaedia both truth and rationality are independent of our apprehensions of or strivings towards them. That such-and-such a person discovered this truth or argued in favor of this thesis is entirely accidental; truth and rationality are both independent of the particularities of the personal. What was uttered is crucial; who uttered it is always a side issue. So the encyclopaedia's own style is that of a studied impersonality. In the Ninth Edition initials, not names, appear at the end of articles, and only with the publication, some time after the substantive volumes, of the Index Volume were contributors named. Of course, among the findings reported in the encyclopaedia is the truth about the history whereby encyclopaedias came to be, that history of development and progress in which figures out of the past are measured by how well or how badly they did in making the present what it is. So the emperor Frederick II, for example, condemned by Dante to hell and praised by Nietzsche as "a great free spirit," as someone unconstrained by the bondage of morality, appeared in the Ninth Edition as one who "wrought to . . . wise purpose in behalf of human progress and enlightenment" (vol. 9, pp. 733). That is, he too helped to make the Ninth Edition possible.

The genealogical deconstruction of the Ninth Edition was in fact already in progress at the time of its first publication, although neither editors nor contributors could have known this. For during the eight years which preceded his death in 1880, Flaubert had been at work on *Bouvard et Pécuchet,* which he described as "a kind of encyclopaedia made into a farce." François Denys Bartholomée Bouvard and Juste Romain Cyrille Pécuchet have never been accorded their deserved place in the history of higher education. They have, after all, a good claim to be the inventors of the core curriculum and the

Great Books program, the remoter ancestors of Robert Hutchins's innovations at Chicago, of the 1945 Harvard report on *General Education in a Free Society,* and of William J. Bennett's *To Reclaim a Legacy,* even although Bouvard and Pécuchet had no one to educate but themselves. Flaubert confronted the encyclopaedia with his own version of Plato's problem in the *Meno:* What must the reader of both great and not so great books already know if he or she is to be able to learn what such books have to teach? Neither Bouvard nor Pécuchet had an inkling of the need to ask this question, and had they been able to formulate it, they would immediately have searched for the book from which they could learn the answer. So Flaubert mocks the encyclopaedia's presentation of itself as an impersonal authority which requires from its readers no more than they bring to a deferential reading and which does not and cannot put to its readers the question of their own incapacity to learn from such a reading, precisely because its assumption is that learning can take place outside a process in which each participant is able to question the other so as to make both him or herself and that other vulnerable and accountable to dialectical and/or confessional interrogation. Abstract the book or the lecture from that process and what you are left with is the impersonal mode of the encyclopaedia.

The impersonality of the nineteenth-century encyclopaedia marked a new stage in the development of a trend which Foucault saw as originating "in the seventeenth or eighteenth century. Scientific discourses began to be received for themselves, in the anonymity of an established or always redemonstrable truth; their membership in a systematic ensemble and not the reference to the individual who produced them stood as their guarantee. The author function faded away . . ." (*Qu'est-ce qu'un auteur,* Paris, 1969, trans. J. V. Harari in *Textual Strategies,* Ithaca, 1974). And Foucault went on to draw a contrast with "literary discourses," which in the same period "came to be accepted only when endowed with the author function." But the way in which the impersonality of the encyclopaedia is put in question, from Foucault's genealogical standpoint, also brings out the depth of the antagonism between that standpoint and the Aristotelian, Augustinian, and Thomistic tradition. There is indeed a certain coincidence in their diagnosis of the lack of substance behind the encyclopaedist's pretensions. But the different grounds from which they make that diagnosis involve each in a rejection of the other, as we have already seen.

Where the Thomist raises the question of the relationship of those who affirm and deny to the truth by which they are measured and by reference to which they are to be held accountable, the genealogist follows Nietzsche in dismissing any notion of *the* truth and correspondingly any conception of *what is* as such and timelessly as contrasted with what seems to be the case from a variety of different perspectives. So one aspect of accountability, that which relates it to the truth, disappears from view. Where the Thomist understands texts in terms of a relatively fixed, even if analogically related and historically developing, set of meanings and genres, the post-Nietzschean genealogist envisages an indefinite multiplicity of interpretative possibilities, so that the speaker or writer is no more tied down by the given determinateness of his or her utterances than by what the genealogist takes to be a fictitious relationship to the truth. Thus a second aspect of accountability is taken to have been discredited. And where the Thomist conceives of appeal to the standards implicit in and partially definitive of dialectical and confessional activity as providing a possibility of rescuing ourselves from those relationships of power through which the rebellious will either masters other wills or is mastered by them, the genealogist understands both Socratic dialectic and Augustinian confession as themselves distorting and repressive expressions—not of the will, for the will is, on Nietzsche's view, just one more metaphysical fiction—but rather of that impersonal will to power whose symptoms are those of a disguised *ressentiment*. So that what looks like someone's rendering him or herself accountable is in fact something very different, an unrecognized exercise of power in the abasement of the self or of others. It is not to Aquinas or to Agnes or to Dominic that we should look for exemplars, but to Frederick II.

Yet in so dismissing the Thomistic mode of understanding and acting, the genealogist poses a problem for him or herself. For in repudiating all the key features of accountability, understood in terms either of Socratic dialectic or of Augustinian confession, the genealogist has perhaps made it impossible to satisfy the preconditions for at least those ascriptions of identity and continuity which involve accountability. Yet the genealogist almost invariably and perhaps inescapably uses language in such a way as to presuppose ascriptions of both identity and continuity to persons. What then is the genealogist to mean by them? We might indeed be tempted to say that the genealogist owes an account of what from his or her standpoint is to be meant by identity and continuity both to us and to him or herself, if he or she is to make him or herself intelligible not only to us but to him or herself, and that in addition the genealogist owes such an account to him or herself in order to ensure that, in ascribing personal identity and continuity, he or she is not covertly presupposing the very kind of metaphysical thesis which it is the central aim of genealogy to discredit. The genealogist, it might seem, owes it to him or herself to be as suspicious of his or her own ascriptions of selfhood as of everyone else's.

This temptation however must be resisted, since the idiom of 'owing' is itself an expression of just that belief in accountability which, so we might be tempted to say, the genealogist must be committed to repudiating. Yet the idiom of commitment also seems to be an expression of the same rejected belief. So that we may at this point stammer in our puzzlement as to how to invite the genealogist to respond. That we are at something of a loss to know what to say is perhaps at least a temporary victory for the genealogist—perhaps of course the genealogist can on his or her own terms have no victory which is not temporary—a victory, since one central and acknowledged problem for the genealogist is that of how to deny what the theologian and the metaphysician assert without falling back into the very mode of utterance which the genealogist aspires to discredit. This is a problem whose inescapability was recognized in the second lecture. And the part of the genealogical solution there briefly expounded was, we shall recall, that the genealogist in confrontation with the theologian or the metaphysician, that is, with those unable to move beyond good and evil, adopts a temporary and provisional stance and wears, for the purpose of this encounter, a mask that can be discarded. So the relation of the genealogist to any theses, arguments, or doctrine which he or she may propose is quite other than that of the theologian or metaphysician.

It would be a mistake to explore and to evaluate this use of the metaphor of the mask without first considering two other respects in which personal identity and continuity are problematic topics for the post-Nietzschean genealogist, one of them most easily formulated in terms of Foucault's work and the other in relation to that of both Deleuze and Foucault. The analysis of discourses and of judgments in *L'Archéologie du Savoir* makes the subject who utters judgments a function of the nature of the discourse rather than vice versa.

The intentions of the person who judges in making some particular judgment are not even in part an independent source of the constitution of the discourse in which the subject participates. So what from an older point of view could have been understood as the creative extension of meaning in saying through the linguistically embodied intentions of those who speak and write, a type of extension involved in the ability of everyday speakers of a language to innovate and to comprehend innovation as well as in the exemplary innovative uses of the poet, must now be characterized as one type of change occurring in a discourse, according to the underlying laws governing the relationship of the elements in that particular type of discourse. Of course from within a particular type of discourse the authorial function of that specific type of discourse will determine how such changes are in fact characterized and to whom in what guise they may be ascribed. And just this was the point of Foucault's contrast between the growing impersonality of scientific discourse and the personalization of literary discourse in the seventeenth and eighteenth centuries. But one question is left unanswered: that of the relationship of the individual who contingently happens to discharge the authorial function in this or that particular case and of the relationship of that individual's intentions to the function and to the discourse. Paul de Man, who in this at least is at one with Foucault, said that "The way in which I can try to mean is dependent on the linguistic properties that are not only not made by me, because I depend on the language as it exists for the devices which I will be using, it is as such not made by us as historical beings. . . ." That language is in crucial and very large part not made intentionally by human beings is not controversial; but de Man's unqualified assertion renders entirely problematic the relationship of the intentional to the nonintentional in linguistic use and more generally the relationship of the person who judges and acts to the preexisting linguistic and social conventions in and through which he or she judges and acts. Notice that the difficulty confronting the genealogist lies not so much in the problem as in the apparent poverty of the conceptual resources of genealogy to formulate, let alone to deal with it.

   This lack of conceptual resources is connected to a second problematic feature of genealogical thought. In a discussion of two books by Gilles Deleuze (*Différence et répetition,* Paris, 1969, and *Logique du sens,* Paris, 1969), significantly entitled 'Theatrum Philosophicum'

(*Critique* no. 282, 1970), Foucault praises Deleuze's conception of the self as multiple and fissured and more generally his rejection of all categorial thinking, a rejection designed to lay bare the multiplicity of differences unorganizable in terms of categories, species, and identity. Deleuze, we may note, in the course of writing an alternative history of philosophy depicts himself as the heir of Duns Scotus and of all those others, including Spinoza, who have understood 'being' as univocal, but as more radical than they in that he has understood that being is and can be nothing more than "the recurrence of difference." So his alternative history inescapably becomes an anti-Thomistic history in which what attracts Deleuze in Bergson's thought is precisely that which led Maritain to reject Bergson.

It is perhaps something of a surprise to find in Foucault's exposition of Deleuze that he moves immediately from discussing the relationship of Deleuze to Duns Scotus and Spinoza to considering the light thrown upon Deleuze's work by Bouvard and Pécuchet, about whom Foucault remarks that their errors are not ordinary mistakes. When they go astray it is because they—in this illuminating Deleuze's project—bring to the world nothing of ordinary categorization or conceptualization. "Bouvard and Pécuchet are acategorial beings," says Foucault. Nonetheless what he calls their "black stupidity" is revelatory. They point us towards larger, more radical possibilities of acategorial thinking, that thought which is "intensive irregularity—disintegration of the subject."

From Foucault's analysis of discourse we had already inferred the difficulty for Foucault of giving any account of the identity, unity, and continuity of the self. But if we thought that in so doing we were confronting Foucault with what he himself might have recognized as a problem, we were, it now turns out, very much mistaken. For, as the phrase 'disintegration of the subject' suggests, the self which can think *différence* cannot be unitary: "we must imagine not the synthesizing-synthesized subject, but an uncrossable fissure . . . the splitting of the self." So we might conclude that there is *no* way of posing questions about accountability or, correspondingly, about the identity, unity, and continuity of the self within a genealogical framework. It is not that there are no shared points of reference, no common ground, with the classical positions of the metaphysician or the theologian. Foucault's use of Flaubert, as well as Deleuze's approach through the critique of Duns Scotus and Spinoza, makes it plain that that is false. But what *is* lacking is any adequately shared way of characterizing such common ground as there is. And this is not so much a conclusion as it is part of the genealogist's starting point. For the project is one of displacing at the outset and even before the outset that scheme which provided metaphysical and theological thought with its measure; hence no common measure with that thought can be acknowledged. Yet if incommensurability with classical thought is thus a prerequisite for the genealogical enterprise, how can there be conversation with it on a topic such as that of personal identity?

This question can be responded to only by moving towards another question. Characteristically, in writing the disclosing and subverting narrative intended to undermine the metaphysics of being and of good and evil, the genealogist not only explores the unacknowledged oppositions and tensions within the texts which he or she aspires to discredit but continually explains to him or herself and to others what he or she is doing by drawing a set of contrasts between how disastrously Socrates or Plato or Augustine or whoever thinks and how insightfully by contrast the genealogist thinks. Behind the genealogical narrative there is always a shadow self-congratulatory narrative. This shadow narrative is characteristically of some familiar but unacknowledged genre. Sometimes it is recognizable as the story of a wandering knight who reads the riddle or discovers the hidden name, so rescuing the imprisoned captive; sometimes it is the story of a magic ring which has to be safely transmitted in order to avert some monstrous fate; sometimes it is the story of a journey into a labyrinth guided by a thread. These are all stories of avowed achievement, achievements not of the masks but of their wearer. All such genealogical utterance contains a strain of what is not quite boastfulness because it rests upon a rejection of any table of the virtues in which humility is accounted a virtue. But the achievement of the narrator behind the masks in the continuity of this rejection requires a stable and continuing referent for the 'I'—the 'I,' for example, of the section headings of Nietzsche's *Ecce Homo:* "Why I am so wise. Why I am so intelligent. Why I write such good books. Why I am a destiny." Heidegger was to claim that Nietzsche's own biography has nothing to do with these utterances, but it was after all Nietzsche himself who insisted upon not detaching his assertions from his biography by writing that "assuming that one is a person, one necessarily also has the philosophy which belongs to that person" (*Die Fröhliche Wissenschaft,* Preface to the second edition, 2).

So, confronted by the incommensurability of the genealogist's theses about the self with metaphysical and theological claims about accountability, we can enquire whether in telling the tale of how he or she came to advance those claims, the genealogist does not have to fall back into a mode of speech in which the use of personal pronouns presupposes just that metaphysical conception of accountability which genealogy disowns. Or to put this question another way: can the genealogist legitimately include the self out of which he speaks in explaining himself within his or her genealogical narrative? Is the genealogist not self-indulgently engaged in exempting his or her utterances from the treatment to which everyone else's is subjected?

Having posed these questions, it is important to remark that it is incumbent upon the genealogist *not* to provide someone like myself with acceptable answers to them. For to do so, he or she would have to engage in a kind of discourse from whose presuppositions he or she claims to have decisively separated him or herself. It is indeed just insofar as the genealogist succeeds in explaining and justifying genealogy to those of us whom he had previously designated as its victims that he or she rejoins those victims. The genealogist *qua* genealogist has to remain unacceptable. Consider in this light the strange behavior of the apologists for Paul de Man.

Paul de Man's writings are certainly not to be assimilated too easily to those of Foucault or Deleuze. But he shares with them an explicit affiliation to Nietzsche and he wrote against what Foucault and Deleuze have also opposed. Behind all three lies what Nietzsche had to say about memory, a topic which furnishes a crucial part of the genealogical case against accountability. In *Morgenröthe* Nietzsche attempted to recast his readers' view of what is and what is not in their or our power, so that he might undermine morality by, as he says in the preface, undoing Kant's work. In the case of memory, although particular acts of recollection are not to be treated as under our immediate control (II, 126), nonetheless the powers of memory can be developed in different ways and "He who ranks high would do well to provide himself with a courteous memory: that is to say, to notice everything good about other people and after that to draw a line . . . A man may deal with himself in the same way: whether or not he has a courteous memory in the end determines his own attitude towards himself: it determines whether he regards his own inclinations and intentions with a noble, benevolent or mistrustful eye . . ." (IV, 278). And earlier, in the second of the *Unzeitgemässe Betrachtungen,* Nietzsche had written that "Cheerfulness, clear conscience, the carefree deed, faith in the future, all this depends . . . on one's being able to forget at the right time as well as to remember at the right time . . ."

Memory, that is, is an instrument either to be used well or to be used badly, to serve the self-assertive and fulfilling aristocratic expressions of the will to power or to be informed by the deformations of the herd. Which it is will depend upon what we take pride in. For pride presides over memory: "'I have done that' says my memory. 'I cannot have done that' says my pride, and remains inexorable. Eventually memory yields" (*Jenseits von Gut und Böse,* 68). And for the post-Nietzschean the divisions and multiplicities attributed to the self render even more problematic the relationships to the past within the self, whether in the form of memory or otherwise. Return with this in mind to the case of the apologists for Paul de Man —not, I hasten to add, that of de Man himself, which is quite another matter.

Those who had been devoted to de Man, not only as the most brilliant and insightful of deconstructive critics but also as colleague and teacher at Yale and elsewhere, late in 1987 were surprised and painfully shocked to discover that in 1940 and 1941 de Man had published articles consonant with and supportive of Nazi and anti-Semitic ideology, especially in their praise of a highly dubious conception of organic community as that from which culture springs, in the Belgian newspaper *Le Soir,* then a journal of pro-Nazi collaborationists. They should not perhaps have been quite as surprised as they were. In the late 1930s and early 1940s a great many people in Europe of right and of left, drawn from almost every point of view, temporarily lost their moral and political bearings, while a great many others of precisely the same points of view exhibited extraordinary heroism. And just because this was so, those commentators who tried to use this discovery to discredit the point of view expressed in de Man's later deconstructive writings were themselves discreditably silly. But the response to these attacks by some at least of de Man's defenders was unfortunate. For recognizing that the charge against de Man is in key part that he failed in his later life to acknowledge his collaborationist past, they have suggested that de Man's later writings, just because they involve a rejection of his earlier, as they like to call it, 'organicist' ideology can be construed as "a form of implicit ideological critique" (Christopher Norris, 'Paul de Man's Past,' *London Review of Books* 10, 2, February 4, 1988) of his own earlier views or even "a belated, but still powerful act of conscience" (Geoffrey Hartman, 'Blindness and Insight,' *The New Republic*, March 7, 1988). What Norris and Hartman seem to imply is that de Man's later writings can legitimately be read as saying "I confess to having acted badly" or perhaps "I acknowledge my past bad actions and I hereby try to make amends." Yet the very same features of de Man's deconstructive work which make it plausible to claim for it what he himself claimed for irony, namely that it effects a "demystification of an organic world postulated in a symbolic mode of analogical correspondences or in a mimetic mode of representation in which fiction and reality could coincide," and which it is *perhaps* plausible to understand as a separation from his earlier thought, make it deeply implausible to suppose that de Man could have from his later point of view asserted this kind of unproblematic identity with his earlier self.

For like Deleuze, like Foucault, like anyone who has taken Nietzsche as his or her teacher about memory, time, and historicity, for de Man the relationship of present to past self surely must have been envisaged as incapable of either Socratic or Augustinian identity. De Man also said of irony that it "divides the flow of temporal experience into a past that is pure mystification and a future that remains harassed forever by a relapse within the inauthentic." How then are the deeds of the past self to be related to the present self? Not certainly by the categories of innocence and guilt; for de Man, writing about Rousseau, also declared that "it is always possible" to "excuse any guilt, since the experience always exists simultaneously as fictional discourse and as empirical event and it is never possible to decide which of the two possibilities is the right one." And in de Man's case this exemption of the self from guilt was reinforced by his agreement with Maurice Blanchot that an author cannot read his own work and that this is bound up with the author's will to forget, which plays a central part, according to Blanchot, in enabling a work to exist. These Nietzschean theses however have as much application to the relation between the self and its past actions as to that between the self and its past literary works.

What I am suggesting, then, is that the genealogist faces grave difficulties in constructing a narrative of his or her past which would allow any acknowledgment in that past of a failure, let alone a guilty failure, which is also the failure of the same still-present self, that within the idiom which the post-Nietzschean can allow there are no words to say what de Man has been interpreted as saying by his apologists, and that therefore the attempt by de Man's apologists to vindicate the moral credibility of de Man's later standpoint has been made on the basis of a conception of moral credibility and accountability itself deeply at odds with what I take that standpoint to be.

It may be of course that it is I who have misread de Man, that his position is less radical in its implications for life as well as for literature than I have taken it to be. But if this is the case, a schism would open up between that part of de Man which was and that which was not genuinely post-Nietzschean. There are certainly hints of such a schism in Foucault, shown by occasional relapses from the genealogical standpoint, especially perhaps when later in life in interviews he succumbed to the temptation to be professorial in too encyclopaedic an explanatory mode. But such schisms only confirm the difficulties arising for the genealogical standpoint in admitting into itself any conception of the person which involves accountability, not to speak of the corresponding inability of the Thomistic tradition to provide any characterization of those difficulties to which the genealogist could give assent. Why then are there at this point difficulties for the genealogist at all? Is it not only from the standpoint of the adversarial critic of genealogy that the questions of the identity and continuity of the self appear to pose difficulties for the genealogist? Is there anything in the genealogist's understanding of his or her own position which makes these questions problems internal to genealogy?

There is indeed. For while genealogy has engendered in its adherents a suspicion of the concept of a genuinely originating act—on the grounds that what makes of an act an event of origin is what happens later, so that its originating character did not belong to it as it happened—there is always in genealogy reference to some act or series of acts, both originating and continuing, which constituted an interruption of the continuity of one and the same life. What acts are these? They are those acts of disowning in and through which the genealogist begins and continues his or her separation from that against which through genealogical enquiry he or she is contending, by disclosing what he or she now takes to be the pretensions and crippling misrepresentations of, as it may be, Christianity, Judaism, the Socratic dialectic, the Platonic metaphysics, the theology of Augustine or Aquinas, the ethics of Kant or whatever. The function of genealogy as emancipatory from deception and self-deception thus requires the identity and continuity of the self that was deceived and the self that is and is to be.

What has been striking about these ruptures in the lives of the most effective genealogists has been the degree to which they have been marked by not only the rejection of some doctrine or mode of argument, but also the refusal of some hitherto conventional academic style of thought and life. So Nietzsche made his exit from the chair at Basel; so Foucault at Vincennes in 1968 made of the study of philosophy something quite other than it had been; so Deleuze has presented a nomadic rewriting of the history of philosophy in which on the one hand Plato is invoked against Plato and Kant against Kant, while a chain of not usually connected thinkers—Lucretius, Hume, Spinoza, Nietzsche and Bergson—are elevated to a new anti-canon in a series of writings which collectively comprise a retort to Sidgwick's *Outlines of the History of Ethics,* perhaps to be entitled *Outlines of the History of Anti-Ethics.*

From the genealogist's standpoint the problems are not ones of discontinuities within continuities so much as of continuities within discontinuities. But they remain, I want to contend, problems and the resources for dealing with them have yet to be summoned up. For if the genealogist is inescapably one who disowns part of his or her own past, then the genealogist's narrative presupposes enough of unity, continuity, and identity to make such disowning possible. To be unable to find the words, or rather to be able only to find words incompatible with the genealogical project, in which to express an unironic relationship to a past which one is engaged in disowning, is to be unable to find a place for oneself as genealogist either inside or outside the genealogical narrative and thereby to exempt oneself from scrutiny, to make of oneself the great exception, to be self-indulgent towards, it turns out, something one knows not what.

The problems of personal identity and continuity and of the avowals which presuppose such identity and continuity are therefore not merely problems posed from an external adversarial stance. They are problems internal to genealogy and it may be that in coming to terms with them a second set of problems for the genealogist will also need to receive attention. The genealogist has up till now characteristically been one who writes *against,* who exposes, who subverts, who interrupts and disrupts. But what has in consequence very rarely, if at all, attracted explicit genealogical scrutiny is the extent to which the genealogical stance is dependent for its concepts and its modes of argument, for its theses and its style, upon a set of contrasts between it and that which it aspires to overcome–the extent, that is, to which it is inherently derivative from and even parasitic upon its antagonisms and those towards whom they are directed, drawing its necessary sustenance from that which it professes to have discarded.

It is of course possible that genealogy can discover within itself, or at least from sources not alien to it, the resources to provide a solution or resolution to these latter problems as well as to the former, one which is adequate in its own terms and that is to say, given the incommensurability between it and its moral and metaphysical rivals, one which makes no pretense to adequacy in terms other than its own. But should it in due time fail to do so–and I formulate these problems at a time which is not yet due time–then the genealogical stance will have shown itself vulnerable to being overcome, whether it recognizes it or not, by any point of view able to explain both the fact and the manner of its breakdown on either or both of these issues. Genealogy will manifestly have failed by its own standards, the same standards by appeal to which the genealogist successfully discredited the stance of the encyclopaedist, something itself unacknowledged by those whose attitudes still, even now, long after it is due time to recognize the defeat of the encyclopaedists, presuppose that stance.

It is therefore the case that in the tripartite hostilities between the heirs of encyclopaedia, post-Nietzschean genealogy, and Thomistic tradition neither argument nor conflict is yet terminated. These are struggles in progress, defining in key part the contemporary cultural milieu by the progress of their dissensions. And we have had to recognize the extent to which what is at issue includes disagreement over how what is at issue is to be characterized and therefore how the progress of those dissensions is to be chronicled. To contribute to writing the history of these unfinished debates is also inevitably to participate in them.

X

Reconceiving the University as an Institution and the Lecture as a Genre

From the *Encyclopédie* of Diderot and d'Alembert to the Ninth Edition of the *Encyclopaedia Britannica* encyclopaedias served two distinct functions. They were all works of reference increasingly indispensable to a growing reading public. And some, but not all, were also the bearers of a unified secular vision of the world and of the place of knowledge and of enquiry within it. What these latter codified was the culture of a series of Enlightenments and their intended audience was a public not merely literate and given to reading, but held to be educable in accordance with enlightened principles. Between the Ninth and the Eleventh editions of the *Britannica*–the Tenth was no more than a set of supplementary volumes to the Ninth–this latter function disappeared. The Eleventh edition was, its editors declared, a work of universal reference and it was certainly no more than this.

Three related changes underlay this transformation. Enquiry had become finally fragmented into a series of independent, specialized, and professional activities whose results could, so it seemed, find no place as parts in any whole. Such medieval and renaissance metaphors as those of a tree of knowledge or a house of knowledge had finally lost their application. And when facts in turn were abstracted from specialized enquiry to be presented to the nonprofessional layperson, what the reader was to make of them was left to that reader. Encyclopaedias had become and were to remain mere collections of facts pragmatically ordered for convenience of reference. Secondly, an encyclopaedia could no longer be a set of canonical books for an educated public, since increasingly such publics disintegrated. What I mean by an educated public is a group which not only shares fundamental assumptions on the basis of which it is able to articulate disagreements and organize debates, which reads to a significant degree the same texts, draws upon the same figures of speech, and shares standards of victory and defeat in intellectual debate, but which does so in and through institutionalized means, clubs and societies, periodicals and more formal educational institutions. Such was the culture of the eighteenth-century Scottish Enlightenment and such also the culture of that second Scottish Enlightenment which was the milieu both of the Ninth Edition and of Adam Gifford's will. And the disappearance of educated publics was a counterpart to and in part an outcome of, the fragmentation, specialization, and professionalization of enquiries.

A third change which made it impossible both for educated publics to survive, let alone to flourish, and for encyclopaedias to be other than works of reference, was one within education itself, a change which mirrored the changes in enquiry but with one crucial additional feature. For it was not merely that academic enquiry increasingly became professionalized and specialized and that formal education correspondingly became a preparation for and initiation into professionalization and specialization but that, for the most part and increasingly, moral and theological truth ceased to be recognized as objects of substantive enquiry and instead were relegated to the realm of privatized belief. So that by our own time that which provided both the *Encyclopédie* and the Ninth Edition with their overall frameworks, with the unity of their respective visions, has been largely, if not quite entirely, expelled from the academic arena. In that arena we systematically debate with as much rigor as we can questions of physics, of biology, of historical causation, of literary interpretation; we acknowledge with stamps of official approval expertise in economics and psychiatry. But questions of truth in morality and theology—as distinct from the psychological or social scientific study of morals and religion—have become matter for private allegiances, not to be accorded such formal badges of academic recognition.

So the Ninth Edition is indeed a monument to a vanished and vanquished culture. Yet the absence of that culture is still, as I remarked earlier, a background fact in the dominant culture of our own time, a present absence, a scheme of belief which may have been disowned but which in the manner of its disowning still shapes contemporary cultural institutions and intellectual dispositions. The absent generalist against whom many among us measure their own specialization, the absent unity by which they judge the heterogeneity and fragmentation of their own enquiries, the absent cultural authority with which they contrast their own academic marginalization, all these are even now surprisingly often ghostly representations of the thinkers and thought of the Ninth Edition. And this is perhaps why our contemporaries so often accept as unremarkable modes of academic and cultural practice which are survivals from, which make no or little sense except in terms of, the beliefs and presuppositions of the Ninth Edition, among them, of course, the practice of continuing to deliver Gifford Lectures.

Yet even this recognition of a continuing relationship to a scheme of beliefs which is no longer inhabited, inescapably brings home the fact of alienation from that scheme of belief, the lack of credibility attaching to the creeds of Baynes and Robertson Smith and Adam Gifford. Their utterances belong to a form of discourse in which no one can now participate and hence derive the doubts which attend any attempt by us to implement their intentions. Yet it would be a mistake to infer from the demise of encyclopaedia as a form of moral enquiry, and from the way in which it has become natural for us to characterize that demise in a post-Nietzschean genealogical idiom, that contemporary academia has become genuinely hospitable to genealogical voices, that this contemporary culture which now excludes the encyclopaedic mode has genuinely made its own that rejection through which Nietzsche disowned what the Ninth Edition celebrated.

It is of course true that genealogists now occupy professorial chairs with an apparent ease which might have discomfited Nietzsche and that even when they praise the aphorism as the genuinely Nietzschean genre, that praise is expressed, as I noted earlier, in conventional academic journal articles and lectures. If and when some post-Nietzschean is finally invited to give a set of Gifford Lectures, his or her academic hosts can reasonably expect the conventional form of his or her utterance at least partially to neutralize its content. Apprehensions that instead of lectures they would be presented with a set of Gifford aphorisms or Gifford prophecies are surely groundless. Yet that those apprehensions should thus be rendered groundless is itself disquieting.

For what it signals is the capacity of the contemporary university not only to dissolve antagonism, to emasculate hostility, but also in so doing to render itself culturally irrelevant. Consider in this light Foucault's inaugural lecture at the Collége de France in 1970. There is a double movement within that lecture. On the one hand Foucault in the radical opening of the lecture catalogues the ways in which protection against the hazards and dangers of discourse has been afforded by organizational devices as different as the conventionalization of the functions of an author, the traditions of commentary upon established texts, and the standards of acceptability for propositions imposed within scientific disciplines. In so cataloguing them and thereby revealing them for what they are, Foucault neutralizes or seems to be about to neutralize their protective power, so that the dangers of the voices of discourse summoning up disorder almost become real—but not quite. For we suddenly realize that this is after all just one more conventional academic catalogue, itself an ordering, protective device, and where at the beginning Foucault had to resist the temptation to allow Beckett's Molloy to displace his own words, by the end he wishes that the voice which is to speak through his might be that of one more professor, his own teacher, Jean Hyppolite. The radical has become a conserver, if not a conservative. Subversion has been subverted through its employment of the very academic mode which it aspired to undermine.

Should we blame Foucault or the university for this outcome? It is worth remembering that we have already had to notice in a quite different cultural milieu another perhaps even more striking example of the organized forms of university utterance imposing constraints upon what can be said and what can be heard within an academic community, that by which in the fourteenth century Aquinas's thought *as a whole* was rendered generally inaccessible and in the diminished versions which replaced the original was rendered marginal. Academic organizational forms can on occasion effectively exclude from academic debate and enquiry points of view insufficiently assimilable by the academic *status quo,* and they characteristically achieve this exclusion not by formally placing the excluded doctrine under a ban or a prohibition, but by admitting it only in reduced and distorted versions, so that it unavoidably becomes an ineffective contender for intellectual and moral allegiance.

Genealogical thinkers have as a result confronted a dilemma which they have been all too reluctant to acknowledge. *Either* they could write and speak from outside academia, as Foucault did for some years, presenting themselves more convincingly as nomadic thinkers but paying the costs of such self-exclusion, notably the cost of isolation from systematic enquiry and debate, *or* they could accept absorption into the university, wearing professorial masks, but saying and being heard to say only what the standard formats of the current academic mode permitted. But this is of course not merely a problem for the genealogist. For if one believes that the genealogist has successfully put in question the whole conventional academic mode, both as it was in the age of the Ninth Edition and it has been since, and that it is therefore crucial to engage in dialogue with the genealogist, so that that putting in question may in turn itself be put to the question, then the problem of where and how, in what forum and what genre, the genealogical case be heard arises as sharply for the antigenealogist as it does for the genealogist. And if that putting to the question of the genealogist is to be from the standpoint of Thomistic tradition-informed thought, then it is also important that the resemblances between fourteenth- and fifteenth-century academic modes and those of the present, especially in philosophy, suggest—what is in fact the case—that the Thomist confronts much the same problem as the genealogist. The presentation of that overall system of thought and practice, which is Aquinas translated into contemporary terms, requires both a different kind of curricular ordering of the disciplines from that divisive and fragmenting partitioning which contemporary academia imposes and the development of morally committed modes of dialectical enquiry, for which contemporary academia affords no place.

It follows then that to try to develop a conversation between genealogical, Thomistic, and encyclopaedic modes of thought within the framework afforded by a series of public lectures is at the very least to mismatch form and content, to deliver what one has to say over to a form well designed to prevent one saying it or to prevent one being heard saying it. We can perhaps think of this outcome as Adam Gifford's revenge upon recalcitrant lecturers. For while it remains true that we cannot any longer share the presuppositions of his will, the attempt finally to free ourselves from those presuppositions in order to engage in moral and theological enquiry not foredoomed to failure—and so indirectly to realize after all what he wished for from us—is to a significant degree always going to be frustrated by the form of the nineteenth- and twentieth-century academic lecture. The question therefore becomes inescapable: ought we to cease and desist from delivering lectures of this kind? And more generally: can we now realize, within the forms imposed by the contemporary university, the kind of and the degree of antagonistic dialogue between fundamentally conflicting and incommensurable standpoints which moral and theological enquiry may be held to require from within one or more of the contending standpoints? Or can fundamental debate on moral and theological questions now only be carried on outside the constraints of the conventional academic system, in the waging of a kind of guerilla warfare against that system?

Were we to have to answer 'Yes' to this last question, our situation would indeed be desperate. For what forced fundamentally dissident thinkers, such as Foucault, into the conformism of the university was in fact the absence of any independent forums for debate, of any organized institutions for enquiry, of any nonacademic genres for communication outside it. The impoverishment of the wider culture presented them with a harder choice than any that Nietzsche had had to make, that between some considerable measure of academic conformity and almost complete ineffectiveness. Happily, however, possibilities seem recently to be opening up within the university system which may afford new points of entry for radical dialogue and new opportunities for recasting older genres, so that they may allow new antagonisms to emerge. These possibilities are a wholly unintended by-product of the variety of social pressures which have recently required of universities that they produce more cogent justifications for their continued existence and their continued privileges than they have hitherto been able to do out of what have suddenly been revealed as the astonishingly meagre cultural and intellectual resources of the academic *status quo*. For when a number of very different external critics of the university—some deeply hostile, some not hostile but still deeply critical—have proposed from outside the universities measures by which the achievements of contemporary universities should be evaluated and in accordance with which from now on resources and privileges should be allocated to them, the official spokespersons of the academic *status quo* have with rare exceptions responded with stuttering ineptitudes. The postencyclopaedic university has thus been confronted and been seen to be confronted with questions which it lacks the resources to answer, and the very features of its life which deprive it of those resources are, so I want to suggest, the same features which have excluded from it the possibilities of both the development of systematic moral and theological or antitheological enquiry, whether in genealogical or in Thomistic terms, and the development of institutionalized conflict between these and other contending standpoints.

The beginning of any worthwhile answer to such questions, posed by some external critic, as "What are universities for?" or "What peculiar goods do universities serve?" should be, "They are, when they are true to their own vocation, institutions within which questions of the form 'What are x's for?' and 'What peculiar goods do y's serve?' are formulated and answered in the best rationally defensible way." That is to say, when it is demanded of a university community that it justify itself by specifying what its peculiar and essential function is, that function which, were it not to exist, no other institution could discharge, the response of that community ought to be that universities are places where conceptions of and standards of rational justification are elaborated, put to work in the detailed practices of enquiry, and themselves rationally evaluated, so that only from the university can the wider society learn how to conduct its own debates, practical or theoretical, in a rationally defensible way. But that claim itself can be plausibly and justifiably advanced only when and insofar as the university is a place where rival and antagonistic views of rational justification, such as those of genealogists and Thomists, are afforded the opportunity both to develop their own enquiries, in practice and in the articulation of the theory of that practice, and to conduct their intellectual and moral warfare. It is precisely because universities have not been such places and have in fact organized enquiry through institutions and genres well designed to prevent them and to protect them from being such places that the official responses of both the appointed leaders and the working members of university communities to their recent external critics have been so lamentable. How did this come about? The central features of the history have all already been noted at some point or other in these lectures, but it may be useful to summarize them. It is a history with three stages.

The first is that of the preliberal modern university and college, most notably in Scotland and the United States, in the eighteenth and early nineteenth centuries. Its achievements were of two kinds.

It was the university of David Gregory and Colin McLaurin in mathematics, of William Cullen and Joseph Black in chemistry, of William Robertson in history, of Hutcheson, Smith, Ferguson, Reid, and Stewart in philosophy, of George Campbell in philosophical theology. But the achievements in rational enquiry symbolized by these Scottish names were matched by a collective achievement in creating and sustaining an educated public with shared standards of rational justification. In North America it was from a college education with much the same structure and content as the Scottish that the most intellectually significant of the founders of the new republic derived their thought – remember that Madison was Witherspoon's pupil – and it was that same college education that had provided them with a public able to respond to that thought. Later in English-speaking Canada similar debts to Scotland would be incurred.

Both types of achievement, those in enquiry and those in creating an educated public, required as a precondition a high degree of homogeneity in fundamental belief, especially as regarded standards of rational justification, within the wider community as well as in the universities and colleges. Creative rational disagreement characteristically takes place against a background of agreement and the agreement required to constitute a community of enquiry always has moral as well as intellectual dimensions – often enough moral-cum-theological dimensions as in both the medieval and the preliberal modern university. How was such agreement arrived at? And how was it maintained? Three features of these processes are notable.

The first was the emergence of agreement upon standards of rational justification through the work of enquiry itself, not only in the explicit discussions of the philosophers but also through the intellectual practice of professors of mathematics and history and law and theology. Such agreement was not of course static; changes of standpoint occurred, most notably first in the transition from Hutcheson and Smith to the common-sense philosophy of Reid and Stewart and then in the further transition which was involved in coming to terms with Kant's achievement. But a changing consensus was still a consensus.

Secondly, there were the enforced exclusions from the universities and colleges of points of view too much at odds with the consensus underpinning both enquiry and education. Most fundamental perhaps were the earlier Renaissance and seventeenth-century exclusions by which astrology had been expelled from astronomy and Aristotelian physicists excluded from the enquiries of natural philosophy. But the use of religious tests and prohibitions, formal and informal, also safeguarded those agreements on the character of moral training and moral experience which underlay the enquiries and teaching of the moral philosophers and the theologians by expelling or excluding naturalistic and skeptical viewpoints, such as that of Hume, on the one hand, and the anti-intellectual enthusiasm of the radical Protestant evangelicals, such as that of the Erskines, on the other. The enforced exclusion of all Catholic thought, moral, theological, or otherwise, from such preliberal universities mirrored of course the exclusions by Catholic universities, colleges, and seminaries, exclusions which provided some of the necessary preconditions for the Thomistic revival and thereby for the reappropriation of Aquinas's dialectical enterprise. In the United States formal and informal pressures ensured that in the antebellum colleges no nontheological utilitarian was ever appointed to a teaching position.

Thirdly, a counterpart to these enforced exclusions was the use of preferments and promotions to ensure that upholders of the consensus, including those who extended, corrected, and otherwise improved the standards of rational justification embodied in it, occupied the relevant professorial chairs. From this point of view Cleghorn was rightly preferred to Hume for the chair in moral philosophy at Edinburgh.

Yet of course both the preferment of those who conform and the enforced exclusion of those who dissent too radically were policies which, like all human policies, were liable to error and abuse, and to consequent injustice. Nonentities were appointed on occasion and sometimes those who deserved preferment were denied it, both types of event, however, which occur with some frequency in every known type of system of higher education. Much more serious was the systematic injustice to whole groups whose members were excluded from colleges and universities, most notably Jews. And it is clear that the modern preliberal university thereby impoverished itself, as well as laying the basis for its replacement by the modern liberal university, not only in Scotland and the United States but also in Germany and England, where the history of the preliberal university, different as it was, was also such that it moved steadily towards its own abolition.

Liberalism, in moving towards that replacement, appealed to two sets of premises, one true and one false. The true premises concerned those injustices to individuals and to groups of which the pre-liberal university was certainly guilty. The false premises propounded the thesis that human rationality is such and the methods and procedures which it has devised and in which it has embodied itself are such that, if freed from external constraints and most notably from the constraints imposed by religious and moral tests, it will produce not only progress in enquiry but also agreement among all rational persons as to what the rationally justified conclusions of such enquiry are. From this liberal standpoint the enforcement of prior agreement as a precondition of enquiry was simply an error, an error resulting in arbitrary constraints upon liberty of judgment.

The subsequent history of the liberal university has been one of increasing disarray generated in key part by this initial error. In the natural sciences quiet, informal, characteristically unstated policies of enforced exclusion, unacknowledged and unnoticed except by sociologists of science, have provided a basis for continuing fruitful enquiry. The success of the natural sciences has conferred prestige upon technique as such, and outside the natural sciences agreement on technique has often been allowed to substitute for agreement on matters of substance. In both the humanities and the social sciences what can be reduced to technique and procedures and to results stemming from technique and procedure has enjoyed its own kind of status, and in those areas, such as analytic philosophy, linguistics, and economics, where there are indubitably fruitful uses for technique, such uses are often accompanied by a mimicking of the technical in areas where it has in fact no application. So the values both of genuine technical expertise and of its simulacra have been accorded a central place.

Where technical expertise, with its often illusory appearance of unconstrained rational agreement, is manifestly not to the point, in matters of literary interpretation, for example, unconstrained and limitless absence of agreement has gradually become the order of the day. And in these areas what is observable is change of fashion rather than progress in enquiry. But the institutional tolerance of limitless disagreement encounters in the areas of morality and theology standpoints which by their very nature cannot accept the indifference presupposed by such tolerance, standpoints which invite rejection rather than toleration. And thus such standpoints have to be at best exiled to the margins of the internal conversations of the liberal university. For those who require sufficient resolution of fundamental disagreements in morals and theology in order that rational enquiry in those areas may proceed, the liberal university can provide no remedy. And by providing no remedy it has successfully excluded substantive moral and theological enquiry from its domain.

It might of course be thought that the recent rise of interest in and the large-scale provision of funding for work in applied ethics within universities and colleges, particularly in the United States, provides an important counterexample to what I am asserting. For here seems to be an example of genuine moral enquiry, flourishing in a milieu in which I have suggested that that cannot happen. But so to construe the rise of applied ethics would be a mistake. Note first that its fields of application are all within the separate modes of professional life of such figures as the physician, the nurse, the accountant, the lawyer, the corporate executive. Every such profession cannot dispense with a code defining appropriate behavior both between professional and client and between professional and professional. The acute need felt in the last twenty years to refurbish these codes has had two distinct sources. One is the degree of change in the issues requiring professional decisions, in medicine often the result of technological innovation; the other is the poverty of the shared morality of liberal, pluralist societies and its consequent resourcelessness to provide what the professions have needed.

Yet it is not only that the shared public morality of modernity has proved to be thus resourceless. Moral philosophy and its theological counterparts, when they have responded to the appeal to supply answers to the questions posed by disquieted members of the professions, have rarely done more than reproduce in new versions the unsettleable disputes upon which their own enterprises have foundered. Rights theorists, utilitarians, universalizability theorists, contractarians, and multifarious protagonists of various blends of these each advance their own mutually incompatible solutions to the problems of each particular profession, yet of course with a notably different outcome from that within moral philosophy itself. For in the realm of professional practice matters which affect problems of immediate action cannot be allowed to go unsettled. One way or another codes must be formulated, choices made, dilemmas resolved, with or without rational justification. Hence in this realm what is in fact inconclusive intellectual debate nonetheless issues in the practical resolution of problems, a resolution the arbitrariness of which it is the function of both philosophical and professional rhetoric to conceal.

The fate of contemporary applied ethics thus confirms rather than disconfirms the thesis that moral enquiry without some kind of presupposed prior agreements is barren. And since the moral diversity of contemporary society and the presuppositions of the liberal university combine to make such agreements impossible, it is unsurprising that moral philosophy has declined in its relative importance within the modern curriculum. In the preliberal Scottish and American university moral philosophy was characteristically the discipline which provided the curriculum with its keystone, furnishing the rationale for the whole as well as completing that whole. So it is not merely the inroads of specialization which are responsible for the disunity of the curriculum; the dethronement of moral philosophy, like the dethronement of theology in an earlier period, would in any case have deprived the curriculum of any but pragmatic principles of ordering. But this loss of order has had two further important consequences.

Insofar as the curriculum, both in respect of enquiry and in respect of teaching, is no longer a whole, there can be no question of providing a rational justification for the continued existence and flourishing of that whole, of the university as the whole that it once was, either in the form of the modern preliberal university or in that of its Renaissance and medieval predecessors. And insofar as the university as an institution could only be justified by appeal to some specific rational understanding of how human goods are to be ordered and the place within that ordering of the goods of enquiry, the absence from the university of any form of rational enquiry providing such a systematic understanding of how goods are to be ordered inevitably deprives the university of any adequate response to its external critics. Hence the failure of universities and colleges to provide such a response is not a failure of individuals. The emptiness and triviality of so much of the rhetoric of official academia is a symptom of a much deeper disorder.

What would be involved in confronting that disorder can perhaps best be brought out by considering the inadequacy of even the most plausible remedy so far advanced by anyone speaking from a position of authority. It has been argued that what we need, so far as teaching at least is concerned, is a curriculum which satisfies three conditions. It must provide students not with a haphazard collection of topics and subjects to be studied but with something intelligently structured and ordered. It must put students in touch with the best that has been said, written, done, and made in the past cultures of which we are the otherwise disinherited heirs. And it must in so doing restore to them a sense of relationship to those past cultural traditions so that they may understand what they themselves say, write, do, and make in the light afforded by that relationship. Different and rival versions of the project of reordering the curriculum in accordance with these conditions have been advanced, by William J. Bennett, by Allan Bloom, and by others, but since my quarrel is with what these versions have in common I do not need to explore their differences. I need only attend to what they share: most notably the prescription that the core of the curriculum should be a study of great books, in a list that typically begins with Homer, Sophocles, Plato, and Euclid, includes some biblical texts and Augustine, and then perhaps runs, by way of a little Chaucer, two Shakespeare plays, Descartes's *Discourse* and Locke's *Essay*, Newton's *Principia*, Voltaire's *Candide*, a novel by Jane Austen, the Odes of Keats, Mill on *Liberty*, and *Huckleberry Finn*, all the way to whatever more recent texts are judged worthy of a place in this particular hall of fame.

It is not of course that such texts are not important reading for anyone with pretensions to education. It is rather that there are systematically different and incompatible ways of reading and appropriating such texts and that until the problems of how they are to be read have received an answer, such lists do not rise to the status of a concrete proposal. Or to make the same point in another way: proponents of this type of Great Books curriculum often defend it as a way of restoring to us and to our students what they speak of as *our* cultural tradition; but we are in fact the inheritors, if that is the right word, of a number of rival and incompatible traditions and there is no way of either selecting a list of books to be read or advancing a determinate account of how they are to be read, interpreted, and elucidated which does not involve taking a partisan stand in the conflict of traditions.

There are two levels of conflict involved. At one we have to give due recognition to the conflicts of the past within and between cultures: Homeric versus Platonic, Judaic versus Christian, biblical versus classical, Aristotelian versus Augustinian, the Enlightenment versus the Christian, and within each of these antagonisms there is to be found a set of subordinate disagreements. Texts have to be read *against* one another if we are not to misread them, and there is no way of reading them in terms of the conflicts in which they participate independently of the reader's participation in these same conflicts or at least in the analogous conflicts of the present.

Yet we cannot identify which conflicts in the present reproduce which conflicts from the past and we cannot indeed characterize those conflicts of the past themselves in a way sufficient to enable us to understand what was and often still is genuinely at issue in them until we have confronted another set of conflicts, that between the systematic interpretations of the past and of its relationship to the present which are embodied in and justified in terms of the three versions of moral enquiry with which I have been concerned: that presented in the great encyclopaedias of the eighteenth- and nineteenth-century Enlightenments, culminating in the Ninth Edition of the *Britannica;* that Nietzschean and post-Nietzschean genealogical mode which undermined the encyclopaedists' moral and intellectual *weltanschauung* in such a way as to make it no longer rationally defensible, yet left it in place in the university community as a set of no longer quite held, not to be explicitly articulated, background presuppositions, a set of almost but not quite believed propositions still informing both the academic curriculum and modes of teaching and enquiry in a number of significant ways; and the Thomistic tradition-informed dialectical enterprise, rejected by both the encyclopaedist and the genealogist but from which emerge arguments of crucial importance that the failures and incoherences of both encyclopaedia and genealogy as judged by their own standards, even if unacknowledged can only be adequately explained from within a Thomistic framework.

The reading of texts would be systematically different from each of these conflicting points of view and the mode of appropriation of the past in terms of selection, acceptance, and rejection correspondingly different. There is not and never was available any single neutral mode of such appropriation and it was indeed one of the illusions of the encyclopaedist's standpoint to believe that there was, an illusion identified by Flaubert in *Bouvard et Pécuchet*. Consider how much has emerged as at stake in the conflict between these opposing and rival views: there is first of all a set of issues concerning truth and being in which an Aristotelian and Thomistic analogically ordered understanding of these confronts Nietzschean perspectivism; there are different and incompatible views of the self, of its place within communities, and of its identity and accountability; there are rival narratives of how the self acts either in recognizing its *telos* or in seeing through and discrediting any notion of *telos;* and inseparable from these three, as well as important in their own right, are rival conceptions of human goods and how and if they are ordered. So we shall have to read the texts that are given a place in our curriculum from whatever point of view we as readers take in these systematic conflicts as well as seeing how the texts themselves contribute to these same conflicts.

What I am suggesting, then, is that any attempt to revive and restore a curriculum in which rational justification received its due would inevitably return us to the conflicts with which I have been concerned in these lectures, conflicts which, so I have argued, are denied adequate articulation within the structures of the liberal university. Yet, if I am right, that element in the liberal university which prevents its acknowledgment of the systematic challenges to its beliefs and presuppositions presented by both Nietzschean genealogy and Thomistic tradition is also that which prevents it from vindicating itself against its recent external critics. Hence the contemporary university can perhaps only defend that in itself which makes it genuinely a university by admitting these conflicts to a central place both in its enquiries and in its teaching curriculum. What kind of change would this involve?

The preliberal modern university was a university of enforced and constrained agreements. The liberal university aspired to be a university of unconstrained agreements and hence its abolition of religious and moral tests and exclusions, and hence also, so I have argued, its present endangered state. Such reformers as those who propose some version of a Great Books curriculum ignore the fundamental character of our present disagreements and conflicts, presupposing possibilities of agreement of a kind which do not at present exist. What then *is* possible? The answer is: the university as a place of constrained disagreement, of imposed participation in conflict, in which a central responsibility of higher education would be to initiate students into conflict. In such a university those engaged in teaching and enquiry would each have to play a double role. For, on the one hand, each of us would be participating in conflict as the protagonist of a particular point of view, engaged thereby in two distinct but related tasks. The first of these would be to advance enquiry from within that particular point of view, preserving and transforming the initial agreements with those who share that point of view and so articulating through moral and theological enquiry a framework within which the parts of the curriculum might once again become parts of a whole. The second task would be to enter into controversy with other rival standpoints, doing so *both* in order to exhibit what is mistaken in that rival standpoint in the light of the understanding afforded by one's own point of view *and* in order to test and retest the central theses advanced from one's own point of view against the strongest possible objections to them to be derived from one's opponents. So systematically conducted controversy would itself contribute to systematically conducted moral and theological enquiry, and both would inform that teaching in which students were initiated into both enquiry and controversy.

On the other hand, each of us would also have to play a second role, that not of a partisan, but of someone concerned to uphold and to order the ongoing conflicts, to provide and sustain institutionalized means for their expression, to negotiate the modes of encounter between opponents, to ensure that rival voices were not illegitimately suppressed, to sustain the university–not as an arena of neutral objectivity, as in the liberal university, since each of the contending standpoints would be advancing its own partisan account of the nature and function of objectivity–but as an arena of conflict in which the most fundamental type of moral and theological disagreement was accorded recognition.

One responsibility in discharging the duties of this second role would be to ensure that the recognition of conflict and disagreement do not blind us to the importance of those large areas of agreement without which conflict and disagreement themselves would necessarily be sterile. So, for example, although no text can be read without rival possibilities of interpretation arising, and no text can be taught without some interpretative possibilities being favored over others, it does not follow and it is not true that students cannot be taught to read scrupulously and carefully in order to possess a text in a way which enables them to arrive at independent interpretative judgments, so that they can on occasion protect themselves against too facile an acceptance of–or indeed too facile a rejection of–their teachers' interpretations. And on the importance of teaching students to read in this way, adherents of rival and conflicting views ought to be able to agree, if only because it is only by means of such reading that rival interpreters are able to identify what it is about which they are in conflict.

Much more needs to be said of course about both the agreements and the disagreements which would be necessary in the type of university I have envisaged. But even so bare an outline invites an obvious response: you may indeed have imagined an alternative to the liberal university, but this is no more than a piece of fantasy, an academic cloud cuckooland, something incapable of existence. To which it must be replied: what I have imagined has already existed at least once. For what I have imagined is after all in some ways nothing other than a twentieth-century version of the thirteenth-century university, especially the University of Paris, the university in which Augustinians and Aristotelians each conducted their own systematic enquiries while at the same time engaging in systematic controversy. What such controversy now requires is not only a restoration of the link between the lecture and the disputation but also a recognition that the lecturer speaks not with the voice of a single acknowledged authoritative reason, but as one committed to some particular partisan standpoint. The lecture, as we have inherited it from the late nineteenth century, is a genre in which characteristically the lecturer invites the assent of his or her audience to his or her propositions and arguments. But in a university thus reconceived a central task of the lecturer, when concerned in any way with issues of rational justification–most obviously in moral and theological enquiry, but also elsewhere–will be both to elicit the dissent of at least some large part of his or her audience and to explain to them why they will be bound to dissent and what it is in their condition which ensures this.

So from a genealogical standpoint what is needed is some way of enabling the members of an audience to regard themselves from an ironic distance and, in so separating themselves from themselves, to open up the possibility of an awareness of those fissures within the self about which and to which genealogical discourse is addressed. But in achieving this the genealogist cannot avoid opening up the question for his or her audience of what mask or masks the lecturer is, has been, and will be wearing. So the lecture will perhaps be transformed into, perhaps abandoned in exchange for, a theater of the intelligence, a theater in turn requiring critical commentary from both its adherents and its opponents. And among the purposes to be served by both theater and genealogical commentary will be the undermining of all traditional forms of authority, including the authority of the lecturer.

By contrast the Thomistic contribution to the re-creation of the university as a place of constrained disagreement would involve much more of a reestablishment of thirteenth-century forms, even if with twentieth-century content. For to reembody this particular tradition it is necessary not only to reread the texts which constitute that tradition, but to do so in a way that ensures that the reader is put to the question by the texts as much as the texts by the reader. In coming to understand him or herself in the light afforded by those texts the reader also comes to understand the different kinds of authority possessed by different types of text. And it is this that the lecture as commentary and the lecture as prologue to disputation are designed to achieve.

Certainly the repertoire of texts would not be the same in the twentieth century as in the thirteenth, even if the Scriptures and Augustine, Plato and Aristotle would still play the same essential parts. For one thing, the authors read and taught by Aquinas and his contemporaries did not and could not include Aquinas and his contemporaries. For another, a tradition is partially constituted not only by those texts which exemplify, advance, correct, and defend its central doctrines but also by those texts which through their hostile criticism enable the adherents of that tradition to understand their own positions better, to identify those problems and issues against which the theses of their tradition now have to be tested and more generally from which they have to learn. Knowing how to read antagonistically without defeating oneself as well as one's opponent by not learning from the encounter is a skill without which no tradition can flourish.

Yet if within one and the same university arena modes of enquiry teaching and learning would have to develop in these very different ways, so that not only was thesis matched against thesis and argument against argument but genre against genre, the subversion of authority against the re-creation of authority, how could the university achieve a genuinely shared conversation? Surely a set of rival universities would result, each modeled on, but improving upon, its own best predecessor, the Thomist perhaps upon Paris in 1272, the genealogist upon Vincennes in 1968. And thus the wider society would be confronted with the claims of rival universities, each advancing its own enquiries in its own terms and each securing the type of agreement necessary to ensure the progress and flourishing of its enquiries by its own set of exclusions and prohibitions, formal and informal. But then also required would be a set of institutionalized forums in which the debate between rival types of enquiry was afforded rhetorical expression.

Earlier in the argument I envisaged an accusation of utopianism leveled against these modest proposals, and now it must seem that my response to that accusation, by amplifying the content of the case for a postliberal university of constrained disagreements, has shown conclusively that the charge cannot be rebutted. The distance between those present political, social, and cultural realities which have made the liberal university so helpless in the face of its external critics and what would have to occur if the university were to put the question of its own justification in a new light by providing a place of systematic encounter for rival standpoints concerned with moral and theological justification must seem too great a distance to be actually traversed. The charge of utopianism, so it must appear, cannot be evaded.

This I am not disposed to deny but only if it is understood that the charge of utopianism, sometimes at least, has a very different import from that which is conventionally ascribed to it. Those most prone to accuse others of utopianism are generally those men and women of affairs who pride themselves upon their pragmatic realism, who look for immediate results, who want the relationship between present input and future output to be predictable and measurable, and that is to say, a matter of the shorter, indeed the shortest run. They are the enemies of the incalculable, the skeptics about all expectations which outrun what *they* take to be hard evidence, the deliberately shortsighted who congratulate themselves upon the limits of their vision. Who were their predecessors?

They include the fourth-century magistrates of the types of disordered city which Plato described in Book VIII of the *Republic*, the officials who tried to sustain the pagan Roman Empire in the age of Augustine, the sixteenth-century protobureaucrats who continued obediently to do the unprincipled bidding of Henry VIII while Thomas More set out on the course that led to his martyrdom. What these examples suggest is that the gap between Utopia and current social reality may on occasion furnish a measure, not of the lack of justification of Utopia, but rather of the degree to which those who not only inhabit contemporary social reality but insist upon seeing only what it allows them to see and upon learning only what it allows them to learn, cannot even identify, let alone confront the problems which will be inscribed in their epitaphs. It may be therefore that the charge of utopianism is sometimes best understood more as a symptom of the condition of those who level it than an indictment of the projects against which it is directed.

If this is the case with the contemporary Western university, as I believe it to be, then it becomes clear that the encounter between those rival types of enquiry with which I have been concerned in these lectures has inescapably a political dimension. For the degree to which it is difficult to envisage the restructuring of the university so as to make systematic debate concerning standards of rational justification between such points of view as the genealogical and the Thomistic a central preoccupation of our shared cultural and social life, is also the degree to which the structures of present society have exempted themselves from and protected themselves against being put in question by such systematic intellectual and moral enquiry. What are accepted as the *de facto* standards of argumentative justification in the established forums of political and bureaucratic negotiation are to a remarkable degree now protected against subversive challenge because the legitimacy of any particular challenge is measured by those self-same standards.

The student radicals of the late 1960s and early 1970s failed to understand many things, and their own intellectual poverty reflected the intellectual poverty of much, if not all, of that against which they rebelled. But they had understood this and those who defeated them by the use of political as well as academic power still fail for the most part to understand it. The rejection of the liberal university which was signaled by that revolt of the 1960s was a response to the barrenness of a university which had deprived itself of substantive moral enquiry, a barrenness already diagnosed in the nineteenth century by Nietzsche and his successors in one way, by Joseph Kleutgen and the thinkers of the Thomistic revival in another. That such philosophical critics still cannot be heard in any authentic and systematic way in the central forums of our cultural and social order is a mark, not of their irrelevance, but rather of the importance of the task now imposed upon us, of continually trying to devise new ways to allow these voices to be heard.

Index